PRAISE FOR THE BOOK

'Sanjay Kaul has seen the challenges of development in all its complexity at the ground level. He has come up with a thoughtful and innovative agenda for meeting them which he articulates and makes immediate through the lives of a typical impoverished family. His wisdom is really worth imbibing.'

Arvind Subramanian, *Senior Fellow, Brown University, and former Chief Economic Adviser, Government of India*

'This book is unique because an economist who has worked in both the public and private sectors has addressed the Gandhian question of how to "keep the poor at the centre". The book, written in a reader-friendly style, shows us how the poor and most vulnerable face the brunt of failures due to too many hurriedly designed Government schemes, poor service quality of everything from toilets to schools, and a rigid bureaucratic mindset that tends to exclude the reality of the over-worked and under paid poor families. The real strength of the book however is the recommendations in each chapter which show us that there is a practical and common sense way to improve what already exists and to ensure that necessary services reach those who need them. And, importantly, the author answers the nay-sayers by demonstrating how a people-centred approach is financially feasible.'

Renana Jhabvala, *Padma Shri, leading social worker and President SEWA Bharat*

'Sanjay Kaul's book is scholarly yet eminently readable, brutally honest but always optimistic, an indictment, and a clarion call for change. The book is a *tour de force* that deserves to be read carefully by elected leaders, policy makers, and concerned citizens.'

Ashok Alexander, *Founder-Director, Antara Foundation, and former India Country Director, Bill and Melinda Gates Foundation*

AN ALTERNATIVE DEVELOPMENT AGENDA FOR INDIA

This book provides a revamped, transformative, and fiscally sustainable developmental agenda for India to radically improve the well-being and livelihoods of its citizens. Grounded in a 'people first' approach, this alternative agenda focuses on seven vital development and inter-connected areas, including health, education, food and nutrition, child development, gender, livelihood and jobs, and urbanization. The book highlights the systemic issues plaguing these sectors and offers pragmatic and implementable solutions to address them. The author takes cognizance of the COVID-19 pandemic and draws attention to the limitations of the current public policies and suggests cost-effective interventions and strategies that focus on the poor. The book discusses crucial issues of universalizing healthcare, battling malnutrition and food insecurity, ensuring quality schooling, unshackling gendered mindsets, enhancing livelihoods, and improving the urban quality of life to spell out a pragmatic and workable development agenda for India.

Accessible and reader-friendly, the book is an essential read for scholars and researchers of development studies, economics, public policy, governance, development policy, public administration, political studies, and South Asia studies. It will also be of interest to policymakers and professionals in the development sector.

Sanjay Kaul is a development policy analyst, a former IAS officer (1979–2007), and corporate leader (2008–21). He has over four decades of rich professional experience in both the government and the private sectors. During his long tenure as a civil servant, Kaul worked in leadership positions across sectors – development, health, nutrition, education, child development, food and agriculture, and industry, including in the Prime Minister's office. He also had a successful long tenure as head of a leading private agri-business company. His current interests include human development concerns. He was recently appointed Chairman of the Government of India Task Force on Early Childhood Care and Education (ECCE). He is a Director at SEWA GRIH RIN Ltd. (SGRL), an affordable housing finance company, a trustee on the Karnataka Health Promotion Trust and on the World Food Programme Trust of India and a member of the Managing Committee of several schools managed by the Delhi Public School Society. He is also closely associated with Mobile Creches, where he has served as its chairperson, and supports other NGOs such as Doosra Dashak and Rainbow Homes.

AN ALTERNATIVE DEVELOPMENT AGENDA FOR INDIA

Sanjay Kaul

LONDON AND NEW YORK

First published 2023
by Routledge
4 Park Square, Milton Park, Abingdon, Oxon OX14 4RN

and by Routledge
605 Third Avenue, New York, NY 10158

Routledge is an imprint of the Taylor & Francis Group, an informa business

© 2023 Sanjay Kaul

The right of Sanjay Kaul to be identified as author of this work has been asserted in accordance with sections 77 and 78 of the Copyright, Designs and Patents Act 1988.

All rights reserved. No part of this book may be reprinted or reproduced or utilised in any form or by any electronic, mechanical, or other means, now known or hereafter invented, including photocopying and recording, or in any information storage or retrieval system, without permission in writing from the publishers.

Trademark notice: Product or corporate names may be trademarks or registered trademarks, and are used only for identification and explanation without intent to infringe.

British Library Cataloguing-in-Publication Data
A catalogue record for this book is available from the British Library

Library of Congress Cataloging-in-Publication Data
A catalog record has been requested for this book

ISBN: 978-1-032-22480-0 (hbk)
ISBN: 978-1-032-38666-9 (pbk)
ISBN: 978-1-003-34625-8 (ebk)

DOI: 10.4324/9781003346258

Typeset in Sabon
by SPi Technologies India Pvt Ltd (Straive)

THIS BOOK IS DEDICATED TO THE MEMORY OF
ANITA KAUL (1954–2016)

CONTENTS

	Preface	x
1	The 'People First' Imperative	1
2	Universalizing Healthcare	14
3	Battling Malnutrition and Food Insecurity	38
4	Caring for the Young Child	57
5	Ensuring Quality Schooling	80
6	Improving Livelihoods, Creating Jobs	109
7	Unshackling Gendered Mindsets	136
8	Promoting Planned Urbanization	159
9	The Way Forward: Principles, Actions, and Sustainability	185
	Select Bibliography	205
	Index	207

PREFACE

The economic liberalization in the early 1990s in India has ushered in many years of relatively high GDP growth rates, which has led policymakers to believe that the prevailing growth-oriented policy approaches backed by a slew of welfare measures have served the country well. However, policymakers seem to have brushed aside some deeply disturbing signs. Over the years, income inequality has risen, making India one of the most unequal societies; this has meant that the poorest two deciles are not much better off than they were in the last two decades. Further, along with a decline in the employment rate, the absolute number of jobs itself dropped for over a decade – a phenomenon of 'job-loss' growth. Since 2016–17, India has witnessed a sharp deceleration in economic growth, a situation further aggravated by the COVID-19 pandemic, and, more recently, by the global impact of the Ukraine war.

While poverty levels have dropped in the last four decades globally, four out of five impoverished South Asian families live in India. Health, nutrition, and education indicators in India are amongst the worst across nations, along with sharp gender disparities. The country also has a rapidly increasing urban population which has a significant section surviving in unliveable conditions. Thus, development policy approaches, straddling various governments, have led to an iniquitous society, soaring unemployment, social strife, and sub-optimal outcomes across vital development indicators. There is, therefore, no better time than now for a major course correction. What has gone wrong? Why have government programmes not obtained the desired results? What are the policy changes that are needed? These are the kind of questions that this book seeks to address.

The book captures learnings from the unique experience I gained during the 28 years that I served in the IAS and also the 14 years in the corporate sector that encompassed most development areas. The ample opportunities I got to closely observe and understand the development and economic landscape of India, both from within as a civil servant and from the outside as a corporate head, have given me several insights into the working of government policies and programmes. My field-level responsibilities, close interaction with the people that I served, animated discussions with

PREFACE

colleagues and peers, and my abiding and continuing interest in economics and development issues have all contributed to my gaining an insight into the key issues and have shaped my views on the working of development programmes and policies. In no small measure, this understanding has been reinforced by the evidence-based scholarly work, both in India and globally, on what works and what can be the possible enablers to achieve positive outcomes on issues that matter most for people.

The book offers an alternate development agenda for India, which is grounded on a 'people first' approach. This alternate policy approach focuses on seven vital development and inter-connected areas that matter most to citizens – health, education, food and nutrition, child development, gender, livelihood and jobs, and urbanization. The starting point in each of these areas is a dispassionate diagnostic of the systemic issues plaguing these sectors, followed by practical and implementable solutions to address them.

The book provides a revamped, transformative, and fiscally sustainable developmental roadmap for India to radically improve the well-being and livelihoods of its citizens. It suggests workable solutions to address the ineffectiveness of current public policies to reduce poverty levels and improve quality of life indicators, while keeping the COVID-19 pandemic in the backdrop. In addition, the book suggests remedies to tackle unemployment and create an economic landscape in potential urban clusters that can create jobs.

The overall approach of the book is based on four connected and fundamental premises to explain why India continues to be a relative laggard in the comity of nations. First, that there is the obsession with conventional approaches to GDP growth which has resulted in unacceptable levels of inequity and unemployment. Second, that there is the failure of successive governments to realize the fundamental tenet that sustained economic development cannot take place without addressing human development and livelihood issues. Third, that there has been over-reliance on agriculture and rural development for enhancing livelihoods, despite overwhelming evidence that only large-scale planned urbanization can create the millions of jobs needed. The final premise is that inadequate understanding of both government structures and the poor results in systemic design issues in many programmes.

The book seeks to break fresh ground in development policy approaches – its central hypothesis is that an alternate development agenda based on implementable programmes that are focused on enhancing people's well-being and livelihoods is an urgent imperative.

Solutions are based on two underlying principles: first, an appreciation of what works in government structures, and second, an understanding of poverty and the poor. While being critical of existing public policies in the identified sectors, the book is constructive in its approach and suggests cost-effective interventions and strategies that focus on the poor and what

PREFACE

I believe have the most likelihood of success. In the book I demonstrate that failures or sub-optimal outcomes often result from systemic design shortcomings in government programmes, owing to an erroneous understanding of the ground realities. The recommendations that I have provided are based on my extensive field-level experience and success stories, and are backed by research and literature in these areas in equal measure. I have tested the emerging solutions by viewing them from the eyes of a typical impoverished family, Birsa and Rasika, and their three children as a connecting narrative. I have also estimated the additional financial provisions for the suggested interventions that will have to be provided by the centre and states. I demonstrate that the required outlays are well within the fiscal capacity of the governments.

I remain indebted to the innumerable people with whom I have interacted in this learning journey. The idea of a book to cover the identified and inter-connected seven development areas was germinated in early 2016. I was emboldened in this venture as I had Anita Kaul, my spouse, as a critical but supportive partner to whom the book is dedicated. Unfortunately, she had a sudden demise in May 2016 and I all but abandoned my writing for a few years. The lockdown in the aftermath of the COVID-19 pandemic that tied me down to the home provided just the right trigger for me to restart and focus on the manuscript.

My brother Ranjan Kaul, with his vast experience as a publisher and author, provided continued guidance and support at all stages of the writing of the book. My son, Rohan, while being candid in his comments, has been a great source of encouragement. I gained immensely from the detailed comments and suggestions on the manuscript from Anuradha Rajivan and Harsh Sethi. Anup Thakur, through our discussions, refined my thinking on several issues. Rita Brara provided me guidance on addressing the vital issue of gender – a recurring thread throughout this book. Rekha Kaul, Gita Kripalani, Divya Venugopal, Nisha Taneja, Anoop Kaul, Vimala Ramachandran, and Vrinda Sarup have been constant sources of backing and encouragement.

Neeraj Kumar gave excellent research support and data backup that was required. Shyama Warner provided detailed editorial developmental support throughout the writing of the manuscript. Jaideep Krishnan undertook efficient and meticulous proofing and copyediting of the manuscript. Finally, I am grateful to the Routledge team, led by Dr. Shekhar Shashank Sinha, who along with Antara Roy Chowdhury and Anvitaa Bajaj provided me with editorial guidance at all the publishing stages.

Without compromising on academic rigour, the book is written in a reader-friendly and accessible style. I am hopeful that it will be of interest to the general reader, concerned individuals, policymakers, economists, developmental experts, civil servants, and the academia.

1

THE 'PEOPLE FIRST' IMPERATIVE

> A clear focus on the well-being of the poorest offers the possibility of transforming millions of lives much more profoundly than we could by finding the recipe to increase growth.
> **Abhijit Banerjee and Esther Duflo**, Nobel laureates

The Indian Constitution enjoins the state to provide 'justice – social, economic and political', 'equality of status and opportunity', and 'liberty of thought, expression, belief, faith, and worship', and to promote 'fraternity' among all sections of society. We focus on the development commitments to see where India stands on them after 74 years of independence. These commitments to well-being are fundamental to India's growth story. As Nobel laureates Abhijit Banerjee and Esther Duflo point out, 'A clear focus on the well-being of the poorest offers the possibility of transforming millions of lives much more profoundly than we could by finding the recipe to increase growth'.[1]

India accounts for nearly a quarter of global poverty. Notwithstanding the economic liberalization of the early 1990s, and the ensuing years of relatively high GDP growth rates, the reality is that four out of five impoverished South Asian families live in India.[2] The country has poor health and education indicators, sharp gender disparities, high child mortality and malnutrition, a significant food-insecure population, declining employment levels, and a rapidly increasing urban population surviving in unliveable conditions.

Over the years, income inequality has only risen with the Gini coefficient of income inequality estimated at 0.54, one of the highest in the world.[3] The richest 10 per cent of people in the country together own close to 77 per cent of the country's wealth.[4] Income inequality is as stark. Thomas Piketty's latest book published in 2020 suggests that the national income accruing to the top 10 per cent in India increased from 32 per cent in 1980 to 55 per cent in 2018.[5] This inequality in income distribution and wealth has

DOI: 10.4324/9781003346258-1

dramatically undermined the expected trickle-down effect of economic growth. Unfortunately, policymakers sometimes suggest that focusing on growth rather than on redistribution has merit.[6]

Moreover, not only has the employment rate declined perceptibly, but the absolute number of jobs has also dropped in India for over a decade – a phenomenon aptly described as 'job-loss' growth.[7] What has further exacerbated the situation is that, since 2016–17, India has witnessed a sharp deceleration in economic growth, a situation further aggravated by the COVID-19 pandemic. Along with the continuing economic distress faced by a large section of the population, what has been equally worrying is the sharp rise in divisive forces rearing their heads in recent years. All in all, the situation is grim and alarming and it is likely to remain so for some time. A NCAER study carried out before the Ukraine war had suggested that the economy would catch up with the 'no pandemic' growth path only by 2029–30.[8] The global impact of the Ukraine war has further strained the economy. And yet, the opportunity that awaits India as it emerges from the pandemic is immense. Several sectors of the economy have done remarkably well. The IT-services industry has doubled in size in the last decade. Digital services linking citizens with an electronic identity have opened up vast opportunities for direct cash transfers. In overall terms as well, India is forecast to be the world's fastest growing economy.[9]

How did the country get into this unfortunate situation of relatively poor human development indicators and high unemployment, even after long periods of reasonably satisfactory economic growth? One of the reasons could perhaps be the mistaken belief of policymakers that economic growth would automatically bring a population-wide distribution of benefits and opportunities. The government's goal must be to enhance each citizen's well-being and quality of life and improve livelihood opportunities. And on these markers, government policies have largely failed to make a significant impact on vast sections of the nation's population. Economic growth can never be an end in itself.

What are the alternatives available to the government? Minor tweaking of current strategies will certainly not help; major interventions are required, which may even entail turning existing policies on their heads. This is a natural consequence of the realization that rather than growth leading to enhanced well-being and livelihoods, it may be the other way around. Improved well-being and livelihoods are the foundation for rapid and sustained economic growth. Without radical changes to policy, we will continue to have unhealthy, uneducated, and low-income families that face multiple deprivations; such a scenario cannot support sustainable and robust economic growth.[10] The COVID-19 pandemic, which may have resulted in the loss of as many as 4 million lives, has exposed the weaknesses in India's healthcare system, worsened the situation of hunger and malnutrition, deprived children of two years of schooling, and led to the loss of livelihood for millions of families.[11]

Against the above dismal background, we posit an alternative economic development plan that proposes a transformative approach to radically improve people's lives. A 'people first' agenda is not an altogether new idea and can yield multiplier benefits to the economy. Amartya Sen alludes to it and views development as an integrated process of expansion of substantive freedoms that are inter-connected.[12] According to Sen, these freedoms include access to healthcare, education, political dissent, economic markets, and equality, and each freedom encourages the development of another. Given the inequality crisis, there is a crying need to ensure freedom and create opportunities for those at the bottom of the income pyramid.

The alternate public policy that is suggested for India's future development is a double-barrelled approach that encompasses both well-being and livelihood, and I suggest that this holistic strategy is the best way forward. Well-being includes 'a state of complete social well-being and not merely the absence of disease and infirmity'.[13] It is directly linked to livelihood as it covers economic well-being and comprises 'the capabilities, assets (including both material and social resources) and activities required for a means of living'.[14]

We suggest that neither mere economic growth nor enhancing financial outlays for vital development sectors can suffice. In looking for solutions, we will analyse conventional paradigms about development. For instance, there is a widespread and mistaken belief that budget inadequacy, misman-agement, and corruption in implementation are the primary reasons for poor outcomes. Similarly, governments view the expansion of facilities as the panacea for poor outcomes. Closer analysis may demonstrate that these conventional attitudes may need review. Many welfare and development schemes fall victim to the faulty design of programmes and policies based on an erroneous understanding of the ground realities.

In this context, we will begin by critically evaluating existing government development programmes to identify the factors that have led to unsatisfactory outcomes. This means that we have to ask some difficult questions: Why have health, education, and child well-being indicators remained so low? Why are a significant proportion of Indians hungry and malnourished? Why do we still have stark gender and income differences? Why aren't there sufficient jobs even when there is high economic growth? It is only by looking for answers to such questions that we can identify an alternate path that may, at first glance, appear counter-intuitive.

Identifying Vital Areas

Let us first acknowledge that the concepts of well-being and livelihood are multi-dimensional. Thus, we look at seven intertwined areas that matter – health, nutrition and food security, school education, the young child, livelihoods, gender, and urban issues. The policies in each of these areas may require a complete overhaul. We must first take cognizance of the major flaws and thereafter find ways to reformulate existing public policies. While recognizing the need to enhance the budgets of these sectors, we must also appreciate that most government programmes would have little impact unless they are re-designed and re-engineered from the perspective of putting people first.

In identifying and focusing on these seven areas, we remain cognizant of the overriding priority that needs to be placed on issues of climate change and the imperative of limiting the global temperature increase to 1.5°C; otherwise, the survival and sustainability of mankind itself would be in jeopardy. Therefore, in development policy, mitigation and adaptation solutions for climate change should occupy centre stage.[15] This is important as India is particularly vulnerable to climate change.[16]

The first area of concern is healthcare; a healthy population is a bedrock for sustainable livelihoods. The health sector in India has long suffered neglect and the COVID-19 pandemic has made it even more apparent that India's public health services are sub-standard and grossly inadequate compared to those of other countries at a similar development stage. Morbidity and mortality rates, especially amongst children, are among the worst even compared with developing countries. Almost half of India's women are underweight, while non-communicable diseases are on the rise and have come to account for over half of India's disease burden. There is also a need to learn from the COVID-19 pandemic. It is possible to build a sustainable and resilient public health system that can effectively battle epidemics through a set of meaningful and cost-effective programmes.

A closely related issue is food insecurity and malnutrition. Even with vast food grain stocks and large and rising food subsidy budgets, India has unacceptable levels of food insecurity and malnutrition. The situation has only worsened since the COVID-19 pandemic. Despite high malnutrition levels, government budgets for mitigating malnutrition are only 10 per cent of those towards food subsidies. At the same time, there has been a disturbing decline in per capita food consumption, and huge nutrition imbalances persist despite a rise in household incomes. Policymakers have also not taken meaningful actions to combat the adverse impact of climate change on food security.[17] We will analyse the reasons for these paradoxes and reformulate strategies that can mitigate food insecurity and malnutrition.

There can be no better way to improve health and nutrition than to focus on the young child. India ranks amongst the worst in the world in early childhood care services. Despite India boasting of the world's most extensive childcare programme, as many as 30 per cent of Indian children are malnourished, underweight, and unable to get full immunization. This neglect of the young child has led to a colossal waste of the country's human capital. Childcare is the right of every child, and there is growing evidence that the more a society invests in the young child, the greater are the economic returns.[18] Apart from the obvious need to dedicate more resources in this area, we will also diagnose what has gone wrong, re-set the agenda, and consider a holistic plan to improve the well-being of young children.

Education is the most vital enabler for the poor to improve their health and nutrition, expand their choices, and lift themselves out of poverty. Education is also critical for human dignity and empowerment and for realizing the economy's productive potential. Thus, the fourth key area is school education, the foundation for all subsequent learning. While school enrolment has increased in India, learning outcomes remain dismal. In addition, the COVID-19 pandemic has deprived children of almost two years of learning. Children of low-income households have been particularly disadvantaged, as the performance of government schools, with rare exceptions, is inferior to that of private schools.[19] We will delineate a set of actions that can radically improve schools, particularly government schools.

We should also acknowledge that, while health, nutrition and food security, school education, and the young child are crucial aspects of human development, human capital by itself cannot materially enhance livelihoods. People get a sense of well-being only when they are productively and adequately engaged. For that to happen, livelihoods and job creation are most vital; in recent decades, employment generation has declined perceptibly. In addition, innumerable livelihoods have been lost in the wake of the COVID-19 pandemic.

Sixty-five per cent of Indians live in rural areas, and large-scale interventions are needed to transform and materially enhance their livelihoods. The government can no longer sit back in the fond hope that jobs will get created through market forces. The situation of women's livelihood is particularly bleak. India is ranked 140 among 156 countries on the Global Gender Gap Index and occupies the 151st position on economic participation and opportunity for women.[20] If women, who constitute half the population, continue to be denied their rights as equal citizens, the country will be unable to realize its full productive potential. We will discuss and set forth a comprehensive set of well-directed public policy initiatives to foster a transformative environment that can enhance livelihoods, particularly of women, and create jobs that the country urgently needs. Based on historical trends and the existing potential, it has become abundantly clear that agriculture cannot create enough jobs for the country's sizeable rural population. Most new opportunities will be created in urban agglomerations and our strategies must recognize this reality.

One of the prime causes of the non-participation of women in the workforce is gender discrimination. This discrimination is not limited to the workplace – it is everywhere, pervading all social contexts, and impacts well-being in its entirety. But our public policies have swept women's issues under the carpet. Owing to deep-seated cultural beliefs and patriarchal mindsets, women have not received their rightful due either at home or in the workplace. Given the alarming gender inequities, women's empowerment is the sixth area that is imperative for us to examine. Existing public policy interventions have been largely cosmetic and have failed to address entrenched social beliefs and practices concerning the role of women.

We consider a few policy actions on a massive scale, which can not only ensure gender justice but also materially improve the working life of women.

As noted, urban settlements are the focus zone for new livelihoods and jobs, and thus, improving the urban landscape is the seventh area that needs urgent action. Forty per cent of urban residents presently occupy areas that would be considered unliveable.[21] For instance, migrant labourers are squeezed into slum settlements and, as we saw during the COVID-19 pandemic, are particularly disadvantaged during an economic crisis. The percentage of poor households in urban areas is set to rise. It follows that it is of crucial importance for the government to improve urban lives and to ensure an enabling environment to support livelihood strategies. Poor living and housing conditions in urban areas are not only a denial of human rights but also adversely impact economic productivity. A near absence of urban planning, poor and unhygienic living conditions, pathetic state of waste management and sanitation arrangements, hugely inadequate public transport, and unsafe streets characterize India's average town or city. We can no longer afford this degree of urban neglect. We will look at strategies to reverse the urban sprawl across all cities and many urban settlements. In identifying solutions for the emerging urban landscape, several out-of-the-box strategies recommend themselves. For example, it may be possible to create an affordable and thriving market in low-income housing to cater to migrant and low-income households.

The solutions that are suggested in these seven areas may go against the grain of existing policies. For example, despite an acute paucity of hospital beds, we suggest deploying resources to strengthen existing facilities rather than establishing new hospitals. Similarly, the government can consider putting a brake on expanding the school network and shifting priority to improving the performance of existing schools. To take yet another situation, we counsel caution in providing cheap loans for the self-employed and the poor; without a supportive and enabling environment, the loan may only mire them deeper into debt.

We should be mindful that a silo approach to these fundamental developmental issues will not work. Success in one sector will catalyze positive change in other sectors. Equally, neglect or failure in one sector could have a cascading effect on the outcomes in the remaining sectors. For example, education leads to improvement in health and nutrition. But the health status of the nation will not show an improvement if families remain malnourished or reside in unclean surroundings. Similarly, gender inequity is pervasive and impedes progress across all aspects of well-being.

The ideas we suggest for redesigning and restructuring the country's priorities rest on two fundamental planks. The first is a robust and clear understanding of the target audience, particularly the neediest households; the second is a fuller understanding of government institutions and implementation structures. We should be solution-oriented and the prescriptions suggested are those that will certainly work.

THE 'PEOPLE FIRST' IMPERATIVE

Understanding Poverty

Let us look at a day in the life of a hypothetical poor family from the deep rural interior of India to understand the effects of poverty on those in that situation.

Birsa Oraon is a 32-year-old tribal who lives in Bamparda village of Deogarh district in Jharkhand, one of India's most backward states. He and his wife Rasika live in a mud hut with their three children, Komal, Bindu, and Shibu. Birsa and his wife work as wage labourers on the farms in the village. The planting season is over, and the family's cash reserves, never more than meagre, are running out. Birsa has already borrowed money from the village moneylender at an exorbitant interest rate. He is now waiting for the promised government-sponsored employment guarantee work of de-silting the village pond and visits the panchayat office every day to find out when the work will begin but in vain. He drowns his woes each evening at the local arrack shop. The local fair price shop has not received the public distribution system (PDS) supplies for the month, and he has had to borrow more money to purchase rice from the market. Komal, his eldest child, is eight years old and goes to school, while the three-year-old Bindu goes to the anganwadi. Rasika has found a part-time job, which means that Komal has to occasionally skip school and stay at home to look after her younger siblings. Every day, the family eats the meagre portions of rice and watery dal that Rasika puts together and goes to sleep, with little hope for a better tomorrow. Rasika has heard of a vaccination camp the following day, and Shibu, their five-month-old, is due for the next shot. However, Rasika is so trapped in her daily struggles that she does not take him for vaccination.

(Note: We will continue unfolding this plausible scenario that reflects the existing situation in a typical impoverished rural Indian household in the subsequent chapters.)

To understand the poor, we need to put ourselves in Birsa and Rasika's shoes. Nobel laureates Abhijit Banerjee and Esther Duflo observe that the poor often do not display what is considered 'rational' behaviour.[22] As in the case of Birsa and Rasika, the poor are less likely to get their children vaccinated or regularly send their children to school. The poor in a village are also most unlikely to treat their water before drinking it. In India, as in other developing economies, the adoption of government programmes by the poor is slow. Not only is the quality of services sub-standard on the supply side, but the 'demand' side is also equally weak. Even if the poor are made aware of the programme's benefits, they do not always access it. Deficiency of service or lack of knowledge does not fully explain such behaviour. Economists Sendhil Mullainathan and Eldar Shafir attribute this behaviour to 'scarcity' and bandwidth: 'poverty is the most extreme form of scarcity'.[23] The scarcity of resources creates a scarcity of bandwidth. When stressed, and in a 'scarcity' mindset, low-income families have a challenging time distilling information and making the right choices.[24] This behaviour has nothing to do with intelligence. If the poor could afford the luxury of devoting careful thought and attention to improving their lives, they would undoubtedly participate in programmes intended to help them. Poverty imposes a hefty attentional 'tax' which, along with the 'scarcity' mindset, is the principal cause of such sub-optimal behaviour.[25]

Struggling with hunger, debt, and work uncertainties, Birsa and Rasika have no time to think of anything else. Birsa wants to work and provide for his family. Rasika wants to have her one-year-old vaccinated. Yet, they do not do so; they are focused on mere survival. This 'scarcity' results in their inability to send children regularly to school or get them vaccinated. At the other end of the spectrum, Birsa always applies to the local moneylender for a loan, because that assures instant money. Expecting Birsa to utilize alternative financing resources would be asking too much; though interest rates are lower at formal financial institutions, the documentation and delay involved are enough to make them an unattractive option for the poor.

Banerjee and Duflo suggest that programmes for low-income families need to be more 'fault-tolerant'. They observe that 'the poor lack critical pieces of information and have some inaccurate deep-rooted biases and beliefs'. All these factors mean the poor end up making faulty decisions. Banerjee and Duflo do not have all the answers, but their work is valuable, and their approach is a radical re-conceptualization of poverty policy. The point is that there is now abundant evidence on strategies that work and form the basis for the recommendations that we will consider.[26]

While poor households should certainly be the focus, there is a fairly complex problem at hand: Who qualifies as poor? How many are there? Where can we find a working list of low-income families that should constitute the government's target group? This is a highly contentious issue. Each government programme – even each state – adopts different criteria to identify eligible poor households for coverage under their schemes. For example, under the public distribution system (PDS), over 70 per cent of all households are covered, much more than the 'below poverty line' (BPL) estimates. The government Economic Survey released in January 2020 recommends that the PDS should only cater to the bottom 20 per cent of families.[27] Similarly, under the Ayushman Bharat health protection scheme, the coverage is 40 per cent of households based on the socio-economic census; that too has many inaccuracies. Again, banks have different criteria for identifying beneficiaries under the Jan Dhan savings account scheme.

The crucial takeaway from this is that lists and inclusion criteria for beneficiary families are extremely variable. Further, the enumeration of the poor by the government machinery has been ad hoc and arbitrary. Multiple categories and lists add to the complexity. Maintaining these various lists for different departments saps the administration's energy and bandwidth, besides creating vested interests. For example, the hard truth is that 'below poverty line' certificates can be easily obtained by greasing palms. Families remain clueless about the schemes for which they are eligible, and low-income families spend a lot of money and time getting their names included in each programme's beneficiary list. Thus the accurate identification of poor households poses a huge challenge. For the strategies that we consider, we will adopt a uniform listing of families to cover the bottom 30 per cent of families for all social protection, poverty, and welfare programmes rather than creating different identification and coverage criteria for each programme. The methodology for estimating the number of poor households in each state must begin with national sample surveys of household expenditure and the list must be finalized by intensive engagement with local communities (see Box 1.1).

Box 1.1   Identification of the Poor

National Sample Survey (NSS) expenditure surveys indicate poverty levels based on household expenditure by the bottom deciles at the country level. The Centre's latest state-wise poverty estimate based on such surveys is 21.92 per cent for 2011–12. It uses the Tendulkar methodology based on a poverty line expressed in per capita consumption terms using NSSO consumer expenditure data. The BPL proportion of families varies vastly from as high as 35 per cent in Jharkhand and Manipur to single digits in Goa (5 per cent) and Kerala (7 per cent).[28] Estimates suggest that since 2011–12 poverty levels may have declined.[29] However, there are estimates to the contrary as well. Also, there is a need to make an allowance for 'exclusion errors'. Therefore, we suggest adopting a uniform list of families to cover the bottom three consumption deciles, i.e., the poorest 30 per cent of households across all development programmes. An expert group in the Centre's policy think-tank, NITI Aayog, could determine the overall numbers across each state for coverage while leaving it to the states to undertake the actual enumeration.

In respect of central schemes, this would mean that the number of target households would vary – states like UP and Bihar with lower expenditure per household in the bottom categories would get a higher number for coverage; states like Kerala and Punjab that have high per capita incomes will have lower numbers. Scheduled Caste (SC) and Scheduled Tribe (ST) households would merit higher coverage. Higher allocations for schemes such as highways and other economic infrastructure projects could be used to compensate states with lower coverage under welfare programmes, due to lower BPL numbers. The central government could also give some flexibility to states to add beneficiaries.

An exercise of this nature is, no doubt, complex. However, an honest, objective survey is possible. There are workable proxy indicators for the easy identification of low-income families. These include households without a pucca house, persons in employment programmes, landless agricultural labourers, SC and ST families, households that send their children to government schools and anganwadis, and slum dwellers.[30] It is also vital that the *grama sabha* (village assembly) in each area vets the list to ensure that the neediest households are not left out.[31]

Understanding Government Policymaking

As critical as it is to have an in-depth understanding and accurate identification of the poor, it is equally crucial to be conscious of governance structures, bureaucratic capacity, and political realities. The government must prioritize as it too has limited 'bandwidth'; its capacity is often needlessly stretched because it tries to do too many things. The government announces new schemes at the drop of a hat; an estimate suggests the central and state governments currently implement as many as 400 welfare schemes, many with tiny budgets! Ever eager to announce new schemes, especially at election time, governments reluctantly discontinue programmes even when they become obsolete or dysfunctional. Further, while the government abdicates its role in vital human development and livelihood sectors, its energy, capacity, and resources are needlessly expended on areas best left to the private sector or civil society.

As repeatedly encountered in the analysis of several programmes, there are design failures. Yet, often because they have created vested political interests, the government perseveres with them. At the same time, policymaking and design reforms in a democratic polity must consider their 'popular appeal'. Schemes that do not resonate with electors and elected representatives are unlikely to be adopted by governments. A fundamental challenge for policymakers is to identify strategies and programmes that both make for good economics and have broad electoral appeal. The recommendations we make will take both these imperatives into account.

In recent years, there has been a disturbing over-centralization in the design of programmes. Given the wide variance in economic and social indicators, geography, culture, and governance capacity across states, one-size-fits-all solutions cannot work. Public policies and programmes must have built-in flexibility to accommodate the requirements of a diverse nation. Implementation has always been and should continue to be driven by the states. Unless states take ownership of them, the programmes will fail.

Finally, a 'people first' agenda must have the people at the centre stage. This can be best achieved by involving them in decision making, empowering local communities, and collaborating actively with grassroots-level civil society.

We aim to offer a transformative, alternate economic development agenda that the country urgently needs. No doubt, there are political and fiscal constraints and competing priorities, say towards defence, infrastructure, and climate change, which need large outlays. Yet, radically overhauling public policies and re-ordering priorities to favour the well-being and livelihoods of people sectors is not an aspirational, impractical dream. Rather, it is an imperative that is practical, implementable, and, as we will demonstrate, well within the fiscal capacity of the state.

Notes

1 Abhijit Banerjee and Esther Duflo, "Good Economics for Hard Times", *Juggernaut Books*, 2019.
2 "Poverty and Shared Prosperity 2018: Piecing Together the Poverty Puzzle," *World Bank*, 2018. https://openknowledge.worldbank.org/bitstream/handle/10986/30418/9781464813306.pdf.;date of access: 15 June 2021.
3 T.N. Srinivasan, Pranab Bardhan and Azad Singh Bali, "Poverty and Income Distribution in India", *Juggernaut Books*, 2017. The Gini coefficient of income inequality for India has been estimated at 0.54, as high as in Brazil.
4 i) "India, Extreme Inequality Numbers," *Oxfam International*, https://www.oxfam.org/en/india-extreme-inequality-numbers; date of access: 10 April 2021. The share of national income accruing to the top 1 per cent income-earners is at its highest level in the last 100 years.
ii) Savvy Soumya Misra and Tejas Patel, "The Inequality Virus," *India Supplement 2021*, Oxfam, 22 Jan 2021. https://www.oxfamindia.org/press-release/inequality-virus-india-supplement-2021; date of access 12 April 2021.
iii) https://www.oxfam.org/en/research/inequality-virus; date of access 12 April 2021. 100 Indian billionaires have seen their fortunes increase by ₹13 trillion since March 2020, enough to give the estimated 138 million poorest Indians a cheque for ₹94,045 each.
5 Ramgopal Agarwala, "Can India Arrest Income Inequality", *Hindu Business Line*, July 26, 2020. Agarwala refers to Thomas Piketty, "Capital and Ideology", *Harvard University Press*, 2020.
6 See, "Inequality and Growth: Conflict or Convergence?" Chapter 4, Economic Survey 2020–21, Ministry of Finance, *Government of India*, January 31, 2021. The Economic Survey attempts to divert the issue of inequality by suggesting that the "relationship between inequality and socio-economic outcomes, on the one hand, and economic growth and socio-economic outcomes, on the other hand, is different in India from that observed in advanced economies." While acknowledging the work by leading economists, Wilkinson and Pickett, Atkinson and Piketty show that higher inequality leads to adverse socio-economic outcomes and that it incorrectly suggests that focusing on growth rather than on re-distribution has merit. No economist suggests mere income re-distribution

would alleviate poverty. What the Economic Survey crucially misses out on is the analysis of the impact of improvement in socio-economic indicators on economic growth.

7 P. Kannan and G. Raveendran, "Jobless to Job Loss Growth," *Economic and Political Weekly*, Vol. LIV No. 44, 9 November 2019.

8 Sudipto Mundle, "Covid's Aftershocks: Why we Need Wide Ranging Reforms Now," *Mint*, July 16, 2021.

9 "India's Next Decade", *The Economist*, May 10–14, 2022.

10 Udaya Wagle, "Rethinking Poverty: Definition and Measurement," *International Social Science Journal*, 19 March 2019. https://onlinelibrary.wiley.com/doi/full/10.1111/issj.12192; date of access 10 November 2020. Wagle highlights the need for meaningful integration of the three dimensions of poverty – economic well-being, capability, and social exclusion.

11 i) www.worldometers.info/corornavirus; date of access March 1, 2022. The official estimate of Covid-19 infections in India till the end of February 2022 was 42.9 million with 514,054 deaths. However, the numbers of both infections and deaths are grossly underestimated. ii) Rhythma Kaul, "Covid death toll in India may be 8 times more: Lancet study", *Hindustan Times*, March 11, 2022. iii) Also see, Abhishek Anand, Justin Sandefur, and Arvind Subramanian, "Three New Estimates of India's All-causes Excess Mortality During the COVID-19 Pandemic," Working Paper 589, 2021, *Center for Global Development*, 20 July 2021. The authors have given three estimates of excess deaths during the COVID-19 pandemic, ranging from 3.4 to 4 million, against the official count of 0.43 million deaths due to COVID-19.

12 Amartya Sen, "Introduction," *Development as Freedom*, Knopf, New York, 1999.

13 WHO Constitution, "Well-being at Work," WHO *Regional Office for Europe*, 2012. ii) Justin Fox, "The Economics of Well-Being," *Harvard Business Review*, 2012. https://hbr.org/2012/01/the-economics-of-well-being; date of access April 9, 2021. Many things of value in life cannot be captured by GDP, but can be measured by metrics of health, education, and freedom.

14 "Livelihood," International Recovery Platform, *UNDP*. ii) Also see, Amartya Sen, "Commodities and Capabilities", *Elsevier Science Publishing Company*, 1985. In Amartya Sen's capability approach, development is a process of enhancing people's capabilities by expanding their real freedoms.

15 "Global Warming of 1.5°C", Special Report, *IPCC*, 2019. https://www.ipcc.ch/sr15/; date of access May 5, 2021.

16 Siraj Husain, Pulkit Khatri, "A Climate Crisis Is Upon Us, And It's Threatening India's Food Security", *Money Control*, May 24, 2022.

17 Siraj Husain, "Climate Change Poses Serious Threats to India's Food Security", *The Wire, September 19, 2019.*

18 Chapter 1, "State of the Young Child in India", Mobile Creches, *Routledge*, 2020.

19 Radhicka Kapoor, "Inequality Matters," *Economic & Political Weekly*, Vol. 48, No. 2, 12 January 2013.

20 The World Economic Forum Global Gender Gap Report, 2021, March 2, 2021. http://www3.weforum.org/docs/WEF_GGGR_2021.pdf.; date of access June 6, 2021. Also see, Mahua Venkatesh, "India Ranks 120th Among 131 Nations in Women Workforce, says World Bank," *Hindustan Times*, 29 May 2017.

21 The 2011 census registered 31 per cent of the population as urban. The census, however, used rigid criteria to classify settlements as urban. Further, with increased urbanization in the last decade, an estimate of 40 per cent is more realistic.

22 Abhijit Banerjee and Esther Duflo, "Poor Economics", *Random House*, 2011.

THE 'PEOPLE FIRST' IMPERATIVE

23 Sendhil Mullainathan, and Eldar Shafir, Chapters 7, 8, *Scarcity*, Penguin Books, 2013.
24 Anandi Mani, Sendhil Mullainathan, Eldar Shafir, and Jiaying Zhao, "Poverty Impedes Cognitive Function," *Science*, Vol. 340, 30 August 2013.
25 Alice G. Walton, "How Poverty Changes your Mindset," *Chicago Booth Review*, 19 February 2019. https://www.wykop.pl/tag/wpisy/hnlive/wszystkie/next/entry-30479559/; date of access June 10, 2021. A study quoted in this paper observed that individuals with low income working through a difficult financial problem experience a cognitive strain equivalent to a 13-point deficit in IQ or a full night's sleep lost. Simply put, poverty damages cognition.
26 Abhijit Banerjee and Esther Duflo, "Poor Economics", *Random House*, 2011. Randomized control trials that have formed the basis of Banerjee and Duflo's thesis have been critiqued by several scholars. Tightly controlled experiments undertaken through a passionate NGO may not be replicable at the state level. Further, what may work in one setting may not work in different geographies and cultures.
27 Sayantan Bera, "Slash Food Security Coverage: Economic Survey," *Mint*, 31 January 2020.
28 "Number and Percentage of Population Below Poverty Line," *Reserve Bank of India*, September 2015. https://www.rbi.org.in/scripts/PublicationsView.aspx-?id=16603; date of access May 10, 2021. The Tendulkar methodology involves an exogenously determined poverty line, expressed in terms of per capita consumption expenditure in a month, based on the class distribution of the NSSO consumer expenditure data.
29 Nushaiba Iqbal, "Explained: Ways to measure Poverty in India – and Why the Numbers Matter," *Indian Express*, 26 February 2020.
30 Seema Gaur and N. Srinivasa Rao, "Poverty Measurement in India, Ministry of Rural Development," WP 1/2020, *Government of India*, September 6, 2020. https://rural.nic.in/sites/default/files/WorkingPaper_Poverty_DoRD_Sept_2020.pdf; date of access April 5, 2021.
31 N. C. Saxena, "The Poor Don't Count So Why Count the Poor," *The Wire*, 24 July 2015. https://thewire.in/economy/not-counting-the-poor; date of access May 7, 2021. Saxena points to the glaring errors in the socio-economic and caste census survey, errors which he ascribed to the fact that *Grama Sabha* approval had not been sought by the government. Saxena himself had recommended to the government earlier that the list be discussed and approved in the *Grama Sabha*.

2

UNIVERSALIZING HEALTHCARE

> Health care is a tale of being upstream or being downstream.
> If you are downstream, you are at the end of the river pulling people out of the current rapids. You can save a good number of people that way.
> But if you are upstream, you stop them from falling into the river in the first place, and you save a good deal more.[1]
>
> **Michael J. Dowling**, a leading advocate for a humane health policy

A Health System in Tatters

India's healthcare is in severe crisis, especially the public health system. The COVID-19 pandemic has exposed fundamental fault lines in the country's healthcare system. The country's health outcomes are poor even compared to nations at a similar development stage with comparable budgets. Ranked 145 amongst 195 countries in quality and accessibility of healthcare, India is way behind Southeast Asian countries and ranks lower than its smaller neighbours Sri Lanka (rank 77) and Bangladesh (rank 133).[2] India's rank has plummeted because of slow developmental progress. Even though the national averages of key indicators – birth rates, death rates, and maternal and child mortality rates – have significantly improved since the early 1990s, they mask the wide divergence in these from state to state. For instance, several states, such as Bihar and Uttar Pradesh, have health indicators worse than sub-Saharan countries.[3]

Inadequate budgets do not fully explain the shortcomings of the Indian public healthcare system. For example, Bangladesh has a far better health system than India, despite having a smaller public health budget and a considerably smaller private sector presence.[4] India's public health expenditure has remained at approximately 1 per cent of GDP for several years – among the lowest in the world. Developing countries in South and Southeast Asia, such as Sri Lanka and Thailand, spend approximately 3 per cent of their GDP on health, while China spends a little more. Developed countries, like the US and Germany, and middle-income countries such as Brazil, spend

14   DOI: 10.4324/9781003346258-2

between 8 and 9 per cent. Even Cuba, which does not have a high per capita income, spends close to 12 per cent of its GDP on health and has health indicators that match those of the First-World countries.[5]

Prioritizing improvement in health indicators is critical as economic growth and well-being require people to be healthy. India's experience during the COVID-19 pandemic has underscored the need for a resilient public healthcare system that can quickly adapt to shocks such as sudden epidemics. As Michael Dowling emphasizes, preventive and promotive healthcare is vital.[6] Given the large percentage of households living on the margin, the government needs to play the primary role in ensuring accessible and affordable healthcare for all. This chapter seeks to identify the central public health policy issues, drawing important lessons from the COVID-19 pandemic, and provides a road map for the transformational reforms needed in healthcare from a public health and community perspective. The suggested reforms include a reimagining of Ayushman Bharat to provide improved access to the poor and wider space for private health insurance providers.

A Well-functioning Health System

We begin by looking at the essential components of a well-functioning health system. For any country, regardless of its level of economic development, a sound and effective health system must necessarily include three types of properly managed components. The core must be a population-wide preventive and promotive service. The COVID-19 pandemic has highlighted the importance not only of prevention but also of the promotion of behaviours such as exercise and nutritional diets conducive to good health. Second, the pandemic has drawn attention to the criticality of an effective system to screen for diseases and to vaccinate people effectively. A set of health and sanitary laws must underpin these two services. Such regulations should aim to ensure environmental health, monitor health conditions, and avert potential health threats. Third, well-managed and accessible curative services must complement the preventive and promotive services. Countries that have focused on preventive and promotive health have seen vast improvements in health outcomes. There is ample evidence to indicate that countries with a well-maintained sanitary infrastructure, efficient waste management, and robust public health programmes have generally tackled disease outbreaks far more effectively.[7]

Unfortunately, in India, the health system's focus has been on curative rather than preventive services, and the former continues to command the lion's share of the health budget. An Indian state typically spends less than 10 per cent of its health budget on preventive healthcare. Most worryingly, it is not merely the inadequacy of funds that has progressively severely devalued preventive healthcare; there has also been ineffective governance. There is no focal point for environmental or public health services at the central level, and only a handful of states have a separate public health department.[8] Given this singular focus on curative services, you would think that these services at least would have performed relatively well. But sadly, the reality is quite the opposite. According to the analysis presented here, borne out by field experience, not only is our primary healthcare system mostly dysfunctional, but the curative infrastructure and related services are also in a sorry state.

Yawning Gaps in Public Healthcare

An investigation into the various levels of healthcare reveals that, while the network is vast and extensive, the quality of infrastructure and services remains extremely poor. The focus of facilities should have been on primary healthcare, to provide a solid foundation for secondary and tertiary healthcare services. The ground reality, however, reveals a dismal picture across all three levels.

The country's primary healthcare infrastructure comprises over 25,000 Primary Health Centres (PHCs). Family planning and tubectomy operations were the initial focus of these PHCs. The entire spectrum of primary healthcare was brought into the ambit of PHCs only much later. Planning Commission mandarins rapidly increased the number of PHCs with each Five-Year Plan but failed to pay attention to the required infrastructure or service quality. It is no surprise that some PHCs function from a single room, that less than three-quarters of them have a delivery room, and that most lack a functional operation theatre.[9] Filthy, overcrowded, rundown PHCs, with little or no attention paid to maintenance and repairs, and with only intermittent electricity and water supply, are not unusual.[10]

This absence of quality infrastructure is typical of the country's planning process across all healthcare levels. Had plans focused solely on adding to the numbers, the government could have, perhaps, later provided budgets for improving maintenance. Instead, the planners compounded the problem by deciding that PHCs could be 'upgraded' to support even higher-level services. Thus, in the 1990s, our planners embarked on building operation theatres at PHCs to cater to complicated caesarean operations, forgetting that the focus was on primary care. I visited a few of these 'upgraded' PHCs in 1999, while I was Commissioner of Health & Family Welfare in Karnataka. The upgradation of PHCs included the establishment of Emergency Obstetric Care (EOC) operation theatres as part of the World Bank–assisted central RCH10 programme, implemented in the states in the 1990s. I was horrified to find that, though the government had built these expensive modern operation theatres, several of these PHCs remained without adequate provision for electricity and water! There was also no plan to recruit the gynaecologists and anaesthetists required to conduct caesarean sections. Thus, these newly created facilities saw no surgeries.[11]

Central government norms require PHCs to have at least one doctor and fourteen paramedical and other staff. However, 2,000 of the 30,000 centres lack even a single doctor, and 75 per cent lack a female doctor. As of 2018, over a quarter of the sanctioned posts for doctors were vacant, and over a third of the sanctioned posts for female and male health assistants remained vacant.[12] Even where staff exists, absenteeism is high and motivation levels are low. Thus, many PHCs often remain closed even during working hours.[13] Worse, even when they are open, they function without the required complement of staff.[14] And in cases where doctors and staff are physically present, most are either not well-trained or are not motivated enough to care.[15] To provide primary care and perform deliveries, PHCs need to function round the clock, but only 38 per cent do so, even on paper. As a result, a large percentage of births occur in private institutions. In a few states, such as Bihar, as many as 15 per cent of deliveries are performed at home by traditional *dais* (midwives) in unhygienic conditions. The sorry state of PHCs is not limited to poor infrastructure and inadequate staffing; even essential drugs are not available in over half of the PHCs.[16]

Each PHC has five to six subcentres (SCs), whose primary role is maternal and child health, and the story here is not any better. Each SC is supposed to have a female health worker, termed auxiliary nurse midwife (ANM), to cater to a population of 5,000. By this metric, India has a shortfall of 30,000 SCs, even though there are already over 1,60,000.[17] Besides chronic understaffing, SCs suffer from terrible infrastructure. Only a tiny proportion of the SCs have living accommodation for ANMs. Even where there is habitable accommodation, only a third of ANMs live in them; the percentage is much lower in several states. For example, in Bihar, only 1 per cent of ANMs reside in their designated accommodation. The government's 'Rural Health Statistics' report for 2018–19 revealed that many SCs also lack electricity and water supply. In Jharkhand, over half of the state's SCs did not have a steady electricity supply, and 65 per cent did not have a regular water supply.[18] Many SCs are dysfunctional and poorly supervised. ANMs cannot ensure essential services, such as antenatal care (ANC), because administrative tasks unrelated to primary care take up much of their time.[19] Ideally, the ANM should be a sick person's first port of call. Low-income families need intensive engagement at the household level for health education and support during illnesses; the SCs have not provided this outreach.

In this failed state of primary healthcare, there is a silver lining in a community-level initiative. Since 2005, the government has been implementing the Accredited Social Health Activist (ASHA) worker scheme under the National Health Mission. An ASHA worker is a trained female health worker and the community and the public health system interface. Her role is vital as she acts as a catalyst and change agent.[20] There are 1 million ASHA workers across India; unfortunately, they are poorly paid and work only part-time.[21]

The ASHA worker scheme drew its inspiration from an interesting experiment conducted in the 1990s in the remote district of Gadchiroli in Maharashtra. Two public health specialists, Doctors Abhay and Rani Bang, conducted a pilot trial that brought down the infant mortality rate in rural Gadchiroli from 121 per 1,000 live births to 30. This field trial showed that newborn care could be brought out of the confines of big hospitals and high-tech units and be so simplified that it could reach any village or home. Their easy-to-replicate home-based model demonstrated that well-informed community women could bring about dramatic improvements in women's health and child health indicators through a well-designed outreach programme. The Bangs published their findings in a landmark paper, published in *The Lancet*, which ignited worldwide interest and changed the medical community's perception of both community health workers and the power of home-based care for neonates. The central government incorporated this model to reduce infant mortality through the ASHA worker scheme in the 12th national Five-Year Plan.[22]

The vital role of the ASHA worker can be exemplified by continuing the story of Birsa and Rasika, whom we introduced in Chapter 1:

> Birsa and Rasika's youngest child, Shibu, is five months old. It is the peak of summer, with temperatures soaring above 40 degrees centigrade. One day, Rasika, in addition to breastfeeding the baby, also gives him little sips of water drawn from the village well through the day. The following day, Shibu is down with bouts of diarrhoea, and Birsa seeks out the local village healer. The healer advises him to stop feeding Shibu until he gets better and gives Birsa a powder for Shibu to take with water. By the next day, Shibu's condition has worsened. Birsa and Rasika take Shibu to the local SC but find it shut. They are now in a panic. The nearest PHC is at the block headquarters, 50 kilometres away, and they get on the only bus that goes there. They reach the PHC but, as the doctor is on leave, they are turned back and told to return the next day.
>
> Birsa and Rasika return disappointed to their village. As they are trudging home from the bus stand, they run into Sitari bai, the village ASHA worker. She examines Shibu and asks them to immediately stop giving him water from the well as she suspects it is contaminated. She asks Rasika to recommence breastfeeding immediately. Sitari bai gives them a packet of oral rehydration salts (ORS), which she asks them to get Shibu to drink using packaged drinking water bought from the local store. Shibu recovers within two days.

This story shows how the poor tend to first approach local practitioners, and that the free primary healthcare system is both difficult to access and unreliable.[23] Had Birsa contacted the ASHA worker first, Shibu may not have got seriously ill and would have recovered faster. But the ASHA worker is a voluntary worker and her stature as a trained health worker is not fully recognized by the village community. Only 30 per cent of India's poor use public health facilities; most poor households prefer to consult unqualified health providers as the first port of call.[24] Little wonder that an average village has around two unqualified healthcare providers.[25]

A similar story of unsatisfactory health services unfolds as we move above the level of PHCs to the Community Health Centres (CHCs), which are expected to cater to around 100,000 persons. The country has 5,700 CHCs; of these, only 350 are in urban areas. India has 0.6 such centres for every 100,000 people with significant variance across states. For example, Bihar has only 0.14, while Kerala has close to 2 CHCs per 100,000 persons. Not surprisingly, only 20 per cent of the CHCs function as per the government's public health standards; most of them are dysfunctional because of massive shortages of specialists, equipment, and infrastructure. Only 7 per cent have all the four specialists required at each centre. There is also a significant shortage of support staff.[26]

The shortage of hospital beds, staffing, and poor quality of infrastructure is not limited to CHCs. India ranks among the lowest in the world in hospital beds, with 0.7 beds per 1,000 people, far below the global average of 3.4 beds.[27] The problem is more acute in some states. For example, Bihar has only 0.11 beds for every 1,000 persons, compared to Kerala, Tamil Nadu, Delhi, and West Bengal, which have over 1 bed per 1,000 persons. Even this limited hospital infrastructure is poorly maintained and managed. The media is awash with horror stories of the abject neglect of public hospitals.[28] These hospitals – whether at the level of block, district, or state – are overcrowded, understaffed, and dangerously lacking in hygiene.[29] The overcrowding at the secondary and tertiary levels is significantly attributable to the neglect of PHC facilities, driving people to seek redressal at higher-level facilities. Further, the functioning of government hospitals is ad hoc and shockingly lacking in standardized protocols and hospital practices.[30]

Hospital mismanagement also manifests itself in other forms. For example, it is often not merely a problem of specialist posts lying vacant but also a problem with their right mix. For example, during a visit to the District Hospital in Mandya in 2000, I observed the absence of anaesthetists and the presence of as many as five gynaecologists. During cadre reviews, I observed that while Karnataka had an acute shortage of anaesthetists, several of them who had been recently recruited had been posted to PHCs because Karnataka had a rule that doctors had to serve seven years at PHCs before they became eligible for posting to hospitals. Posting anaesthetists at PHCs, which are not equipped to perform operations, was a futile exercise. When I proposed relaxation of this rule to overcome the shortage of anaesthetists and other specialists at hospitals, the state government doctor's association protested citing cadre rules; the principal reason for the resistance was because doctors occupying the posts in hospitals, even without the required specialization, would then have to be replaced and packed off from the comfort of the District Hospital.

Unsurprisingly, due to glaring instances of gross mismanagement and poor quality of care, fatality rates are high in government hospitals. Deaths in family planning camps or of children in hospitals due to negligence are commonplace.[31]

Given the utter neglect and poor state of public health facilities, the private sector has quickly moved in to fill the gap.[32] The dilapidated state of the public hospital system is also due to India's GDP-focused fiscal policy (discussed in Chapter 1), which has consistently limited investments in the social sector. India's health policies have contributed to this shift by limiting the government's involvement in delivering health services and promoting the private sector rather than restoring faith in public healthcare.[33] The National Health Policy 2017 recommends 'strategic purchasing' from the private sector. This shift in focus to the private sector is in line with the thinking of right-wing economists such as Arvind Panagariya. They argue that no additional allocation of India's limited budget should be used to expand public health services further because their quality is poor! Instead, it is suggested that any budget increase should allow more purchasing power to low-income families, say through health insurance or cash transfers, and they should then choose between public and private health providers.[34] According to the data compiled by the Centre of Disease Dynamics, Economics and Policy (CDDEP) report published in 2020, out of 69,265 hospitals in India, as many as 43,487 hospitals are private hospitals, while public hospitals number 25,778.[35]

The co-existence of the public and private sectors has been a key structural aspect of the Indian healthcare system. The rationale that a limited public sector would serve the poor and disadvantaged, while the private sector would cater to those better off, is flawed. The harsh reality is that well-off individuals often get the best service from both sectors, while the poor struggle to access basic healthcare from either. The private healthcare industry does not provide access to those who cannot pay, and quality care is limited to major metropolitan cities. Within these cities, we have seen the rapid rise of large, for-profit chains like Fortis, Apollo, Max Healthcare, and Manipal. There has been rapid market-driven growth of the private healthcare industry, due to the poor quality of services in public facilities, and the commercial pull of an aggressive private sector healthcare industry. In respect of consultations sought with health providers, only 30 per cent of Indians currently access government facilities, with the remaining preferring private providers, many of whom are unqualified. Similarly, the private sector accounts for close to 60 per cent of hospitalization.[36]

The neglect of the public hospital system has increased the overall cost of improving people's health.[37] Estimates suggest that 5 per cent of all household expenditure in India is on health, of which out-of-pocket spending is the dominant part. Such out-of-pocket spending has risen over time and now accounts for between 50 and 60 per cent of total health expenditure.[38]

Prioritizing Public Health

With the private sector occupying a progressively larger space, there has been limited focus on prevention and screening; curative care is fast becoming the norm. Unfortunately, the challenges presented by COVID-19 have not resulted in the required impetus by the government towards prevention, screening, and the early management of health issues.

With persistent overcrowding in government hospitals, the not unexpected clamour for establishing new hospitals continues. But when new hospitals get added to the system, they suffer the same sorry neglect. The government does not consider prioritizing either the upkeep of existing institutions or the prevention and strengthening of primary healthcare to reduce the pressure on public hospitals.

In the context of strengthening the public health system, it is also critical to revisit the regulatory framework that underpins public health services. In 1955, and then again in 1987, the central government had developed a 'model Public Health Act' but could not encourage states to adopt it. A public health Act may well be the need of the hour as it would enable proactive measures to prepare for public health crises before they occur. Any health legislation should set standards for sanitation, environmental health, food hygiene, and water quality. The COVID-19 pandemic serves as a grim reminder of the need for an overarching legislative framework to deal with public health emergencies. In the absence of a unified public health Act, the central government used various Acts to manage the COVID-19 pandemic. These included the Epidemic Diseases Act 1897, the Disaster Management Act 2005, the Clinical Establishments Act 201, the Essential Commodities Act 1955, and the Indian Penal Code 1860. Each of these Acts has its limitations and flaws and is not appropriate for pandemic management. A comprehensive health Act would enable the government to derive all the powers required to manage epidemics, including regulating the private health sector.

In developed countries, environmental health services form the core of the healthcare system, underpinned by a set of public health regulations. Focus on these services, backed by law, has resulted in rapid improvements in health outcomes in these countries. In contrast, a series of measures have systematically devalued preventive services in India over the past four decades. The first, based on the Bhore Committee's recommendation, was the decision to amalgamate the medical and public health services, which marginalized public health services. The Jungalwala Committee recommendation in 1967, that health services should have a unified cadre, further opened the way for public health services to be eclipsed by medical specialists.

I resisted this trend during my tenure (2000–01) as Commissioner Health & Family Welfare in Karnataka. It was ensured that doctors with a public health specialization were valued over medical specialists and occupied the top spots in the health department hierarchy. However, public health services have gradually fallen off the radar of most state health departments, and their capacity for public health policy and planning stands weakened.

The second significant change came with the focus shifting to single-disease programmes – such as those for malaria, tuberculosis, and blindness control – instead of broader public health services. The third factor for devaluation of the public health cadre was the decision, in the 1970s, to separate public health engineering services from the health department, which undermined the health department's capacity to undertake environmental health interventions.[39]

States now spend less than 10 per cent of their health budgets on public health programmes, compared to 40 per cent on tertiary and secondary care services, reflecting the curative sector's power to capture health budgets.[40] Budgetary allocations for public health and health education have remained meagre, with a relatively higher share of the spending being on curative health facilities. The COVID-19 pandemic has demonstrated that the government must shift its focus back to public health. The government should also establish a focal point for public health in the Health Ministry, which should coordinate public health and monitor services provided by other essential agencies, such as drinking water and sanitation infrastructure, and set and implement public health standards and regulations.

Rapid urbanization has increased the urgency for building a robust public health system because of the massive potential for rapid disease spread in urban areas, as seen during the COVID-19 pandemic. Urban areas are crowded, generate vast quantities of waste, and have a high density of marketplaces, leading to health hazards. There is a need to develop as well as maintain sanitary infrastructure in compliance with essential health standards. The central government cannot remain a mute spectator and leave critical issues of municipal health, sanitation, and waste management to poorly resourced urban local bodies. (We will revisit this issue and the strategies that cities and towns need to implement in Chapter 8.)

Transforming Primary Health Facilities

By renewing the focus on public health, it is possible to ensure comprehensive primary healthcare services with effective community outreach. The COVID-19 impact showed that the lack of community engagement and the decentralized response at the primary healthcare level were critical gaps in managing pandemics. But even in non-pandemic conditions, it is only a well-functioning primary healthcare system that can help Birsa and his ilk when trying to get help for their families.

UNIVERSALIZING HEALTHCARE

Three steps are critical for this transformation of the primary healthcare system. First, PHCs must work 24/7. This would require each PHC to have a full complement of doctors and trained staff nurses in three shifts to handle deliveries and emergencies round the clock. The government must mount a national campaign to fill all vacant posts of nursing staff, doctors, and paramedical personnel. Second, infrastructure and equipment at PHCs must meet the government's own Indian Public Health Standards (IPHS) standards. A sample study shows that the average PHC scores only 52 per cent in its compliance with government standards. The states of Uttar Pradesh, West Bengal, and Manipur are the worst performers.[41] Over the decades, successive governments and programmes have added new PHCs but failed to provide adequate infrastructure and staff. Planning for new centres has been an ad hoc and random engineering exercise. Thus, it is imperative to have comprehensive plans and budgets that fully consider staff salaries, maintenance, infrastructure, and consumables.

Third, the government must ensure PHCs have adequate quantities of essential medicines. Essential drugs are not available in over 50 per cent of PHCs.[42] The non-availability of medicines at government facilities is a primary cause for households seeking care from private providers. Currently, medicine supplies by the government account for only a tiny percentage of the health budget, though medicine purchase is a significant proportion of the household expenditure of low-income households.[43] According to one estimate, as many as 30 million people could be impoverished annually by spending on medication alone whereas they could have got treated merely by providing essential medicines.[44] Over half of this out-of-pocket healthcare spending is on unnecessary medications or investigations. The wide availability of medicines in the open market has also led to widespread misuse.[45] The experiences of Tamil Nadu, Kerala, and Rajasthan indicate that the supply of free medicines is eminently possible – these states supply free, quality generic medicines to patients in public health facilities.[46]

Ensuring round-the-clock operation, proper staffing and equipment, improved infrastructure, and adequate drug supplies are good starting points. However, for most rural low-income families, accessing the more centrally located PHCs is challenging. Therefore, the critical next set of actions is to incorporate an intensive engagement at the household level with the primary healthcare system to support poor households when they need it. As stated earlier, ANMs are not providing this outreach. Their description as 'Auxiliary Nurse Midwife' is, in any case, a misnomer – they hardly undertake deliveries. ANMs could be re-christened 'female health workers' and viewed as community health workers rather than be tied to dysfunctional SCs.

Instead of strengthening the capacity of its frontline health workers, the central government has sought to continue its centre-based approach through the upgradations of subcentres and PHCs to 'Wellness Centres' as part of its 'Ayushman Bharat' scheme launched in 2018, which was touted as the 'mantra' for universal health coverage. On paper, by August 2020, the government had converted 45,000 centres into 'Wellness Centres'. However, the entire exercise has been cosmetic, as budget allocation for each centre has been meagre.[47] In any case, if ANMs could work as female health workers, there would be little need to 'upgrade' SC infrastructure. Rather than spreading resources thinly across a large number of SCs, it would be way more cost-effective to provide budgets for strengthening PHCs.

Even with a redefined role, ANMs will have multiple responsibilities. They need support at the village level from ASHA workers, who are currently compensated only through small incentives and a tiny honorarium, and that too is not regularly disbursed.[48] The poor compensation is typical of the discriminatory treatment of women workers, especially in care work. Even anganwadi workers, the backbone of childcare programmes, are not adequately compensated. ASHA workers were at the forefront of the battle against the COVID-19 pandemic. Their productivity would increase manyfold by professionalizing them with commensurate compensation, making them full-time community workers and accountable to the community. States with a well-functioning Panchayati Raj system would do well to have ASHA workers report to the village panchayat. The country may require an additional half a million ASHA workers for community coverage of the entire poor and vulnerable population. Apart from vastly higher compensation, ASHA workers need intensive training. Importantly, they also need improved supervision and guidance through regular visits by ANMs.[49]

The health system must also actively engage with panchayats, local bodies, NGOs, and civil society institutions that have been largely missing in government policy. A fundamental error in COVID-19 management was the government's failure, at least in the initial phase, to take into confidence citizen groups and NGOs. In the beginning, the government treated the pandemic as a law-and-order problem, rather than a public health issue, and failed to gauge the potential economic and social distress which would be caused by its actions. In any case, police could not have achieved the public health imperatives of contact tracing and testing for new infections, which required active community engagement.

Women and Child Health

The entire gamut of issues relating to women's health needs special attention. The typical female advantage in life expectancy, seen across most countries, had been absent for a long time in India, suggesting that the mortality rate for Indian women is high, particularly during childhood and reproductive years. Female life expectancy at birth is only now more favourable to women as compared to their male counterparts at 70.7 years as compared to males, which is 68.2 years.[50]

Also, violence against women, low nutritional status, the unequal treatment meted out to girls, and the subordinate position accorded to women in our patriarchal society, negatively impact women's health. Women's poor health has repercussions not only for themselves but also for their families. Women in poor health are more likely to give birth to low-weight infants. They are also less likely to be able to take adequate care of their children. A woman's poor health also affects the family's economic well-being, as she is less productive.

Though women's health programmes have centred on fertility control, even these services have significant gaps. The latest NFHS-5 survey results released in November 2021show a worsening of the situation relating to anaemia among women, with those aged 15–49 years being anaemic having increased almost 4 percentage points from 53.1 per cent to 57 per cent since NFHS-4. The percentage of pregnant women in this age group who are anaemic has also increased from 50.4 per cent in NFHS-4 to 52.2 per cent in NFHS-5.[51] Similarly, complete antenatal care, comprising four visits to the PHC, is at an abysmal rate of 21 per cent.[52] The government's maternity benefits programme also has several shortcomings.[53]

The obsession with fertility control is because an influential section of politicians and the middle class continues to harbour the perception that reducing fertility rates should be the overriding priority, even though, in reality, there has been a sharp slowdown in population growth. The NFHS-5 survey has indicated that the fertility level at the national level is down to 2, even below the population replacement fertility level of 2.1. India now has only five states which have a total fertility rate (TFR) higher than 2.1. These are Bihar (3.0), Meghalaya (2.9), Manipur (2.2), Jharkhand (2.3), and Uttar Pradesh (2.4) and even these states have seen a significant decline in fertility rates.[54] Overall, the unmet demand for family planning services is higher than 14 per cent, which clearly shows that women are desirous of having fewer children, thus precluding the need to impose restrictions on the number of children people can have.[55] Further, in contrast to popular perception, the decline in fertility rate and unmet demand for family planning services persists across all religious groups; for instance, the decline in fertility rate is higher amongst Muslims, compared to Hindus, while their unmet demand for family planning is 12 per cent, not much lower than the country average.[56]

The need to prioritize child health is as vital as women's health. Child health indicators continue to be a matter of concern; for example, the NFHS-5 survey results indicate 35.5 per cent of children are stunted, only a marginal improvement from 38.4 per cent recorded under NFHS-4.[57] Simple interventions through ANMs and ASHA workers can significantly improve child health indicators. For example, three simple remedies could save many child deaths: immunization, chlorine bleach for purifying water, and ORS. Even when low-income families are aware of these remedies, they are slow to adopt them despite ingredients being well within their reach.[58] To bring about behaviour change, health workers need to engage closely and intensively with families. The healthcare system needs to work closely with the women and child development department in strengthening the Integrated Child Development Services (ICDS), the central programme to benefit young children. (Chapter 4 evaluates the current approaches to child health and nutrition and suggests transformative strategies.)

Disease Prevention, Management, and Health Education

Another systemic change required relates to the prevention, early detection, and management of diseases. The health system must detect and interpret local warning signs and isolate threats. A well-functioning disease surveillance programme must form the backbone of an epidemic preparedness plan for managing both infectious and fast-rising non-communicable diseases (NCDs) through a dedicated cadre. ANMs already have their hands full with a host of functions relating to maternal and child health. A separate cadre of multi-purpose male health workers, supervised by a cadre of epidemiologists – as initially envisaged in the health policy – is vital for effectively managing diseases. Over time, the central government stopped supporting the salaries of this multi-purpose male cadre. Consequently, this cadre has seen increasing vacancies in most states, which has led to disease-control programmes being bereft of dedicated frontline workers.[59] The government must fill these vacancies on priority.

Health education and promotive health, especially, require this cadre of multi-purpose health workers. There is ample evidence that the financial returns on investment in health education can be exceptionally high. Public health campaigns are critical to raising awareness about NCDs and the vital need for immunization. There is a need for the government to counter irrational beliefs in non-proven remedies that cause immense harm. Faith in traditional theories and convictions is an essential part of how the poor navigate the health system. For example, there is a perception that only medicines administered via injections work.[60] Health education is vital to dispel such beliefs. Low-income families need repeated messages to foster responsible and rational health behaviour. New challenges, such as obesity among the non-poor, also need dedicated awareness campaigns; obesity prevalence rates increased from 11 to 20 per cent between 2005 and 2015.[61] Innovative health education programmes with sizeable budgets, in place of stereotyped media outreach efforts, are required for early screening for NCDs. The COVID-19 pandemic has also highlighted the need for resilient information infrastructure. We saw how, in the early stages of the pandemic, poor communication and a lack of transparency and openness created tremendous confusion, panic, stigma, and distress among people, especially the poor.

A reworked community-based primary healthcare strategy founded on a responsive, dedicated, and well-trained public and primary healthcare staff, supported by well-maintained infrastructure, can do wonders for health indicators in a short time. A similar strategy has significantly improved health outcomes in Sri Lanka and Bangladesh.[62] Countries that have put in place institutional mechanisms for well-functioning primary healthcare and intensive community engagement show good health status, even at relatively low levels of per capita incomes. Cuba is one of the best examples of this. Its per capita income is less than 15 per cent of that in the US, yet its health indicators match those of the US. In the Cuban healthcare system, at the community level, a team of local staff comprising one physician and a group of nurses live in the communities they serve and are available 24/7. This team makes a home visit to each family in the community at least once a year. At the next level are community-based polyclinics, with 20–40 doctors and nurses, who attend to severe cases and support the local staff.[63] India must transform its PHCs and CHCs into similarly vibrant and fully functional community-level institutions. We do not even have to look at evidence from other countries – we have seen such success in Kerala, which has a smooth and efficient primary healthcare system.

The transformation of primary healthcare services as outlined above would reduce the pressure on public hospitals. Currently, cases that should be managed at PHCs land up at district hospitals and tertiary institutions, such as one of the All India Institutes of Medical Sciences. Patients that cannot be handled at PHCs should be referred to CHCs and other block-level hospitals, and not be forced to go to hospitals at the district level or higher. As noted, though India already has close to 25,000 government hospitals, they lack proper infrastructure and equipment and have a chronic staff shortage. These first-level referral hospitals, if adequately equipped, would take care of most patients that PHCs cannot treat.

There are success stories of referral strategies that have worked. For example, Karnataka successfully implemented a project to strengthen its referral system by upgrading *taluk* hospitals and CHCs. The Karnataka project, supported by the World Bank and implemented between 2000–05, focused on the upgradation, refurbishing, and modernization of all CHCs and other hospitals up to the district hospital. The project comprised four components: (i) refurbishing of the buildings, including structural repairs; (ii) replacement and procurement of essential diagnostic equipment; (iii) ensuring at least four specialists at each facility – general physician, surgeon, gynaecologist, and anaesthetist – supported by staff nurses, technicians, and para-medical staff; and, (iv) capacity development and putting in place a hospital quality management system. I was fortunate to have been part of the planning and implementation phase of the project. The successful completion of the project, broadly within the timelines and costs estimated, demonstrates that it is possible to completely overhaul the government hospital system through careful planning and execution.

The height of the COVID-19 pandemic highlighted the chronic shortages of critical equipment, staff, and hospital beds in the country. During this period, the functional bed capacity in government hospitals was much below the official number because of these shortages. Therefore, rather than adding new hospitals, the government needs to prioritize the refurbishment, modernization, and redesign of the existing hospital infrastructure, while replacing obsolete equipment and augmenting hospital personnel. These measures would be cost-effective and could improve bed strength and optimize capacity utilization. By merely adding more doctors, nurses, and support staff, government hospitals can handle more patients, run outpatient departments for 16 hours a day, and significantly reduce patient overload. Each hospital must have an Emergency Response Plan that should include a contingency plan for quickly adding bed capacity in times of an emergency. Many of the 25,000 PHCs have the building infrastructure for 4–6 beds, mostly lying unused. Ensuring that PHCs function around the clock, strengthening existing infrastructure, providing adequate diagnostic equipment, and supplying essential medicines must get prioritized. Prioritizing existing PHCs will take pressure off higher-level facilities and, more critically, give relief to patients in rural areas where public hospitals are few and far between.

Unfortunately, rather than the suggested cost-effective strategy of strengthening existing hospitals and PHCs, the conventional government strategy has been to go on a mindless spree of adding new hospitals at the expense of improving existing hospitals. New hospitals are hugely capital intensive and have long gestation periods. For example, under the 'Pradhan Mantri Swasthya Suraksha Yojana', in operation since 2003, 20 new All India Institutes of Medical Sciences and 71 state government hospitals have been planned. As with several government programmes, implementation has been tardy, with massive budget over-runs from ₹6.5 billion in 2010–11 to ₹60.2 billion in 2020–21.[64] Such unplanned addition to the hospital network has further shrunk the budgetary outlays for maintaining the existing institutions.

Halting hospital infrastructure expansion does appear counterintuitive; after all, there are already too few hospital beds per person. Abhijit Banerjee, too, has suggested that the government prioritize building a second district hospital.[65] However, should such new facilities be set up while starving the existing hospital capacity of resources for their upkeep and functioning?

There are other innovative and efficient ways to improve hospital effectiveness. For example, doctors have extensively used video conferences and digital platforms for diagnosis and online monitoring of patients who were isolated at home during COVID-19.

Health Insurance and Private Sector Regulation

We have already noted the central government's poor implementation of Ayushman Bharat in the context of Wellness Centres, ostensibly in aid of the country's push towards universal health coverage. However, the principal component of Ayushman Bharat is not the Wellness Centres but the insurance coverage of ₹5,00,000 for accessing secondary and tertiary care, primarily from private hospitals. The programme aims to cover 40 per cent of households, comprising 107 million poor families or 530 million beneficiaries; however, by March 2021, only 145 million Ayushman cards had been issued. In its actual implementation, much like the older health insurance programmes that it replaced, Ayushman Bharat does not address the needs of low-income households. Instead, there is evidence that this ambitious programme is likely to divert public funds to private players. Estimates suggest Ayushman Bharat, if fully funded, could gobble up 75 per cent of the central government's health budget, raising a fundamental question about the scheme's financial viability. Further, while the insurance only covers hospitalization, most of the out-of-the-pocket expenditure made by households is for buying medicines.[66] Ayushman Bharat should have seen higher spending during the COVID-19 pandemic; however, on the contrary, utilization of funds fell during the lockdown period.[67]

The primary systemic design flaw with Ayushman Bharat is that it requires the government to adjudicate claims and fix the price for each medical treatment and service. The scheme has several unanswered questions: How should a hospital respond when it gets *prima facie* evidence that a doctor in the hospital carried out unnecessary procedures or made false diagnoses? How do patients know what they are entitled to and what goes beyond their entitlement? And how will disputes be settled? In fact, due to these issues, good private hospitals may not want to participate in the scheme.

Rather than expend additional resources on an unviable, costly scheme, a better approach would be to shift the first claim on resources and time to the public healthcare system. In designing a health insurance scheme, the government should not become a micro-manager for settling claims or determining the cost of each treatment. Insurance design is a very specialized, complex job requiring extensive studies and professional actuaries to assess health risks and determine premiums. Therefore, insurance companies should be left free to design and implement their health insurance scheme, including claims settlement. Accreditation of private hospitals is also best left to insurance companies. If left to government structures, vested interests get created, and poor quality institutions begin queuing for inclusion. The eligible beneficiary families should be the 30 per cent poorest households, identified based on the guidelines set out in Chapter 1, rather than a separate list of beneficiaries being drawn up by the health department. The beneficiary households should have the freedom to choose any insurance scheme.

In public facilities, hospitalization and treatment should be free, though the insurance scheme should cover other expenses that the family needs to spend on. Reducing the pressure on private provisioning of hospital care by strengthening public hospitals would also make the government's health insurance budget manageable. Failure to strengthen public hospitals on priority would, over time, lead to a rise in healthcare costs and the cornering of the health sector industry by a few corporate entities, as has happened in the US.

In the light of the private sector's rapid expansion and the policy push through Ayushman Bharat, one would have expected the central government to establish a well-designed regulatory framework and comprehensive legislation for the industry. Sadly, regulation continues to be a neglected aspect of policymaking; we are yet to have comprehensive legislation to regulate the industry. The central Clinical Establishments (Registration and Regulation) Act, 2010, meant to oversee private hospitals, has been adopted only by 11 states and mostly on paper. The National Medical Commission Act, 2019, setting up the medical education regulatory authority, has been recently enacted to oversee medical education and practice. The National Medical Commission has replaced the Medical Council of India. The government has called this Act the 'biggest reform' in the medical profession, terming it a 'pro-poor legislation' that would make quality medical care more accessible to the people. Paradoxically, the Act has run into severe resistance from the very profession whose lot it was supposed to improve. A detailed study of the Act reveals that its provisions make it a case of the 'cure being worse than the malady'.[68] Quite apart from the inadequate regulation of private hospitals, practices relating to prescribing medications and investigations also have little regulation; only 10 per cent of the medicine market is under price control.

The Clinical Establishments (Registration and Regulation) Act of 2010 is an essential regulatory reform and needs to be adopted and fully implemented by all states. Private practice regulation is also necessary to arrive at consistent pricing norms for consultations and treatment procedures. Non-transparent and price-inefficient provisioning of drugs and diagnostic services is a systemic flaw, particularly impacting the poor. There is considerable scope to standardize pricing protocols across various pharmaceutical drugs and diagnostic services. In the absence of such regulations, several private hospitals took advantage of the shortage of hospital beds during the COVID-19 pandemic and resorted to charging exorbitant fees, profiteering from the situation.

Regulation of the private health sector does not mean that government should not leverage the strengths of the private sector. The government relied entirely on the private sector for vaccine development against COVID-19. In the initial phase of the pandemic, the government policy of limiting testing to only government centres did not utilize the capacity of the private sector; subsequently, once many private laboratories got accredited, testing infrastructure radically improved country-wide. An expanded system of laboratory networks, including private laboratories and all government health centres, is a priority. The government must also ensure the active participation of private hospitals in disease surveillance.

One question concerning the private sector remains: How should the government deal with local unqualified private health providers? Declaring them illegal and ignoring their existence would break their close connection with households. Instead, the government can implement simple strategies to use such providers productively. Local health providers should be recognized as partners in the health system and reoriented to provide responsible health extension services at the community level. Studies in West Bengal suggest that training private sector health providers improve their performance significantly, and the state has already begun to train thousands of private health providers. A helpful strategy could be to create a set of digital checklists of treatment protocols that these practitioners can save on their phones to use when faced with the common symptoms they would encounter. Following a round of intensive training, the government could introduce a simple test that allows it to certify these practitioners as health extension workers, who can be permitted to deliver various public health interventions. However, we should be cautious as these providers can be a public health hazard, often incorrectly administering antibiotics and steroids, contributing to drug resistance in the population.[69]

Enhancing Health Budgets

The shift of focus from the private sector to public health will mean a re-engineered 'bottom-up' approach, beginning with primary healthcare. Central health budgets are not only inadequate; there are also enormous distortions in health financing.[70] Financing the fast-rising insurance component of Ayushman Bharat is at the expense of essential primary healthcare and public health. As a result, we have seen sharp cuts in budgets earmarked for the National Health Mission covering primary healthcare, including the critical component of reproductive and child health services. Similarly, there is a misplaced focus on a clinical health and curative approach to disease management rather than health promotion and outbreak prevention. States have also not accorded priority to health expenditure.[71] All this must change.

It would be unrealistic to expect health budgets to rise dramatically to reach the levels in Cuba and Brazil. During India's fight against the COVID-19 pandemic, the 15th Finance Commission announced, in June 2020, that it was working towards a financing model to raise central public-health spending to over 2 per cent of GDP.[72] Even if this were to occur, the country might not be able to ensure universal health coverage. The experience of comparable countries such as Thailand and Sri Lanka suggests that health expenditure must rise to 3 per cent of GDP to ensure universal health coverage.[73] Universal coverage is achievable provided we reorient our policies, plan correctly, and adopt cost-effective strategies such as those outlined in this chapter. The budget hike to 3 per cent of GDP would mean a significant jump from the 1 per cent of GDP currently spent. We have estimated that the implementation of the recommendations made in the chapter may not require such a huge hike in the health budget; a modest increase of the central health annual outlay by ₹678 billion may be adequate (as detailed in the appendix to Chapter 9). States with low health indicators would, of course, need a concerted push and disproportionate budget enhancements.

There is much to be done to reform the healthcare system. This chapter has outlined the critical elements of this redesign. The COVID-19 epidemic has exposed the limitations of our health services. The essential components of a reworked strategy would include a focus on preventive and promotive care on the back of a dedicated, efficient, well-trained, and adequately resourced primary healthcare cadre. It is imperative to focus on improving the quality of services in hospitals and primary health centres. The immediate priorities must be refurbishing and modernizing the existing hospital infrastructure, optimizing utilization, implementing a referral system to reduce overcrowding, strengthening disease surveillance and screening, and implementing a hospital quality management system with rigidly enforced standards operating protocols.

Finally, we need to remind ourselves that the healthcare system does not exist in a vacuum. Education plays a prominent role, as do sanitation and access to clean drinking water. Equally, impoverishment and malnutrition impinge on health. Primacy has to be given to women and child health. Physical well-being is much more than just health – another essential element is food security and nutrition for every citizen, the subject of our next chapter.

Notes

1 Michael Dowling, "Moving Care Upstream, Addressing Social Determinants," Health Care Reboot, 10 May 2019. https://healthcare-reboot.com/2019/05/10/moving-care-upstream-addressing-social-determinants/; date of access, May 20, 2021.

2 Fullman N, Yearwood J, Abay SM, Abbafati C, Abd-Allah F, Abdela J, Abdelalim A, Abebe Z, Abebo TA, Aboyans V, Abraha HN, et al. "The Lancet's Global Burden of Disease Study. Measuring Performance on the Healthcare Access and Quality Index for 195 Countries and Territories and Selected Subnational Locations: A Systematic Analysis from the Global Burden of Disease Study, 2016" *The Lancet*, Vol. 391(10136), pp. 2236–2271, 2018.

3 i) The Health Ministry's Data Set, "NRHM MIS (HMIS) Data Base – Rural Health Statistics, 2019," Department of Health and Family Welfare, *Government of India*. https://hmis.nhp.gov.in/downloadfile?filepath=publications/Rural-Health-Statistics/RHS%202019-20.pdf; date of access June 8, 2021.
ii) Economic Survey, Table 1, Chapter 10, p. 294, Ministry of Finance, 2019–20. https://www.indiabudget.gov.in/economicsurvey/doc/vol2chapter/echap10_vol2.pdf; date of access June 10, 2021.
iii) "World Bank Data Indicator," *World Bank*. https://data.worldbank.org/indicator; date of access May 12, 2020. The country average for maternity mortality (MMR) for 2018 is 113 per 100000 births, down from 374 in 2000. However, MMR in Assam, UP, and MP are as high as 215, 197, and 173, respectively. India's MMR is high in contrast to less than 60 in the several middle-income countries, and is still some distance away from the UN's sustainable

development goal of 70. The infant mortality rate (IMR) has dropped to 32 in 2019 from 66.7 in 2000, while child mortality has fallen from 26.5 to 8.9 in the same period. While infant mortality in states such as Kerala and Goa are now comparable to middle-income countries, Uttar Pradesh has an IMR above 60, on par with several sub-Saharan countries. The life expectancy at birth (LEB) has increased from 60.3 years to 69 years but is much lower in comparison to countries such as Sri Lanka, Malaysia, Thailand, and Brazil which boast of LEB of over 76 years. For the same group of countries, IMR is less than 8, and even Bangladesh scores better with an IMR of 25. Only a few states, such as Kerala, Delhi, and Jammu & Kashmir, have LEB comparable to the middle-income group; LEB is less than 66 in Madhya Pradesh, Uttar Pradesh, and Assam, comparable to sub-Saharan countries.

4 Sadhika Tiwari, "India Spent 1% of GDP on Public Health for 15 years. Result is Vulnerability to Crisis," *IndiaSpend*, 26 June 2020. https://www.indiaspend.com/india-spent-1-of-gdp-on-public-health-for-15-years-result-is-vulnerability-to-crises/; date of access June 10, 2021.

5 Álvaro Fuente, "How does Cuba Manage to Achieve First-world Health Statistics?" *El País*, Feb. 10, 2017. https://english.elpais.com/elpais/2017/02/10/inenglish/1486729823_171276.html.; date of access June 10, 2021. As per World Bank Data, Cuba spent 11.71 per cent of its GDP on health in 2017, higher than the global average (9.88 per cent). Cuba's child mortality rate is on par with some of the world's richest countries. With six deaths for every 1,000 births, Cuba is level with New Zealand. Cuba's average life expectancy (79 years) matches that in the US.

6 Michael Dowling, "Moving Care Upstream, Addressing Social Determinants," Health Care Reboot, 10 May 2019. https://healthcare-reboot.com/2019/05/10/moving-care-upstream-addressing-social-determinants/; date of access, May 20, 2021.

7 Monica Das Gupta, B.R. Desikachari, Rajendra Shukla, T.V. Somanathan, P. Padmanaban, and K.K. Dutta, "How might India's Public Health Systems be Strengthened? Lessons from Tamilnadu," *Economic & Political Weekly*, Vol. 45, No. 10, pp. 46–60, 6–10 March 2010.

8 Ibid.

9 Reply given to Lok Sabha starred question, dated 22 November 2019. http://164.100.24.220/loksabhaquestions/annex/172/AS88.pdf; date of access May 5, 2020.

10 Shyam Kumar Sriram, "Availability of Infrastructure and Manpower for PHCs in a District in Andhra Pradesh," *Journal of Family Medical Research*, Nov-Dec 7(6), pp. 1256–1262, 2018.

11 I served as Commissioner, Health and Family Welfare, Karnataka, when the RCH 10 programme was under implementation.

12 "National Health Profile," Central Bureau of Health Intelligence, *Government of India*, 2019.

13 Abhijit Banerjee, "A Note on Healthcare," What the Economy Needs Now, *Juggernaut Books*, 2019. Banerjee quotes a study conducted in Udaipur that showed that the centres remained closed over half the time.

14 "NRHM MIS (HMIS) Data Base – Rural Health Statistics," *Government of India*, 2019.

15 Kavvya Agarwal, "Rural Healthcare in India – a Boon or Bane?" *Oxfam India*, 25 July 2019 https://www.oxfamindia.org/blog/rural-healthcare-in-india?gclid=Cj0KCQjwvvj5BRDkARIsAGD9vlL9dJy6bW_Yfd9g6zq9k7VI7_BRkCjmupz869ah-KsldUthI8T5bssaAh1SEALw_wcB; date of access May 15, 2020.

16 "NRHM MIS (HMIS) Data Base – Rural Health Statistics," *Government of India*, 2019.

17 "Part I, Rural Health Care System in India, Rural Health Statistics 2018–19," Ministry of Health and Family Welfare, *Government of India*. https://nrhmmis.nic.in/RURAL%20HEALTH%20STATISTICS/(A)%20RHS%20-%202014/Rural%20Health%20Care%20System%20in%20India.pdf;. date of access June 10, 2021. ii) "National Health Profile 2019", Central Bureau of Health Intelligence, Government of India. http://www.cbhidghs.nic.in/showfile.php?lid=1147; date of access May 5, 2021. The number of subcentres and PHCs saw modest growth of 8 and 11 per cent over the period from 2006 to 2018. with the number of subcentres rising to 158,417 and primary health centres to 25,743. The number of CHCs, however, increased by nearly 70 per cent to 5,624 over this period. Overall, there are 25,778 government hospitals (including CHCs) in India. The numbers appear impressive, but in terms of norms, there is a shortfall at each of these levels. For instance, as of 2018, there was a shortage of 2,188 CHCs, 6,430 PHCs and 32,900 subcentres.

18 "Rural Health Statistics, 2018–19," Ministry of Health and Family Welfare, *Government of India*. https://main.mohfw.gov.in/sites/default/files/Final%20RHS%202018-19_0.pdf; date of access May 5, 2021.

19 (i) Prachi Salve, "Mothers Education Household Wealth Decide Survival of Infants in India," *IndiaSpend*, 16 January 2018. https://www.indiaspend.com/mothers-education-household-wealth-decide-survival-of-infants-in-india-51235/.; date of access May 12, 2021. A survey carried out survey found that only 51.2 per cent of mothers had the four antenatal care (ANC) visits. (ii) Bhombe I, Raut A.V., Taywade M, and Deshmukh P, "Time motion study of ANMs of a PHC from Wardha District, Maharashtra," *International Journal Adv. Medical Health Research*, vol. 6, pp. 18–23, 2019.

20 Ramila Bisht and Shaveta Menon, "ASHA Workers Are Indispensable. So Why Are They The Least of Our Concerns?" *The Wire*, 1 May 2020. https://thewire.in/rights/asha-workers-coronavirus; date of access May 2, 2020.

21 Arrefa Johari, "Why Women Serving as Frontline Health Workers in India Do Not Even Get the Minimum Wage," *Scroll*, 14 November 2018.

22 Abhay and Rani Bang, *Wikipedia*. https://en.wikipedia.org/wiki/Abhay_and_Rani_Bang; date of access May 10, 2021.

23 Meeta, Rajivlochan, "Inequities in Health, Agrarian Distress and a Policy of Avoidance," *Economic and Political Weekly*, 2010. https://www.researchgate.net/profile/Mn_Rajivlochan2/publication/289203033_Inequities_in_health_agrarian_distress_and_a_policy_of_avoidance/links/572acc8308ae057b0a0796e4.pdf; date of access May 21, 2021.

24 Indrani Gupta, "Relying on Serendipity is not Enough," *Indian Economic Review* 55, 125–147 (2020). https://link.springer.com/article/10.1007/s41775-020-00091-5; date of access July 2, 2021. NSS 75th round data quoted in Gupta's paper shows the heavy dependence on the private sector. In respect of ailments, only 30 per cent accessed public facilities, while in respect of hospitalizations, 42 per cent accessed public facilities.

25 Jishnu Das, Benjamin Daniel, Monisha Ashok, Eun-Young Shim, and Karthik Muralidharan, "Two Indias: The Structure of Primary Health Care Markets in Rural Indian Villages with Implications for Policy," *Social Science and Medicine*, 15 June 2020.

26 Indrani Gupta, "Relying on Serendipity is not Enough," *Indian Economic Review* 55, 125–147 (2020). https://link.springer.com/article/10.1007/s41775-020-00091-5; date of access July 2, 2021. Each CHC is required to have a surgeon, physician, gynaecologist, and paediatrician. Only 55 per cent have functional X-ray machines, 45 per cent lack habitable accommodation for

specialist doctors, and less than 40 per cent have specialist doctors staying in them. There is also a 65 per cent shortage of radiographers (which means that diagnostic equipment lies idle) and a 45 per cent shortage of lab technicians (which means that several diseases go undetected) at these centres.

27 "Social Infrastructure, Employment and Human Development," Chapter 10, *Economic Survey, 2019–20*, Ministry of Finance, *Government of India*, 2020.

28 See for examples i) "Government Rajendra Hospital Lies in Utter Neglect", *The Tribune*, 12 August2018 ii) "Neglected by Authorities, this Government Hospital in Bihar is on the Verge of Collapse," *ANI*, 22 June 2019. iii) "Government Hospital in Utter State of Neglect," *The Hindu*, 19 April 2019.

29 Payal Hathi and Nikhil Srivastav, "Why a Dangerous Lack of Hygiene Persists in Government Hospitals – Caste Prejudice and Infection," *Economic & Political Weekly*, vol. 55, Issue no. 16, 18 April 2020. The paper concludes that a major contributory factor for this malaise is the deep caste prejudice against cleaners. This prevents the professionalization of their work, leaving them overburdened and under-equipped to maintain standards of hygiene. Casteist notions of cleanliness also weaken the rigorous implementation of infection control measures by hospital staff.

30 Meeta, Rajiv Lochan, "Need for Protocols in Public Health," *Economic & Political Weekly*, Vol. 150, Issue no. 12, 21 March 2015.

31 Anne Mills, Arnab Acharya, and Timothy Powell-Jackson, "An Assessment of the Quality of Primary Health Care in India," *Economic & Political Weekly*, Vol. 48, Issue No. 19, 11 May 2013. Also see, Priyanka Pulla, "Why are Women Dying in India's Sterilization Camps?" *Family Planning BMJ*, 2014.

32 Gupta, I., 2020.

33 (i) Vikas Bajpai, "National Health Policy, 2017 – Revealing Public Health Chicanery," *Economic & Political Weekly*, Vol. III, no. 28, 14 July 2018. (ii) Also see, "Atmanirbhar Bharat Package Subsidises Private Sector and Plans for the Rich," Oxfam India, 20 May 2020. https://www.oxfamindia.org/press-release/ atmanirbhar-bharat-package-subsidises-private-sector-and-plans-rich; date of access May 10, 2021.

34 Arvind Panagariya, Chapter 19, "India – The Emerging Giant", *Oxford University Press*, 2008.

35 Oomen C. Kurian, "Running to Stand Still: Healthcare in India in 2021," *Health Express, ORF*, 4 January 2021.

36 Abhay Shukla, "Public Health systems and Privatised Agendas," *Economic & Political Weekly*, Vol. LIV, No. 17, 27 April 2019.

37 Vikas Bajpai, "National Health Policy, 2017 – Revealing Public Health Chicanery," *Economic & Political Weekly*, Vol. III, no. 28, 14 July 2018.

38 Indrani Gupta, "India: International Health Care System Profiles," *The Commonwealth Fund*, June 5, 2020. Out-of-pocket payments have been the primary means of funding healthcare, accounting for 65 per cent of total health expenditures. Also see, "Household Health Expenditures in India (2013–14)," December 2016, Ministry of Health and Family Welfare. https://main.mohfw. gov.in/sites/default/files/38300411751489562625.pdf

39 Monica Das Gupta, et al, "How might India's Public Health Systems be Strengthened? Lessons from Tamilnadu," *Economic & Political Weekly*, Vol. 45, No. 10, pp. 46–60, 6–10 March 2010.

40 Expert bodies including the High Level Expert Group set up by the Planning Commission (2011) and the High Level Group of Health Sector (2019) have observed that a focus on prevention and early management of health problems can reduce the need for complicated specialist care provided at the tertiary level.

41 "National Health Profile," Central Bureau of Health Intelligence, *Government of India*, 2019.
42 Abhijit Banerjee, *Juggernaut Books*, 2019.
43 Indrani Gupta, *The Commonwealth Fund*, 2020. The paper estimates that out-of-pocket payments have been the primary means of funding health care, accounting for 65 per cent of total health expenditures.
44 (i) Kavvya Agarwal, "Rural Healthcare in India – a Boon or Bane?" *Oxfam India*, 25 July 2019.
https://www.oxfamindia.org/blog/rural-healthcare-in-india?gclid=Cj0KCQjwvvj5BRDkARIsAGD9vlL9dJy6bW_Yfd9g6zq9k7VI7_BRkCjmupz869ah-KsldUthI8T5bssaAh1SEALw_wcB; date of access May 10, 2021 (ii) Also see, Sakthivel Selvaraj, Habib Hasan Farooqui, and Anup Karan, "Quantifying the Financial Burden of Households' Out-of-pocket Payments on Medicines in India: A Repeated Cross-sectional Analysis of National Sample Survey Data, 1994–2014," *BMJ Open*, 2018. https://bmjopen.bmj.com/content/8/5/e018020; date of access May 15, 2021.
45 Gillian Porter and Nathan Grills, "Medication Misuse in India: A Major Public Health Issue," *Journal of Public Health*, Vol. 38, Issue 2, pp. e-150 – e-157, 2016.
46 Abhijit Banerjee, "A Note on Healthcare," What the Economy Needs Now, *Juggernaut Books*, 2019.
47 Shailendra Kumar Hooda, "Decoding Ayushman Bharat, a Political Economy Perspective," *Economic & Political Weekly*, Vol LV, No. 25, 20 June 2020. The allocation towards the Wellness Centres constitutes a meagre share of 3–4 per cent of the National Health Mission budget.
48 Rochana Kamawanee, "ASHA's Health Services – Social Service or Care Work," *Economic and Political Weekly*, Vol. LIV, No. 49, 14 December 2019.
49 Nilanjan Mondal and Manoj V. Murhekar, "Factors Associated with low Performance of ASHA Workers Regarding Maternal Care in Howrah District, West Bengal, 2015–16: An Unmatched Control Study," *CEGH*, Vol. 6, pp. 21–28, 1 March 2018.
50 National Family Health Survey, "NFHS-5 (2019–21) Factsheets," Ministry of Health and Family Welfare, *Government of India*, http://rchiips.org/nfhs/; date of access March 9, 2022.
51 National Family Health Survey, "NFHS-5 (2019–21) Factsheets," Ministry of Health and Family Welfare, *Government of India*, http://rchiips.org/nfhs/; date of access March 9, 2022.
52 Prachi Salve, 2018.
53 "Pradhan Mantri Matru Vandana Yojana (PMMVY)," Government of India, 2017. https://wcd.nic.in/sites/default/files/PMMVY%20Scheme%20Implemetation%20Guidelines%20._0.pdf; date of access April 5, 2020.
54 National Family Health Survey, "NFHS-5 (2019–21) Factsheets," Ministry of Health and Family Welfare, *Government of India*, http://rchiips.org/nfhs/; date of access March 9, 2022.
55 "National Family Health Survey (NFHS-4), 2015–16: India," International Institute for Population Sciences (IIPS) and ICF. http://rchiips.org/NFHS/NFHS-4Reports/India.pdf.
56 Y. Quarishi, The Population Myth, *Harper Collins*, 2021.
57 National Family Health Survey, "NFHS-5 (2019–21) Factsheets," Ministry of Health and Family Welfare, *Government of India*, http://rchiips.org/nfhs/; date of access March 9, 2022.
58 Dasgupta, R., Chaand, I., and Barla, K. R., "The Slippery Slope of Child Feeding Practices in India," *Indian Paediatrics*, Vol. 55, pp. 284–86, 02 May 2018.

https://www.indianpediatrics.net/apr2018/apr-284-286.htm; date of access May 12, 2021.

59 Monica Das Gupta, et al, 2010.

60 Abhijit Banerjee, 2019.

61 Indrani Gupta, 2020.

62 Sanjiv Kumar, Vinay Bothra, and Dilip Singh Maireban, "A Dedicated Public Health Cadre: Urgent and Critical to Improve Public Health in India," *Indian J. Community Medicine*, 41: 253–55, 3 November 2016.

63 i) Alvero Fuento, "How Does Cuba Manage to Achieve First-World Health Statistics?" *El Pais*, 10 February 2017. ii) C. William Keck and A Gail Reed, "Lessons for the Margins of Globalization: Appreciating the Cuban Health Paradox," *Journal of Public Health Policy*, 25(10) pp. 85–110, 2012.

64 This was noted by the Comptroller & Auditor General (CAG).

65 Abhijit Banerjee, "A Note on Healthcare," What the Economy Needs Now, *Juggernaut Books*, 2019.

66 Abhay Shukla, 2019.

67 Dipa Sinha, "Rs 1.3 Lakh Crore – a.k.a. What's Expected of the Health Budget This Year," *Wire*, 25 January 2021. https://thewire.in/health/budget-2021-health-expectations. Ayushman Bharat utilization (for hospitalization among the poor) declined by 64 per cent during the early lockdown, and by 51 per cent during the full 10-week lockdown. The National Health Mission data suggests immunization, routine check-ups of pregnant women and care for serious conditions and communicable diseases also declined during the lockdown period.

68 Vikas Bajpai, 2020.

69 Abhijit Banerjee, 2019.

70 Amit Sengupta, "Universal Health Care in India," Occasional Paper, No. 19, *Municipal Services Project*, 2013.

71 Zia Haq, "Finance Panel Focus on Raising Health Spending," *Hindustan Times*, 8 July 2020.

72 Union Budgets, 2006–07 to 2020–21, Ministry of Health and Family Welfare, *Government of India*.

73 Shankar Prinja, Pankaj Bahuguna, Andrew D. Pinto, Atul Sharma, Gursimer Bharaj, Jaya Prasad Tripathi, Manmeet Kaur and Rajesh Kumar, "The Cost of Universal Health Coverage in India: A Model-based Estimate," *PLOS*, 7(1), 2013. The model estimates that the cost of universal healthcare delivery would be ₹1,713 per person per annum in India. Also see, "Dead Weight of Health Care," *Economic & Political Weekly*, Editorials, Vol. 51, Issue 36, 3 September 2016.

3

BATTLING MALNUTRITION AND FOOD INSECURITY

> The dual scourge of hunger and malnutrition will be truly vanquished not only when granaries are full, but also when people's basic health needs are met and women are given their rightful role in societies.
>
> **Gro Harlem Brundtland**, former Director-General, WHO, and former Prime Minister of Norway

The Context

India suffers from serious levels of hunger – amongst the worst in the world. The Global Hunger Index (GHI), 2021, ranked India 101st out of 116 countries in hunger severity.[1] It is, therefore, unsurprising that the capacity to resist and recover from disease gets compromised when nutrition is taken for granted; a significant contributory factor for poor health outcomes that we discussed in Chapter 2. The COVID-19 pandemic has added millions to those impoverished, worsening the hunger situation and pushing many more away from nutritious food.[2] Even countries with significantly lower per-capita incomes in sub-Saharan and East Africa, such as Ethiopia and Kenya, or countries in South Asia – Pakistan, Bangladesh, and Nepal – perform better than India on most hunger-related indicators.[3]

India's abysmal performance on hunger and nutrition-related indicators violates human rights and hugely impacts health, resulting in low productivity. Poor nutrition affects economic productivity directly as adults cannot work to their potential, and indirectly through lower cognitive development. Lower cognition and productivity take an immense toll at the individual, household, community, and country levels.[4] It is estimated that the annual loss in GDP associated with inadequate nutrition can be as much as 12 per cent in low-income countries.[5]

The stakes for India and its people in tackling food insecurity are high, and the COVID-19 pandemic has posed grave challenges. Improved health outcomes through strategies suggested in the previous chapter will come to nought if we fail to deal with the vital issues of food insecurity and hunger. So, we must ask why India has been singularly ineffective in combating

38   DOI: 10.4324/9781003346258-3

malnutrition and food insecurity. What has been going wrong? Why has the Targeted Public Distribution System (TPDS), the world's most extensive and one of the most expensive food security programmes globally, failed to bring down malnutrition levels? We seek answers to these questions, unravel the causes for the ineffectiveness of existing strategies, and suggest a set of transformative reforms to attain our nutrition goals.

High Malnutrition and Nutrition Imbalance

The harsh reality of malnutrition and hunger that emerges from the NFHS-5 survey is the grim picture of child malnutrition in India: as many as 35.5 per cent are stunted, 19.3 per cent 'wasted', while 32.1 per cent are underweight.[6] These results show little change from the data that emerged from the Comprehensive National Nutrition Survey, 2019 (CNNS).[7] The outcomes sharply contrast with indicators in other emerging economies such as Brazil, China, and Mexico, where these percentages are in the single digits.[8] Moreover, stunting in early life has long-term deleterious effects on health, physical and cognitive development, learning, and earning potential.[9]

Though malnutrition lessens somewhat as the child grows, it persists into adolescence and adulthood. Therefore, there is little surprise that the CNNS survey shows that 23 per cent of women and 20 per cent of men are underweight.[10] There are urban-rural differences and wide variances across states, socio-economic groups, and income levels – for example, Jharkhand and Bihar have the highest proportion, over 30 per cent, of underweight women.

In contrast, obesity is increasing among higher-income groups – around 20 per cent of women and men are overweight.[11]

It is not only malnutrition that is a cause for worry; massive nutritional and diet imbalances also exist. Close to 60 per cent of children have some degree of anaemia, while over 50 per cent of women and over 20 per cent of men in the age group of 15–49 years in India are anaemic. The prevalence of anaemia among women is 60 per cent or more in Jharkhand, Haryana, West Bengal, Bihar, and Andhra Pradesh.[12] An unexpected finding of the latest National NFHS-5 survey is the high prevalence of iron deficiency leading to anaemia even among wealthier households and cutting across all age groups.[13]

Apart from anaemia, there are other significant nutritional imbalances in the Indian diet. Less than half the population consumes leafy vegetables, pulses, or milk. Very few consume chicken, meat, fish, or eggs daily. The most prominent deficiency in the diet is fruit and milk or curd.[14]

One would have expected that, as incomes rise, nutritional imbalances would begin waning. But, on the contrary, as households get affluent, they abandon unprocessed foods and healthier cereals like millets, which are considered 'inferior' foods, for processed foods.[15] A complex set of inter-related factors can explain this shift in dietary intake – lifestyle changes, more eating outside the home, changes in expenditure patterns and occupation structure, and demographic changes.[16]

These dietary shifts in India reflect the trend the world over and should not surprise us. However, India's giant puzzle is not this dietary transition but that nutrition indicators have seen little improvement over recent decades. As Angus Deaton and Jean Drèze observe, despite an increase in incomes and steady growth over 25 years, ending in 2010, there was a decline in the calorie intake of India's average household. And, since then, the country has seen only a modest increase.[17]

Along with the slow improvement in food-intake indicators, calorie deficiency is of particular concern. The average Indian consumes about 2,225 calories a day, about 10 per cent less than recommended. The bottom 25 per cent consume only 1,800 calories and are thus undernourished. Nutrition imbalances compound the problem of calorie deficiency. While Indians should be getting 850 calories from carbohydrates, they consume 1,200 calories, and while they should be obtaining 900 calories from protein sources, they get only 310 calories. Generally speaking, Indians consume too much rice and flour and not enough complex carbohydrates or protein.[18] One reason for this dietary imbalance is the vast amounts of rice and wheat distributed through the public distribution system. This imbalance may also partially explain the high percentage of underweight children, wasting, stunting, and anaemia.

These large calorie deficits result in one of the world's worst anthropometric indicators. Stunting levels are so acute that children in India remain among the shortest in the world.[19] Malnutrition and nutrition imbalances alone may not explain this short stature; neither do genetic factors. Two scholars in the UK measured the heights of young Indian children born and raised in England and compared them with children in India, and found they were taller; in fact, as tall as white British children.[20] An improved environment shows dramatically improved results in child development. A recent study by Diane Coffey and Dean Spears points out that open defecation, leading to frequent gastrointestinal infections, is a significant factor that keeps children from growing to their full height potential in India.[21]

The poor indicators among children continue into adulthood. Underweight, stunted, and wasted children grow up to be adults who do not reach their height potential. The adult height of Indians has improved very slowly, even in comparison with most emerging countries. Women have fared particularly poorly. Income alone does not explain this poor outcome; stunting and wasting in sub-Saharan Africa are only half of that in India. Indians tend to be small because they and their parents did not get as much nourishment as required and did not have the advantage of general environmental health.

There are other disturbing signs. For example, maternal nutrition is so poor that the average Indian woman completes her pregnancy weighing less than the average woman in sub-Saharan Africa does at the beginning of pregnancy. Moreover, even though adult height is generally increasing (though very slowly in India), men in India are becoming taller faster than women. This divergence strongly suggests discrimination against the girl child in health and nutrition.

India's pathetic nutritional outcomes reflect poor early-life health, maternal malnutrition, environmental conditions, and people's choices. Failure to reach one's genetic potential as a child leads to a range of adverse consequences throughout life. A child who gets proper nutrients in utero or during early childhood will earn more money every year of his or her life. Taller, healthier individuals are likely to be more productive in environments – such as in agriculture – where physical strength matters.[22]

Inextricable Linkage of Poverty and Malnutrition

We have noted that Indian household diets have the twin problems of calorie deficits and eating the wrong foods, especially in low-income households. Why are low-income families not getting adequate nutrition and balanced diets? Is income poverty the main factor? To understand this better, let us go back to Birsa and Rasika and see what is happening in their lives.

> Birsa and Rasika work as agricultural labourers, and by its very nature, the work is intermittent. They, along with their three children, are acutely malnourished. The family's staple diet consists of rice and watery lentils spiked with chillies. The quantities they eat are what they are used to, and they do not particularly crave more food, though they miss the sweets consumed at festival times. Nobody has told them that they are undernourished; they look about the same as others in their local community. In the last three months, Rasika got over 80 days of wages under the government's employment guarantee programme. The agricultural season was also good, which meant that Birsa earned well. So, after paying off their loans, they were able to save ₹5000. But they spent this extra money very quickly. They spent a portion on new clothes to wear at the harvest festival. Birsa also bought sweets from the local shop. Some of the extra money went into buying alcohol, a little more than usual. A significant purchase by Birsa was a second-hand mobile phone. It did not occur to either Birsa or Rasika to buy extra food or ensure better nourishment for the family.

So, why did Birsa and Rasika not spend the extra money on nourishing their family? Nobel laureate economists Abhijit Banerjee and Esther Duflo explain this phenomenon. They suggest that hunger and poverty are, perhaps, incorrectly assumed to go hand in hand. The inability of the poor to feed themselves properly is one of the most frequently cited root causes of a poverty trap. The idea is simple but powerful: the poor cannot afford to eat enough, making them less productive and keeping them poor. But one hidden assumption is that the poor eat as much as they need to. The reality is that they do not. The typical poor household could spend 30 per cent more on food than it does if it completely stops expenditure on alcohol, tobacco, and festivals. Yet, this is impossible and unrealistic to expect. In times of stress (e.g., unemployment), 'healthy' or 'wholesome' food is not high on anyone's list of priorities. Instead, you crave tasty food. Even ordinarily, people often choose food based on taste rather than nutritional value. The poor also have other overriding priorities and spend their money on non-food items. For example, as life can be pretty dull in a village, it is easy to see why a poor person like Birsa may prefer to spend on a TV or a cell phone rather than more food. This behaviour may explain why food spending has not been going up in lower-income households.[23]

Most adults, even the indigent, may, in theory, be outside the nutrition poverty trap zone: they could eat as much as needed to be physically productive if they spent their money on food and with the right nutritional mix. But, as we saw in Birsa's case, the poor do not always eat more or any better when their income goes up; there are too many other pressures and desires competing with food. Some economists have characterized such behaviour as 'voluntary hunger' or 'squeezing' the food budget.[24,25] However, a squeeze should have led to the poor shifting to cheaper foods, while the opposite occurred. Instead, Birsa and Rasika buy expensive sweets when they get additional income.[26] Though there may be some merit in the 'squeeze' argument, other contributory factors exist, such as the perception of low-income families, like Birsa's, of different 'pressing' needs. The fact remains that, despite increased food availability, the poor seem to be eating less or, at best, only marginally more when incomes rise. 'Hidden' hunger is what, in my view, best describes the behaviour that Birsa's family exhibits. This discussion should not lead us to incorrectly conclude that income poverty is not a key factor to explain the calorie energy deficits in poor households; we are only suggesting that low-income families have other pressing needs besides food. The causality could also be the other way around; undernutrition perpetuates poverty by adversely impacting the productive capacity of individuals.

As we move beyond Birsa's family to those with higher incomes, we have noted that they face different nutritional deficits due to the rising consumption of processed foods and refined food grains. This change in the food basket results in an epidemiological transition from infectious disease dominance to the rise in non-communicable diseases like cardiovascular diseases, strokes, diabetes, and cancer.

An Ineffective PDS

In the face of such acute and continued prevalence of malnutrition and hunger, the government response through the supply of vast quantities of food appears, at first glance, to be the correct strategy. India has the world's most extensive food security programme globally – the Targeted Public Distribution System. This programme has been the mainstay of the government's effort to boost the food intake of poor households. The legal underpinning for the TPDS, the National Food Security Act, 2013, provides coverage for about two-thirds of the population, or as many as 250 million households. This coverage is far beyond the FAO's estimate of the under-nourished population at 194.6 million or roughly 40 million families, even after accounting for the additional number of families that may have been malnourished following the COVID-19 pandemic.[27] But, even with this extensive coverage, why has the programme not provided food security?

The focus of TPDS has been on the provision of large quantities of cereal, premised on the belief that the poor would get food security and become productive members of society with adequate supplies of cheap grain. Households identified as the neediest are covered under the Antyodaya Anna Yojana and are provided 35 kg of food grains per month. Households with higher income but possessing Below the Poverty Line (BPL) cards are entitled to receive 5 kg of food grain for each family member per month. Both Antyodaya and BPL households are supplied grains at heavily subsidized prices: ₹3 per kg of rice, and ₹2 per kg of wheat. The annual allocation under TPDS is a massive 60 million tonnes of food grains (including the allocation to Above Poverty Line (APL) households).[28]

India spends an enormous amount for subsidizing this massive quantity of food grains.[29] It should come as no surprise that food budgets have risen exponentially. The 2020–21 budget allocation for the scheme was ₹1,900 billion. If fully accounted for, independent estimates suggest the annual fiscal requirement is closer to ₹3,000 billion.[30] The food subsidy budget has grown over ten-fold in just about 12 years from a relatively modest ₹250 billion in 2007–08. This is especially worrisome because there is no clear evidence that this monumental increase has significantly contributed to enhancing the food security of poor households. The growing mountains of food stocks and food budgets are increasingly becoming fiscally unsustainable.

More critically, the TPDS suffers from chronic inefficiency and corruption. The food procurement and distribution system are wasteful and needlessly gobbles up a lot of money. Surjit Bhalla, a vocal critic of the TPDS, estimates that the government spends ₹7 to transfer ₹1 to the poor.[31] According to Ashok Gulati, a prominent agriculture economist, the quantum of TPDS grain stolen and diverted to the open market could be as high as 40–50 per cent.[32] While there is no recent evaluation of PDS leakages, there is anecdotal evidence that at least in some states, leakages may have come down.[33] However, at the country level, leakages and diversion of PDS grain into the open market remain sizeable.

Apart from corruption and leakages, there are other significant problems with the TPDS. Such wide coverage of households can hardly be termed 'targeted'. And even with such high coverage, the government even in normal years sit on a mountain of grain, and the media continues to report on the humungous quantity of food grains stored and rotting in the open.

More worryingly, the programme's impact on nutrition has been negligible. According to a study by the government's NITI Aayog, the public distribution system has negatively impacted the dietary composition of households, by promoting excess cereal intake to the detriment of other essential nutrients. The study further concludes that the programme does not substantially influence food expenditure among low-income families.[34] Other studies have corroborated this conclusion. For example, Neeraj Kaushal and Felix Muchomba have demonstrated that the programme has a negligible impact on micro-nutrient consumption.[35]

Other fundamental problems have emerged in recent times. Critics argue that the present Minimum Support Price (MSP) procurement regime has led to an imbalance in cultivation, especially in states like Punjab and Haryana. Rice and wheat occupy less than 30 per cent of the country's food basket but are the most important focus of MSP support. As the entire MSP benefits only 30 per cent of farmers, the remaining 70 per cent of farmers who grow pulses, oilseeds, spices, fruit, vegetables, cotton, sugar cane, and the like, do not derive any benefit from food subsidy. Moreover, the present procurement system has MSPs fixed at well above the market prices. Under the TPDS, the supply of grains is at highly subsidized prices, which results in depressing open market prices, which means that the gap between the MSP and market prices has progressively widened. Consequently, the government has been caught in a vicious cycle, needing to procure larger quantities of rice and wheat each year, much above the TPDS requirement, leading to excess food grain stock.[36] However, the year 2022 has been exceptional. The heatwave resulted in significantly lower wheat production. Further, the global wheat supply chain disruptions caused by the Ukraine war led to an increase in market prices, resulting in higher private sector procurement and consequently significantly reduced procurement of wheat under MSP. And yet the government ended the season with wheat stocks above the buffer stock norms.

In summary, several TPDS elements have created a singularly pernicious and perverse market impact. It was largely to address this crisis arising from progressively higher food grains procurement leading to humungous and unmanageable stocks and mounting food subsidies that the central government had notified three farm laws in May 2020. Several farmer groups had vociferously opposed these legislations. In their view, the laws would have only paved the way for a few select large corporates to dominate the market and squeeze them. The government argued that the three legislations would expand farmers' choices and make transactions more open and transparent. The unvoiced expectation of the government was that opening up the market to private players would reduce the procurement burden of the government. However, whatever their merits, the new farm laws would not have fundamentally increased farm incomes.[37] In the face of persistent and sustained farmer protests, the government repealed all the farm laws in December 2021.[38] We will address the issue raised by the farm laws again in Chapter 6.

Moreover, MSP's core issue will remain unresolved as long as there is a wide divergence between the MSP and market prices. At the same time, we should not conclude that, ideally, the government should abandon the TPDS. Undoubtedly, access to food at affordable prices is a vital element of the strategy for tackling food insecurity. Critical reforms can make the system efficient and transparent and release much-needed funds for neglected nutrition interventions.[39] We explore these strategies in the subsequent sections.

Changing Policy Mindsets

The first step in the reform process is for our policymakers to rid themselves of the mindset that grain supply alone can tackle malnourishment and instead use evidence-based mechanisms to determine policy interventions. We need a comprehensive and robust strategy. While overt hunger is well understood, the prevalence of hidden hunger, especially among young children, requires more detailed analysis. The typical Indian diet is very frugal and based heavily on cereals and legumes. Relatively expensive items such as milk, eggs, meat, fruit, and vegetables are the principal sources of vitamins and minerals. While calorie deficiency is an essential aspect of nutritional deprivation, we need to pay close attention to other food deprivation aspects, such as lack of vitamins and minerals, fat consumption, and diet diversity. Nutrition requires a host of additional inputs not adequately measured by total calories, including a range of micronutrients and a varied diet. For example, children in poor households have a substantial fat deficit. Contrary to the general view that fat is unhealthy, it is well-established that fat helps children achieve adequate calorie intake; it is calorie-dense, facilitates the absorption of various nutrients, and is helpful for brain development.[40]

In contrast to the costly cereal distribution system, some other ways to improve nutrition would be way more cost-effective. Around 25 per cent of both men and women are anaemic. Providing iron supplements would help men in labour-intensive work, and a reduction in anaemia can quickly improve maternal health. Other cost-effective measures include fortifying foods, domiciliary counselling, the widespread use of the four-in-one package (de-worming, vitamin A, iron, and iodized salt) in schools and anganwadis, and promoting the consumption of locally grown green leafy vegetables. However, a word of caution: too much focus on micronutrients and fortification should not allow the fundamental issue of poverty to drop away from our policy discourse. Indeed, the sociologist Aya Kimura argues that 'nutritionism' could make a complex food problem seem manageable and controllable by looking at it only as a nutrition problem. The central focus must remain on the general lack of food and calories, especially the right kind of calories.[41]

Focusing on Child and Mother

As we explore alternate cost-effective strategies for combating malnutrition, we need to recognize that the societal returns of investing in young children and women are disproportionately high. Therefore, there is considerable merit in strengthening the POSHAN Abhiyan, the central government's flagship programme to improve nutritional outcomes for children, pregnant women, and lactating mothers. For the implementation of POSHAN Abhiyan the four-point strategy/pillars of the mission that have been set are:

- Inter-sectoral convergence for better service delivery
- Use of technology (ICT) for real-time growth monitoring and tracking of women and children
- Intensified health and nutrition services for the first 1,000 days
- Jan Andolan (people's movement).

The POSHAN Abhiyan has set ambitious goals.[42] It recognizes the need to go beyond the food-centric approach and includes healthcare measures, birth spacing, exclusive breastfeeding, and complementary foods.

While the POSHAN Abhiyan's strategic direction is on the right track, budgetary allocations have remained minimal and must be enhanced manyfold to make an impact. In this context, there is a need to review the Integrated Child Development Services (ICDS) programme in its entirety. This world's most extensive child services programme has remained food-centric and has neglected service quality and other critical factors impacting nutrition. A significant limitation in implementing nutrition programmes is that we do not know how successful interventions have been until we get survey results. Credible information forms the fulcrum for informed implementation. Official data is voluminous but lacks credibility, and programmes like POSHAN Abhiyan will continue to be ineffective until they can access the actual ground situation. To better understand the ground reality, third-party surveys are needed. Civil society institutions working at the grassroots and who know the ground reality must be viewed as partners to improve the quality of services. Prompt dissemination of feedback received would enable programme managers to correct performance in poorly performing areas. (We discuss ways to improve the effectiveness of the ICDS and POSHAN Abhiyan in Chapter 4.)

Communication Is the Key

A vital issue impacting the service quality of nutrition programmes is the lack of awareness among households on improving the quantity, quality, and diversity of their diets. Spending on communication and awareness is mostly considered peripheral to these programmes. Funds for such activities often remain limited; apart from budget inadequacy, there is a failure to realize that communication is serious business and requires professional expertise. Development programmes have often fallen short of their targets, as the fundamental ideas could not be 'sold' to the people. Much greater effort is required to change the attitudes and behaviour of the target population, as well as policymakers and agenda setters. As in health education, we need an imaginative and substantial 'Information, Education, and Communication' (IEC) campaign on a sustained basis to effect the required change in the nutrition behaviour of households. There is evidence that intensive communication and awareness-building programmes can significantly improve nutritional outcomes. For example, a six-month campaign on a typical rural audience found that intensive communication resulted in a dramatic rise in the frequency of health check-ups of children and mothers, improved participation in supplementary nutrition, Vitamin A consumption, and increased immunization. This success was remarkable as, in the past, this very same audience had more belief in faith-based healing, had multiple prejudices, and had little understanding of the link between the diet/activity of mothers and children's health.[43]

In addition to an IEC campaign, community engagement through front-line workers – ANMs, ASHA, and anganwadi workers – is also required. They must carry out a mandatory annual health-nutrition screening across the country for each poor household. Those identified as being affected by low nutrition levels, such as households with stunted children, anaemic women, and chronically underweight adults, should receive continuous follow-up visits. In addition, nutrition counselling, guidance, and nutrition monitoring must become part of the nutrition strategy. Besides household screening and home visits, school-based health check-ups could identify anaemic and underweight children and encourage them and their parents to adopt healthy food habits. Along with this, there is a need for counselling parents and the education of adolescent girls.

Non-poor households also need counselling and education. India is in the throes of a double burden of malnutrition. This malnutrition paradox, the coexistence of undernutrition and obesity, primarily due to unhealthy dietary practices, can be addressed through sustained IEC campaigns. Well-designed, effective social media campaigns and regular home visits are cost-effective and can substantially improve nutritional outcomes.

Transforming the TPDS

Our food and nutrition strategies must address our public distribution system's flaws, which gobbles up a sizeable chunk of our food and nutrition budget. We have noted that, with such extensive coverage, the present 'targeted' system targets nobody. For that reason, and because of exclusion errors, experts have recommended reverting to the near-universal public distribution system that India had in place until 1997. Importantly, such a universal system is unlikely to cost the exchequer considerably more than it does now.[44] This arrangement would mean going back to a system where ration cards are issued to all households who request them. In tandem, 30 per cent of the poor households – identified based on our Chapter 1 guidelines – would continue to be supplied rice and wheat at very highly subsidized rates.[45] The government could issue grain to poor households at 20 per cent of the economic cost: around ₹5 and ₹7 per kg for wheat and rice. All other families could enrol themselves and become part of the TPDS system and be issued grains at 50 per cent of market prices, say at ₹10 and ₹15 per kg for wheat and rice, respectively.

Restoration of the universal system, but at higher issue prices to the non-poor households, will also reduce the arbitrage with market prices and decrease the propensity to cheat and divert grains. Another benefit would be that higher issue prices would positively influence market prices, leading to higher cash realization for farmers and reducing pressures on the government to purchase grain. An increase in issue prices is unlikely to negatively impact the food grain offtake by households; there is evidence that cereal consumption does not fall when prices rise.[46]

Food grains procured under this reformed TPDS should be at a 'floor price' to reduce cropping distortions, resulting in a more balanced and sustainable agricultural cropping system, besides freeing up sizeable food subsidy budgets. These suggested reforms for a universal public distribution system, including guidance on the procurement price, align with the Abhijit Sen Committee's recommendations on the long-term grain policy.[47] Over time, the aim should be to better align the MSP to Market prices, so that the present system which leads to excess procurement leading to huge mountains of surplus food grain stocks becomes manageable. To compensate farmers for rationalizing the MSPs of wheat and rice, the government may have to provide additional cash transfers – beyond the existing PM Kisan Samman Nidh – to rice and wheat farmers. In the short term, the government must also reduce its excess stocks through the following three measures, provide a portion of the remuneration under the National Rural Employment Guarantee programme in the form of food grains, export all three-year-old food grains stock through tenders as a large portion of these grains would have deteriorated in quality, and sell the remaining excess stocks in the open market. These steps would also result in an estimated savings of ₹1,500 billion in the food subsidy budget. Another way to increase private sector participation and limit government procurement would be to implement a modified version of the Bhavantar Bhugtan (price difference compensation) scheme piloted by the government of Madhya Pradesh in 2017, where private procurers got reimbursed the difference between the market price and the MSP.[48] The scheme was discarded by the next government although – with tweaking of the protocols to prevent misuse – this approach has considerable merit. Promoting private sector participation would significantly reduce the procurement and storage cost of government operations.

To streamline the TPDS, we also need to ensure all eligible households are covered. The expectation that the introduction of Aadhar cards would correct the exclusion errors and make it easy for families to access ration cards, and curb the menace of 'bogus' cards, has not been fulfilled. One difficulty is that, while ration cards are family cards, Aadhar numbers are identities given to individual persons. However, the introduction of digital ration cards containing Aadhar numbers would enhance the system's transparency. Once the database is digitized, it should be possible for any individual to get an entitlement irrespective of where she is residing. This system is technologically feasible and only requires the ration card to be adapted to permit both portability and divisibility of entitlements.[49] The exclusion of migrant labour from TPDS, a major issue observed during the COVID-19 pandemic, would also be resolved with such digitization.

Radical reforms in the TPDS are long overdue. A few economists, such as Surjit Bhalla, Ashok Gulati, and Bharat Ramaswami have even suggested conditional cash transfers to replace the TPDS. However, while there may be theoretical justification favouring cash transfers, there is no road map advocated by them on the way forward to dismantling the well-established TPDS. Global experience suggests cash transfers have to be viewed in context and may not be a silver bullet in all situations.[50] We do not advocate such a radical measure as, in any case, abolishing the TPDS is unlikely to get support in Parliament.

Furthermore, cash transfers tend to erode in value over time. Therefore, a re-worked near-universal public distribution system may work best in the present Indian context. Meanwhile, many improvements in the TPDS are possible, as shown by a few states such as Tamil Nadu and Chhattisgarh. Both these states have reduced leakages to only around 10 per cent against an average of 40 per cent at the national level through introducing transparency in distribution.

In re-designing food security programmes, the experiences of other countries are valuable. Bangladesh is an excellent example of a cost-effective food grain distribution system with a targeted approach.[51] It has adopted a broad food-nutrition strategy within a wider enabling environment of pro-poor economic growth that focuses on improving incomes, family planning, parental – particularly women's – education, and broader health access.[52] Brazil's Bolsa Familia Cash Support is one of the world's most extensive and successful cash transfer programmes to combat hunger through guaranteed food access. The programme has three main pillars: first, direct cash to poor and deprived families; second, linkage of the cash transfer to school attendance of children and health check-ups; and third, strengthening family-based agriculture to enhance food supply. Mexico's Progressa Cash Transfer Programme is another successful conditional cash transfer programme linked to human capital development. The programme gives mothers cash as an incentive to send their children to schools and health centres and conducts small group sessions on health and nutrition education.[53]

The poorest of the poor households, due to their income poverty, are not able to afford their family's food and nutrition requirements even after receiving the PDS supply of 35 kg per month. Therefore, there is considerable merit in providing such vulnerable households with a monthly basic income transfer.[54] We, therefore, strongly advocate that the entire savings in food subsidy be reallocated to providing ₹5,000 per month to households comprising the bottom consumption decile. In practical terms, these could comprise families identified under the Antyodaya Anna Yojana. We will discuss this income transfer further in our chapter on livelihoods.

A Multi-pronged Approach

The government must look at food and nutrition strategies with other related interventions. This is the crucial learning from successful cross-country experiences. More than just a reform of the public distribution system, India needs a multi-pronged approach to meet its Sustainable Development Goals, rather than the current food-centric sectoral approach. There are many facets to nutrition, as research shows. For instance, one study in India shows a positive association between education and calorie intake and underlines that small family size and experienced family members improve nutrition status.[55] Similarly, a large body of work has documented the interaction between nutrition and infection. Recurrent infection episodes without sufficient food or adequate recovery time are primary causes of stunting among children; if infections are less frequent or less severe, lower child malnutrition rates will prevail even if food intake is inadequate.

Access to clean and safe drinking water and sanitation is another crucial determinant of improved nutrition outcomes. The country is on the right track on drinking water, though there is a long way to go before we can ensure safe and adequate drinking water facilities at each home. Regarding sanitation in rural areas, official data suggests that over 90 per cent of rural households have a toilet in their homes. However, surveys show that toilet usage remains low even in villages declared 'open defecation free'. Many household members continue the practice of open defecation due to notions of ritual purity. The Swachh Bharat programme has focused on latrine construction without addressing the attitude towards latrine pits.[56] Communication campaigns for behaviour change on toilet use have been inadequate; as in the case of nutrition programmes, they must become integral to the programme. In urban slums, most households do not have toilets in their homes and, where they exist, are unconnected to a sewerage system. (We discuss the solutions to urban sanitation in Chapter 8.)

Other cross-sectoral interventions are necessary. There is strong evidence that if women are educated up to the secondary school level, they can improve the nutrition status of children and other household members. Conversely, women's disempowerment is a significant barrier to improving nutrition outcomes. Gender imbalances in India – as reflected in our adverse sex ratio, the subordinate social status of women, and prejudices leading to neglect of the girl child – must be urgently addressed. These gender issues also undermine the nutrition status of children in the household. Cultural attitudes militate against improved opportunities for women. (We discuss these vital gender issues in Chapter 7.)

Our strategy on multiple connected areas impacting malnutrition and food insecurity must remain centred around poor households and on programmes that can get families such as Birsa's out of the poverty trap. Abject poverty is associated with high levels of food insecurity and malnutrition. Had the decline in poverty been faster, calorie intake would likely have risen among underprivileged households, perhaps even on average. Growth in incomes must be significant and rapid for the country to see calorie energy deficits going down without any other major intervention. Thus, improved livelihoods for low-income families must occupy centre-stage in policy discourse and programmes designed for such targeted interventions. (We look at the design of such strategies in Chapter 6.)

Re-prioritizing Nutrition Budgets

We round up our discussion on this complex and intractable issue of food insecurity and malnutrition by focusing on reordering our priorities. Let's take a look at what research indicates. For example, a study finds that food transfers through public schooling are more useful than those through the public distribution system.[57] Yet, there is no social cost-benefit analysis or discussion in Parliament on the impact of existing schemes or the extent to which they have met their objectives.[58] By making the right choices in nutrition interventions, health, and education, and broadening the scope of our food security system, we can put to better use what we can save in food subsidies. Through reforms in the public distribution system, the savings in food subsidy can provide additional income to the poorest households who face acute food insecurity, enhance the POSHAN Abhiyan, provide nutrition education, and focus on other areas where nutrition interventions are sorely needed.

In allocating budgets, we must direct our attention on priority to states and districts with high malnutrition levels. Government capacity and bandwidth must be employed where it is most needed. Focusing on, say, the 200 worst-affected districts in the country will yield better returns than spreading resources thinly across the country. These districts must be allocated disproportionately higher budgets, enhanced human resources, and be closely monitored. Urban slums also need particular focus.

Our discussion has shown that issues of food security and nutrition are complex. The COVID-19 epidemic has sharpened the need to tackle hunger and malnutrition on an emergency footing. We need to change nutrition-related behaviour and dietary practices through education, nutrition information, and awareness. Additionally, we need to enhance incomes overall to ensure that all poor households have access to food with the required diversity. And the starting point for improving health and nutrition to ensure improvement across generations is the young child, the subject of the next chapter.

Notes

1 "India – Global Hunger Index, 2021", https://www.globalhungerindex.org/results.html; date of access December 8, 2021.
2 i) Rakesh Kochhar, "In the Pandemic, India's Middle Class Shrinks and Poverty Spreads While China Sees Smaller Changes," *Pew Research Center*, 18 March 2021. ii) Parthasarathi Biswas, "Covid-19 has Pushed Half of India's Poor Away from Nutritious Food: Report," *The Indian Express*, 14 April 2021.
3 "Global Hunger Index 2020: India Ranks 94 out of 107 Countries, Under Serious Category," *Indian Express*, 29 January 2021. Also see, Welthungerhilfe and Dublin, "2019 Global Hunger Index: The Challenge of Hunger and Climate Change," *Bonn: Concern Worldwide*. https://www.globalhungerindex.org/results.html.
4 Cesar G. Victora, Linda Adair, Carolin Fall, Pedro C. Hallal, Renaldo Martorell, Linda Riter, Harshpal Singh Sachdev, "Maternal and Child Undernutrition: Consequences for Adult Health and Human Capital," *Lancet*, Vol. 371 (9609) pp. 340–357, 2008.
5 Horton and Steckel, "Malnutrition – Global Economic Losses Attributable to Malnutrition, 1900–2000 and Projections to 2050," Assessment Paper, *Copenhagen Consensus on Human Challenges*, 2011. https://www.copenhagenconsensus.com/sites/default/files/malnutrition.pdf.
6 National Family Health Survey, "NFHS-5 (2019–21) Factsheets," Ministry of Health and Family Welfare, *Government of India*, http://rchiips.org/nfhs/; date of access March 9, 2022. Also see, Deshpande and Bhardwaj, "Here is What NFHS-5 Tells us About India", *Ashoka University*, 2021. https://ceda.ashoka.edu.in/here-is-what-nfhs-5-tells-us-about-india/, date of access March 8, 2022.
7 "Comprehensive National Nutrition Survey (CNNS), National Report," Ministry of Health and Family Welfare (MoHFW), *Government of India, UNICEF, and Population Council*, 2019. The CNNS survey showed little progress since the National Family Health Survey (NFHS-4) of 2015–16. Stunting declined from 38.4 per cent to 34.7 per cent, wasting from 21 per cent to 17.3 per cent, and underweight from 35.7 per cent to 33.4 per cent.
8 "Nutrition," Chapter 31, Strategy for New India @ 75, NITI Aayog, *Government of India*, November 2018. The comparative figures are: Brazil, stunting – 6.1 per cent, wasting – 1.6 per cent, China, stunting – 6.8 per cent, wasting – 2.1 per cent, and Mexico, stunting – 13.6 per cent, wasting – 1.6 per cent.
9 McGovern Mark E, Aditi Krishna, Victor M Aguayo, and SV Subramanian, "A Review of the Evidence Linking Child Stunting to Economic Outcomes," *International Journal of Epidemiology*, pp. 1171–1191, 2017. https://academic.oup.com/ije/article/46/4/1171/3095890.
10 CNNS, 2019.
11 Ibid.
12 Ibid.
13 National Family Health Survey, "NFHS-5 (2019–21) Factsheets," Ministry of Health and Family Welfare, *Government of India*, http://rchiips.org/nfhs/; date of access March 9, 2022.
14 Angus Deaton and Jean Drèze, "Food and Nutrition in India: Facts and Interpretations," *Economic & Political Weekly*, Vol. 44, Issue No. 7, 14 February 2009.

15 Prabha Pingali, Anaka Aiyar, Matthew Abraham, and Andaleep Rehman, "Transforming Food Systems for a Rising India," Chapter 4, Open Access, *Palgrave Macmillan*, 2019.
16 Angus Deaton and Jean Drèze, 2009.
17 Ibid.
18 Sanjiv Mehta, "To Get Health Right, India Must Focus on Nutrition," *Hindustan Times*, 2 April 2020.
19 Diane Coffey and Dean Spears, "Where India Goes", *Juggernaut Books*, 2017.
20 Caterina Alacevich and Alessandro Tarrozi, "It's Not Just the Genes: Ethnic Indians Grow Taller in the UK," *Scroll.in*, 24 January 2017.
21 Diane Coffey and Dean Spears, "Where India Goes", *Juggernaut Books*, 2017.
22 Caesar G. Victora, Linda Adair, Carolin Fall, Pedro C. Hallal, Renaldo Martorell, Linda Riter, and Harshpal Singh Sachdev, "Maternal and Child Undernutrition: Consequences for Adult Health and Human Capital," *Lancet*, Vol. 371 (9609) pp. 340–357, 2008.
23 Abhijit Banerjee and Esther Duflo, "A Billion Hungry People?" Chapter 2, Poor Economics, *Juggernaut Books*, 2011.
24 Pronab Sen, "Of Calories and Things," *Economic & Political Weekly*, Vol. 40, Issue No. 43, 22 October 2005. Pronab Sen suggests that that the food budget may have got squeezed out because the cost of meeting the minimum non-food requirements increased. Deaton and Drèze, however, point out that in the event of such a squeeze, one would expect low-income households to switch towards cheaper calories. But the opposite occurred with poor families making a modest switch towards more expensive calories, away from cereals and other sources of cheap energy.
25 S.K. Srivastava and Ramesh Chand, "Tracking Transition in Calorie Intake Among Indian Households: Insights and Policy Implications", *Agricultural Economics Research Review*, Vol. 30 (No.1), pp 23–35, January–June 2017. This paper suggests that a squeezed food budget, due to "voluntary hunger" has been the major factor responsible for the decline in calorie intake from 1993–94 to 2004–05, while a sufficiently large increase in total and food expenditure along with improvement in the PDS after 2004–05 triggered an uptick in energy intake.
26 Angus Deaton and Jean Drèze, 2009.
27 "The State of Food Insecurity in the World," *FAO*, 2015.
28 "TPDS", Department of Food and Public Distribution, *Government of India*. https://dfpd.gov.in/pds-pds.htm.; date of access May 8, 2021. APL households are also issued food grains at highly subsidized rates of ₹8.30 per kg for rice and ₹6.10 per kg for wheat.
29 Siraj Hussain and Jugal Mohapatra, "Once Again the Centre has Excess Wheat, Rice Stocks: What Are its Options?" *The Wire*, 10 April 2021. https://thewire.in/agriculture/once-again-the-centre-has-excess-wheat-rice-stocks-what-are-its-options; date of access April 11, 2021.
30 Data sources: Ministry of Finance, Government of India budget documents, and information obtained from the Food Corporation of India. The food subsidy budget grew exponentially from a relatively modest ₹250 billion in 2007–8 to ₹1,137 billion in 2014–15, and to ₹1,900 billion in 2020–21. Two decades ago the economic cost of procuring wheat and rice was ₹853 and ₹1,098 per qtl., respectively. This roughly doubled by 2011–12. By 2020–21 the economic cost had shot up to ₹2,624 per qtl. for wheat and ₹3,727 per qtl. for rice. The increase since 2001–02 has been 2.7 times for wheat and 3.7 times for rice. During this period, there has been a rapid increase in the quantum of rice and wheat procured under minimum support price operations. Procurement of rice increased from 16.4 million tonnes in 2002–03 to 44.4 million tonnes in 2018–19; a 170

per cent increase. Procurement of wheat was 19 million tonnes in 2002–03 and moved up to 35.8 million tonnes representing an 88 per cent increase. To finance these higher levels of procurement, and as food subsidies have not been released in time, borrowing by the Food Corporation of India has also grown exponentially. A major contributor to the high subsidy levels is the cost of borrowing. The average borrowing was limited to ₹288.3 billion in 2001–02, which shot up to a whopping ₹3,322.8 billion in 2019–20.

31 Bhalla, Surjit S., "Food, Hunger, and Nutrition in India: A Case of Redistributive Failure," Frontier Issues Brief submitted to the Brookings Institution's Ending Rural Hunger project, *Brookings Institution*, 2016 https://www.endingruralhunger. org/.; date of access April 15, 2021. By comparing food subsidy with estimates obtained from the National Sample Survey household expenditure in 2011–12, Bhalla estimates that the amount of the subsidy that made its way to the poor was less than 15 per cent.

32 i) Ashok Gulati and Shweta Saini, "Leakages from Public Distribution System (PDS) and the Way Forward," Working Paper, No. 294, *Indian Council for Research on International Economic Relations (ICRIER)*, New Delhi, 2015. https://www.econstor.eu/bitstream/10419/176312/1/icrier-wp-294.pdf; date of access August 2, 2021.
ii) A. Ganesh-Kumar, Ashok Gulati and Ralph Cummings Jr., "Food Grains Policy and Management in India: Responding to Today's Challenges and Opportunities," *Indira Gandhi Institute of Development Research, Mumbai and IFPRI, Washington, DC*, PP-056, 2007.

33 Siraj Hussain, Jugal Mohapatra, Labharthis can help Modi win UP. If that happens, PDS coverage is unlikely to shrink in India. https://theprint.in/opinion/labharthis-can-help-modi-win-up-if-that-happens-pds-coverage-is-unlikely-to-shrink-in-india/856240/; date of access March 11, 2022.

34 "Evaluation Study on Role of Public Distribution System in Shaping Household and Nutritional Security in India," Development Monitoring and Evaluation Office, NITI Aayog, Report No. 233, *Government of India*, 2016. https://niti. gov.in/writereaddata/files/document_publication/Final%20PDS%20Report-new.pdf; date of access May 2, 2021.

35 i) Neeraj Kaushal and Felix Muchomba, "Effect of Food Subsidies on Micronutrients Consumption," *Indian Journal of Human Development*, Volume 10, issue 3: 317–335, December 2016. https://journals.sagepub.com/doi/10.1177/0973703016685668?icid=int.sj-full-text.similar-articles.2; date of access July 5, 2021.
ii) Neeraj Kaushal and Felix Muchomba, "How Consumer Price Subsidies Affect Nutrition," *World Development*, Volume 74, pages 25–42, October 2015. https://www.sciencedirect.com/science/article/abs/pii/S0305750X1500090X? casa_token=3FftOZAt8IsAAAAA:WTvXkwJ5urkO50kFki7_ oQuYgHTPDOzZM1GUhOig1EyBSMK3QGZESr8WrKEvyCcel6RtdDGw1ms; date of access March 2, 2021.
iii) Neeraj Kaushal and Felix Muchomba, "Free Lunch? Effect of India's Food Subsidy Programme on Nutrition," Voxeu, 24 December 2013. https://voxeu. org/article/nutritional-impact-india-s-food-subsidy-programme; date of access March 5, 2021.

36 The TPDS was designed to serve twin objectives: provide a remunerative price to farmers and provide food grains at affordable rates to poor households. The logic of fixing an MSP higher than the market rate is contentious. Despite high coverage of households, there are complaints galore of needy households not being able to get Antyodaya or below poverty line cards. Distribution of grain at such highly subsidized prices depresses market prices. There are other ways of reducing the pressure on procurement and food stocks. A committee led by

Dr S.S. Johl, a Punjab-based agriculture economist, had recommended a shift from the unsustainable paddy-wheat rotation, through cash compensation to farmers to move away from paddy cultivation in Punjab. This issue has required urgency and the FCI has also been debating this proposal with seriousness. The FCI has estimated that farmers could be incentivized to shift from paddy cultivation in Punjab and Haryana if they were given cash compensation equivalent to one-third of the MSP of paddy. The compensation quantum has been calculated at ₹150 billion (for shifting 24 million tonnes of rice currently procured from Punjab and Haryana at a compensation of ₹633 per qtl.). The total subsidy on rice for 24 million tonnes currently being procured is ₹612 billion, which would mean a saving of ₹460 billion if a complete shift takes place. This measure alone would give multiple benefits apart from the huge saving in food subsidies. A visible benefit would be the total elimination of stubble burning, a major cause of pollution in Delhi and several cities of Punjab, Haryana, and UP. The depleted ground-water table would have a chance to replenish itself. The shift from paddy would lead to higher production of oilseeds, reducing our import dependence. Finally, reduced procurement levels will mean a lower requirement of warehousing capacity.

37 Sanjay Kaul, "Farm Laws: Unlikely to Bring Transformative Change," *Ideas4India*, 14 October 2020. The first law frees a host of agricultural commodities from the Essential Commodities Act. The second seeks to open agricultural markets to the private sector, while the third provides a framework for buyers to directly enter into contracts with farmers.

38 "Its Official. Three Farm Laws Repealed", *The Hindu*, December 2, 2021. https://www.thehindu.com/news/national/president-gives-assent-to-farm-laws-repeal-bill/article37802828.ece; Date of access, March 11, 2022.

39 Vijay Paul Sharma, "Food Subsidy in India: Trends, Causes and Policy Reform Options," *W.P.* No. 2012-08-02, *IIM Ahmedabad*, August 2012.

40 Angus Deaton and Jean Drèze, 2009.

41 Aya Hirata Kimura, "Hidden Hunger; Gender and the Politics of Smarter Foods", *Cornell University Press*, pp. 162–172. 2013.

42 i) "SDG India, Index and Dashboard," NITI Aayog, *Government of India*, 2019–20. India has set itself stiff targets to meet the Sustainable Development Goals relating to hunger and nutrition (Goal 2). It has resolved that by 2030 it would bring down stunting among children below five years to 2.5 per cent, reduce the percentage of anaemic children to below 14 per cent for the 1 to 6 years cohort and to 0.9 per cent for those below four years, and the percentage of pregnant women who are anaemic to below 14 per cent. ii) "Nutrition", Strategy for New India @ 75, Chapter 31, NITI Aayog, *Government of India*, November 2018.

43 S. Y. Quarishi, "Role of Media in Addressing Issues of Nutrition," National Food Security Summit, *World Food Programme*, 2004.

44 Vijay Paul Sharma, 2012.

45 The government could issue grain to the poorest households at 20 per cent of the economic cost; all other families could enrol themselves in the TPDS system and be issued grains at 70 per cent of the cost.

46 Praduman Kumar, Anjani Kumar, Shinoji Parappa, and S.S. Raju, "Estimation of Demand Elasticity for Food Commodities in India," *Agricultural Economics Research Review*, Issue No. 24(1), January 2011. Cereals have been observed to have highly inelastic demand, close to zero, and even negative for coarse cereals.

47 "Report of High Level Committee on Long Term Grain Policy," *Government of India*, July 2002. https://www.domain-b.com/economy/ecosurvey2003/pdf/prices_and_food_management/report_of_the_high_level_committee_on_long_term_grain_policy.pdf.; date of access July 2020. A high-level committee headed

by Abhijit Sen made major recommendations in 2002 on the grain policy. I served as a Member-Secretary to this committee. The committee had voiced concern on the rapid increase in the food subsidy budget and recommended measures for a more sustainable program. The most significant recommendation was to introduce a system of universal PDS, with the central issue prices set at the average acquisition cost of the grain. The committee also recommended that the MSP should be at no more than floor prices based on C2 cost of production, i.e., all costs paid plus imputed cost of family labour. The food subsidy could be cut by around ₹500 billion annually through an increase in issue prices, fixing procurement prices at 'floor' prices and by providing food grains at heavily subsidized prices only to the poorest 30 per cent households.

48 Milind Ghatwai, "Explained: Why MP Farmer Scheme is Talking Point Again", *Indian Express*, 23 January 2019.

49 Devesh Roy and Mamata Pradhan, "Improving India's Public Distribution System: What Can We Learn from COVID-19?" *Consultative Group on International Agricultural Research*, 17 June 2020. https://a4nh.cgiar.org/2020/06/17/improving-indias-public-distribution-system-what-can-we-learn-from-covid-19/; date of access June 5, 2021.

50 Sudha Naryanan, "A Case for Reframing the Cash Transfer Debate in India", Vol. 46, Issue no. 21, *Economic & Political Weekly*, 21 May 2011.

51 O. Banerjee, T. Darbas, P. R. Brown, and C. H. Roth, "Historical Divergence in Public Management of Foodgrain Systems in India and Bangladesh: Opportunities to Enhance Food Security," *Global Food Security*, Vol. 3, Issues 3–4, pp. 159–166, November 2014.

52 Nicholas Nisbett, Peter Davis, Sivan Yosef, and Nazneen Akhtard, "Bangladesh's Story of Change in Nutrition: Strong Improvements in Basic and Underlying Determinants with an Unfinished Agenda for Direct Community Level Support," *Global Food Security*, Volume 13, Pages 21–29 June 2017. https://www.sciencedirect.com/science/article/pii/S2211912416301018; date of access March 5, 2021.

53 P. K. Joshi, "Pathways to Improve Food Security and Reduce Poverty in Emerging India", *Agricultural Economics Research Review* Vol. 29 (No.2), July-December 2016, pp 171–182. DOI: 10.5958/0974-0279.2016.00045.8. https://ideas.repec.org/a/ags/aerrae/254053.html; date of access April 2, 2021.

54 Abhijit Banerjee, Esther Duflo, "Cash and Care", Chapter 9, "Good Economics for Hard Times", *Juggernaut Books*, 2019. Banerjee and Duflo have suggested a much wider coverage under a Universal Basic Income to cover all poor households.

55 S.K. Srivastava and Ramesh Chand, 2017.

56 Diane Coffey and Dean Spears, 2017.

57 i) Anders Kjelsurd and Rohini Somanathan, "Poverty Targeting through Public Goods, Poverty and Income Distribution in India" ii) N. Srinivasan and Azad Singh Bali, "A Postscript to Income distribution, Poverty and Income distribution in India," *Juggernaut Books*, 2017.

58 Van de Walle and Kimberly Nead, "Public Spending and the Poor: Theory and Evidence for a Review of Public Spending and the Implications for the Poor," *World Bank*, 1995.
   https://documents.worldbank.org/en/publication/documents-reports/documentdetail/404991468778782212/public-spending-and-the-poor-theory-and-evidence; date of access May 5, 2020.

4

CARING FOR THE YOUNG CHILD

Many of the things we need can wait. The child cannot. Right now is the time his bones are being formed, his blood is being made, and his senses are being developed. To him, we cannot answer 'tomorrow', his name is today.

Gabriela Mistral, Chilean poet, educator, and
Nobel laureate, excerpt from 'Su Nombre es Hoy'
('His Name Is Today')

The Well-being of the Young Child Is Paramount

Not only is holistic well-being the right of every child, but investment in the health and nutrition of the young child (0–6 years of age) gives enormous returns to society. This is a phase of life when significant human growth takes place. Further, as we noted in the previous chapters, the young child's physical well-being is critical for the health and nutrition of the country's citizens; neglect during this stage limits the productive potential of future generations. Thus, at the current stage of development of India, the government must play a pivotal role in ensuring the well-being of every young child, especially those who most require help: the girl child, children in low-income households, and other disadvantaged children.

In India, the situation of the estimated 160 million children under 6 years is grim in each of the four vital elements of a child's well-being – health, nutrition, cognitive development, and care. India ranks 114th of 132 countries in stunting prevalence, and 120th of 130 countries in wasting.[1] As noted in Chapter 3, 35.5 per cent are stunted, 19.3 per cent 'wasted', while 32.1 per cent are underweight. The recent 'State of the Young Child in India' report published in 2020 provides a detailed account of the situation of the young child in India. I was a member of the core group that brought out this report.[2] India accounts for the highest number of neonatal, infant, and under-five deaths in the world. Of the 20 million infants born every year globally with low birth weight, an estimated 7.5 million births take place in India.[3] Many children are born with congenital defects and disabilities, and many are vulnerable to infections. Though the infant and child mortality

DOI: 10.4324/9781003346258-4

57

rates have come down, the picture varies widely across different states and economic and social groups. In overall terms, the situation of the young child needs urgent attention, and as Gabriela Mistral, the Chilean poet, famously said: 'Many of the things can wait. The child cannot'.

Though India has the world's most extensive childcare programme – the Integrated Child Development Services (ICDS) – improvements in the health, nutrition status, and cognitive development of the young child have been slow and not been commensurate with the size and scale of this programme. Child health and nutrition indicators remain low in comparison to many countries at the same developmental level as India. Moreover, the COVID-pandemic has caused significant disruptions in the ICDS, resulting in the worsening of the situation for young children. So why have the ICDS and other government interventions been unable to deliver the desired outcomes?

We identify the systemic and structural gaps in the ICDS and suggest cost-effective and workable strategies for improving its effectiveness. Based on analysis, we recommend a multi-sectoral approach and identify priority areas for attention across each vital component for the development and care of the young child.

Sluggish Progress in Children's Well-being

To improve our understanding of what could be going wrong with government interventions, we begin by looking at the situation of Birsa and Rasika's children.

> Birsa and Rasika's three children Shibu, Bindu, and Komal, are malnourished, anaemic, and stunted. The couple had a fourth child who died when she was only three months old. The eldest, eight-year-old Komal attends the local government school. At school, she gets a mid-day meal, though intermittently, whenever the school receives its rations. Three-year-old Bindu is taken to the anganwadi, though not regularly. Shibu, the youngest who is only five months old, is taken along by Rasika when she goes to work in the fields but is occasionally left at home in the care of Komal, who at such times must skip school. Birsa and Rasika are not sure if their children are fully immunized, though they remember them having received some shots.
>
> The parents are not consciously aware that their child is not getting adequate nourishment as their only comparison is with other children in the same age group in their community, who in physical appearance are on par with Shibu. However, they have noticed that a few of the children of 'high caste' and better-off families are taller and look healthier. They have built a toilet next to their hut with the money given by the government, but they continue to defecate

in the open. As a result, their children have frequent bouts of diarrhoea, and other infections, like most children in their village.

The children don't get age-appropriate diets and eat the same food as their parents. The bulk of each meal of the family consists of rice, most of which is obtained from the local ration shop at a subsidized price. The rice is accompanied by small quantities of locally available lentils – they seldom consume vegetables, milk, or meat. The children do not demand more food and seldom claim they are hungry, except when their rice rations run out.

Birsa does not involve himself much in caring for or nurturing the children, because he does not see that as his responsibility.

A young child's nutrition requirement is minimal, and even though the family is impoverished, it is not beyond what Birsa and Rasika can manage with their income. Yet, their children are malnourished. What is the reason for this? Are they not caring parents? Or is there something more fundamental at work? To understand their behaviour, we go back to our discussion in Chapter 1 on the limited bandwidth of poor households. Rasika's engagement in household chores and the struggles of day-to-day life leave her little time to ensure a nourishing diet for her children or to regularly send them to the anganwadi or the school. She is also not aware that children require age-appropriate balanced food in the right quantities.

Malnutrition levels in the country have stagnated and even worsened in some states.[4] As noted in Chapter 3, as many as one in three children are stunted and underweight, over 15 per cent are 'wasted'. Less than 10 per cent of children between six months and two years receive an adequate diet.[5] Micronutrient deficiencies among children are widely prevalent and act as significant impediments to their overall development. Anaemia prevalence among children is high – over 70 per cent in several states.[6] Though children from poorer households are beset by malnutrition, those from well-to-do families have the opposite problem – that of obesity. The country has the second-highest number of obese children globally.[7]

Birsa and Rasika lost their second child, but infant deaths are no longer a widespread occurrence. India has witnessed a significant decline in infant and child mortality rates in the past two decades – currently, 33 and 39 per 1000 live births, respectively.[8] Yet India has the highest number of neonatal, infant, and under-five deaths globally. Around 600,000 children in India die within a month of their birth.[9] Though the mortality rate has declined, a child in a remote rural area or an urban slum has a lower chance of survival than a child in a well-to-do household. The picture also varies widely across different states and amongst economic and social groups.[10]

A contributing factor to the continued high levels of mortality and malnutrition is that children living in poverty are acutely vulnerable to infectious diseases. Most children in low-income families suffer from multiple illnesses through early childhood and are particularly susceptible to respiratory infections, diarrhoeal diseases, measles, meningitis, and other viral diseases. Mosquito-borne diseases – malaria, dengue, chikungunya, and encephalitis – remain significant public health challenges. Poor sanitation, non-availability of safe drinking water, and poor environmental hygiene exacerbate the situation.[11] An alarmingly high percentage of infants (between 61 and 70 per 1,000 live births) are born with congenital disabilities, or structural and functional disorders, which lead to infant mortality or disability.[12] Immunization, so vital for the prevention of childhood illnesses, stands at a low 62 per cent and raises questions about the effectiveness of the country's universal immunization programme.[13]

Neglect of Girls and Disadvantaged Children

As noted in Chapter 2, gender discrimination favouring male children leads to differentials in the food distribution within households, as well as access to healthcare, which adversely impacts the mortality and nutrition of girl children. Patriarchal social norms have also led to modern diagnostic technologies being misused for aborting female foetuses, resulting in a skewed gender balance in the population.[14] The enactment of the Prenatal Diagnostic Techniques Act in 1994 has had limited impact as it does not change social perception.[15] The 'Beti Bachao, Beti Padhao' campaign to address gender discrimination has not been as successful either.[16] A report by the Department of Women and Child Development noted positive outcomes in less than 50 per cent of the 100 programme districts. Moreover, budgets for the campaign have been inadequate, and even these meagre funds have been under-utilized.[17]

Apart from the girl child, several other categories of children face disadvantages – children of impoverished households, SC/ST children, children with disabilities, children in urban slums, homeless children, street children, and children in pathetically run state institutions. Thirty million young children belong to low-income families.[18] Children in such families and other disadvantaged children fare very poorly on child indicators and are victims of abject neglect by the government.[19]

The Absence of Early Child Care and Education

We have discussed two of the vital components of early childhood development (ECD) – health and nutrition. Early Child Care and Education (ECCE) or preschool education constitutes the third critical component. While there cannot be a substitute for parental inputs to early learning, well-designed ECCE enhances the young child's early cognitive, physical, social, and emotional development. Young children acquire proficiency in language at a rapid pace. Their brains are wired for making sense of the sounds in their environment and adults can ease language learning for infants. ECCE should support this learning of the mother tongue.

As noted, most of the time of anganwadi workers is consumed in routine administrative activities and in providing supplementary nutrition, leaving them with little or no time for ECCE. Anganwadi workers are also poorly ill-equipped and lack the training to handle ECCE. Further, ECCE play materials supplied to anganwadis are neither age-appropriate nor available in adequate quantities. Anganwadi workers seldom utilize even the materials provided, fearing that they will be held accountable for any damage to the materials. As a result, the children do not develop a school-readiness foundation before entry into school.

The ICDS is the largest preschool education provider, followed by private preschools, private day care centres and crèches, and NGO-run facilities. However, in the 5–6 age cohort, only slightly more than a quarter of children are in anganwadis, with many children attending private nursery schools, some even entering schools directly in class 1, unprepared to face the rigour of formal schooling.

Most children do not have access to preschools; government preschool sections have low enrolments and few teachers. The NFHS-5 survey shows only 13.5 per cent children have access to pre-schools.[20] Government data itself shows a low 11 per cent enrolment in pre-primary classes, close to the UNESCO estimate of a 14 per cent pre-primary gross enrolment ratio.[21] Only one in four primary schools has a pre-primary section; this figure varies widely across states.[22] In addition, the preschool curriculum is neither well-designed nor standardized: there is a staggering variance in the curriculum across states and education boards.[23]

But there is a more fundamental problem concerning the cognitive development of the young child. Due to early learning being equated with formal preschool education (rather than from birth), the existing preschool education system, at best, only serves the older childhood age group (3–6 years) and results in the neglect of infants and toddlers. Early learning should begin at birth, initially through stimulation, play, interactions, non-verbal and verbal communication, and gradually through observation and cues from the immediate environment and increasingly structured activities. Unfortunately, due to the chronic ill-health of children, the lack of awareness of parents, and day-to-day stresses, very little learning takes place in the home environment in impoverished households.

Even joint families, which have dominated the Indian family system, do not always create conducive conditions for young children as they do not value the importance of ECCE. They want the best for their child but have a blinkered view of early learning. They view preschools as a medium for children to learn reading, writing, and arithmetic, and due to lack of guidance, know-how, and time, fail to recognize the importance of engaging appropriately with children. They only value formal education and do not recognize the importance of play with their children; in many cases, work demands also leave most parents little time and energy to engage constructively with their children.[24]

Low-income families have also begun to send their children to affordable preschools that have mushroomed up in response to rising demand, but most have a flawed teaching and learning approach.[25] In most preschools, poorly trained teachers use outdated learning techniques and rote-based teaching methods that parents value but which fail to ensure conceptual understanding.[26]

As the Annual Status of Education Report (ASER), 2019, declares, this lack of a developmentally appropriate pre-primary education system in both the government and the private sector has 'ballooned into a nation-wide learning crisis'.[27]

Absence of a Caring Environment

The fourth and, perhaps, most crucial component of ECD is a caring environment both at home and outside for young children. The family is the best place for a child to grow up in. However, extreme poverty and lack of education combined with a situation in which both parents are working undermine the ability of families to provide a caring environment at home. In the country's traditional patriarchal system, the mother is alone responsible for nurturing infants and young children. Therefore, the mother's well-being and ability to care for her children are particularly vital, as she becomes the sole caregiver of her infants and young children. With the emergence of nuclear households and the joint family's disintegration, the pressure on women has increased even further. Working women face a triple burden – work-related pressures, household chores, and childcare responsibilities. Impoverished families are unable to provide a caring environment for the child.[28] Those working in the unorganized sector have even weaker support systems, compromising their ability to provide quality nurturing and stimulating care.[29] Urban migrant families especially face multiple challenges. SC/ST families such as Birsa and Rasika's family, who face social discrimination, find it even more challenging to take care of their children. In poor households, it is often the elder girl child who is roped in to look after her younger siblings. According to a study, the proportion of children involved in childcare is as high as 23 per cent in the 3–6 years age group, as childcare arrangements for low-income families are virtually absent.[30] In many Indian homes, mothers are beaten or abused; children in such homes are not only vulnerable to violence but lack the emotional support they need. All children have the right to grow in a conducive environment where parents provide care and nurturing support. Low-income families require supportive measures. In this context, childcare arrangements through day care are vital. Childcare in institutional settings can provide young children, especially those between six months to three years of age, nurturing care along with adequate nutrition and healthcare for a firm foundation of life. This would also release older girl siblings from childcare responsibilities. Equally, women in the informal sector who bear a disproportionate burden of work both within and outside the home need childcare provisions.

The only central childcare programme, the Rajiv Gandhi National Crèche Scheme, is a grant-in-aid scheme run and managed by NGOs and monitored by the states. The programme has had a minimal impact – it is only superficially reviewed, and the scheme's budgetary allocations have remained meagre.[31] An NGO running a crèche is required to bear 10 per cent of the annual running costs. But the costing norms are unrealistic, which deters NGOs from setting up many crèches. It is, therefore, no surprise that barely 8,000 crèches under this scheme are functional across the country.[32]

The private sector has been mandated under the Maternity Benefit Act, 1961 (amended in 2017), and under labour laws to provide for crèche facilities for their employees. However, enforcement is weak, and quality of service norms are rarely followed even where crèches are set up.

In the absence of government support for crèches, random and informal childcare arrangements have mushroomed, especially in the growing urban and peri-urban areas. Working women in urban slums pay their neighbour sizeable amounts for taking care of the children when the parents go out to work. These day care arrangements are ad hoc and unregulated.[33] The children are deprived of play, learning, and bonding opportunities and are at the risk of violence or even abuse. Government support through trained childcare workers is essential for children who are left in the care of an untrained caregiver or a sibling. Such children are much more likely to be undernourished and prone to illness and developmental deprivation.[34]

Better-equipped private day care facilities have also sprung up in towns and cities to cater to those that can afford them. However, persons handling such facilities have only a superficial understanding of child development principles and the protocols required to run them, resulting in poor service quality. Only a handful of corporates, mandated by the Maternity Benefit Act, 1961, have taken steps to provide well-planned crèche facilities, and that too mainly to attract and retain their employees. Third parties manage these or tie up with other companies that have set up crèches.[35] Most small-scale and mid-sized enterprises find ways to evade their statutory obligations, as a crèche is usually not a priority for them.

Systemic Challenges to the ICDS

Close to 80 million children, or nearly 50 per cent of the 159 million children under six years, are enrolled in anganwadis.[36] However, the ICDS programme's effectiveness has been way below potential due to severe systemic deficiencies. As in health facilities, the priority has been to expand coverage rather than ensure service quality. Moreover, rather than a community-based programme as originally envisioned, the ICDS at best mainly caters to children that come to the anganwadi; there is minimal outreach to households and only sporadic home visits. During the COVID-19 pandemic, most anganwadis shut down for long durations. As a result, child health and nutrition worsened during this period.

Anganwadi workers spend a lot of time administering supplementary nutrition, yet despite this focus, ICDS has been unable to significantly impact child malnutrition. There appears to be little or no association of an anganwadi in a village with a child's nutrition status.[37] There is also anecdotal feedback that households often view the supplementary nutrition component at the anganwadi as a substitute for a child's regular meal at home, resulting in the impact being diluted.

Anganwadi workers are overburdened with routine administrative tasks. Apart from being required to maintain at least 12 different types of records, they are often given other responsibilities outside of ICDS, such as teaching Class 1 students or managing family planning targets. As a result, home visits, advice on antenatal care, promoting breastfeeding, timely immunization, regular weighing, and ECCE are neglected tasks. The focus on providing a meal at the anganwadi has led to the neglect of several vital child development indicators. For example, until recently, stunting was not even being measured and monitored under ICDS. The programme has also not achieved its goal of improving specific child health interventions such as deworming and Vitamin A supplementation. Frequent bouts of diarrhoea, infections, and water-borne diseases neutralize the beneficial impact of supplementary nutrition.

The neglect of the youngest age group (under-3s) has been the most severe deficiency of the ICDS. This age group is the most vulnerable and could have benefitted most from ICDS interventions. Parents face immense logistical challenges in bringing children of this age group to the anganwadi. Anganwadi workers with just one helper also find it challenging to cope with children in this age group. Government guidelines permit 'take-home ration' for this category. But the number of households accessing 'take-home ration' is limited. Even when taken home, the supplement often gets distributed to other children.

The ICDS design envisages the anganwadi worker as an 'honorary' part-time community worker recruited locally. Consequently, anganwadi workers' remuneration, even though enhanced in recent years, in most states, remains below the minimum wages of unskilled labour. Further, many anganwadi workers are not from the village and commute daily from long distances. A study indicates that a significant 40 per cent of anganwadi workers do not reside in the place of their posting.[38] Finally, the selection of anganwadi workers is fraught with many errors as there is no formal consultation system with the local community. Not surprisingly, the programme's extension and outreach activities are thus severely restricted.

The required coordination between the departments of Women and Child Welfare and Health and Family Welfare has also been missing. The anganwadi workers view immunization as a health programme. Conversely, malnutrition is looked at by health functionaries as the responsibility of the ICDS. As a result, both health and nutrition outcomes have been sub-optimal.

Apart from the weak ECCE component, the absence of day care arrangements is another significant reason for the failure of the ICDS. After an initial thrust in the Twelfth Five-Year Plan (2012–17) of converting five per cent of anganwadis into anganwadi-cum-crèches, in 2018, the centre reversed its commitment. A few states – Rajasthan, Madhya Pradesh, and Delhi – had rolled out these crèches in some districts. However, lack of clarity from the central government on the scheme's continuation, operational challenges, and the reluctance of states to allocate additional resources have led even the crèches set up to gradually close. This closure has meant that the young children of women workers in informal work are deprived of childcare. Recently, however, a few states have taken initiatives to improve childcare. For example, Karnataka has extended the timing from the earlier three hours to seven hours in many anganwadis and provided budgets for an additional worker, while Odisha has piloted a few community-run crèches.

There are numerous governance issues in the ICDS as well that undermine its effectiveness. Many posts of anganwadi workers and supervisors remain vacant, urban slums hardly have anganwadis, and discrimination, especially based on caste, is widely prevalent.[39] Training and capacity-building processes are also weak. To make matters worse, the ICDS suffers from severe funding deficits across the country. The poorest states, which are also those with the highest malnutrition and the lowest child health indicators, have the least programme funding – the principal factor being the weak finances of such states.

The Need for Coordinated Cross-sectoral Action

We have noted the failure in service delivery and systemic deficiencies in the ICDS across all the four vital components of ECD – health, nutrition, cognitive development, and day care. While millions of low-income families cannot care for and nurture their children, even families with resources do not adequately fulfil this responsibility. In a solutions-oriented approach, it is vital for the government to have an integrated ECD policy and not take a silo approach. The ECD policy must involve all stakeholders interacting with the young child – parents, caregivers, the local community, and government agencies. The impressive improvement in the overall child health indicators in Southeast Asian countries such as Malaysia, Laos, Vietnam, and the Philippines has demonstrated the effectiveness of a multi-pronged approach. These address the child's entire environment, including sanitation, safe drinking water, maternal health, and poverty alleviation programmes.[40]

The following sections suggest a road map for improving child development outcomes across each of the four vital elements of ECD. We begin by recommending specific strategies for improving child health and nutrition outcomes through a multi-sectoral approach. In this context, we specifically delineate the measures to strengthen the health and nutrition components in the ICDS by addressing its design deficiencies. Following this discussion, we turn our attention to the remaining two ECD components: ECCE and day care, at present, the weakest links in the young child ecosystem.

Improving Child Health

We begin by identifying policy reforms to improve child health and reduce child mortality. WHO has identified pre-term birth complications, acute respiratory infections, delivery complications, congenital anomalies, and diarrhoea as the leading causes of child deaths. Preventive measures can address all these factors. Such actions would include immediate and exclusive breastfeeding, access to skilled health professionals for antenatal, birth, and postnatal care, adequate nutrition and micronutrients, access to water, sanitation, immunization, and knowledge of danger signs to seek immediate medical or emergency intervention.[41]

In the Indian context, four cost-effective, workable strategies to improve infant and child health need prioritization. Chapter 2 has already outlined these strategies. The first of these strategies is to ensure maternal health and nutrition, as this has major implications for the health and nutrition status of the young child. Antenatal care (ANC) and adequate and appropriate nutrition for pregnant women can be radically improved by close monitoring through regular home visits by full-time and well-trained ASHA workers. Full ANC coverage and education and counselling of both parents to ensure mothers get proper nourishment would reduce the percentage of low-birth-weight babies, a major reason for child mortality.

The second step would be to ensure safe deliveries by getting the PHCs to work 24/7. PHCs should carry out a mandatory health check-up of all newborns within a day of their birth. Currently, only a paltry 24 per cent of newborns get a check-up in the first two days. Perinatal and neonatal care is weak, even in the relatively better-served southern states, and deaths in this cohort can significantly decline by introducing a home-based natal care system overseen by ASHA workers. Home-based care protocols must emphasize exclusive breastfeeding for the first six months as it is the best for the young child's nutrition and guards against illnesses caused by contaminated food and water.

The third strategy is the full implementation of the Universal Immunization Programme (UIP), for eliminating vaccine-preventable deaths.[42] The UIP is cost-effective. The target of 90 per cent full immunization coverage is entirely realizable.[43] The Department of Health & Family Welfare has taken several initiatives on the supply-side of the UIP. These include the rollout of the Electronic Vaccine Intelligence Network and the National Cold Chain Management Information System for monitoring vaccine coverage, and cold chain equipment stock management and logistics, as well as temperature tracking.

The principal reason for inadequate immunization coverage is on the demand side. As we saw in the case of Birsa and Rasika, impoverished households are so preoccupied with their day-to-day struggles for survival that immunization may not be at the top of their minds. They are also unlikely to keep a complete record of the vaccination schedule. For such families, frontline workers – anganwadi and ASHA workers – in coordination with ANMs must regularly monitor and take responsibility to ensure no child is left out. As we have already emphasized, a precondition is that anganwadi and ASHA workers be made full-time workers with better pay. They will then have both the motivation and the time they need to reach out to each household, maintain records, and ensure each child is immunized. There is also a need for sustained communication on immunization to reach each household. The success of the polio vaccination campaign provides ample evidence of how a well-conceptualized campaign can reach the most remote corners of the country. Involving village panchayats and offering them suitable rewards is a possible method to keep the local community engaged and motivated.

The fourth strategy to address child illness and deaths is to accord priority to the related areas of sanitation awareness, drinking water availability, and overall environmental hygiene. Close monitoring of drinking water sources and mosquito-breeding sites, followed by timely corrective measures through a well-trained and fully manned male health worker cadre that we discussed in Chapter 2, would make a difference. As in immunization, sustained awareness communication campaigns to foster behaviour change on matters such as purifying drinking water by boiling and toilet use could significantly reduce diseases amongst children.

Child Nutrition

For a child, the first 1,000 days – 270 days in the mother's womb and 730 days after birth – are critical for its development. Therefore, focused attention on the mother's nutrition and well-being during pregnancy and prioritizing proper feeding (from breastfeeding to complementary feeding) can significantly reduce child malnutrition. A child's brain develops rapidly until the age of three, and adequate nutrition at this stage is essential to ensure age-appropriate cognitive development.

As in child health, vast improvements in child nutrition are possible by prioritizing home-based interventions. As already noted impoverished families have the means to meet the child's nutrition requirement, but what is lacking is awareness of the child's food requirement. In many households, mothers provide inadequate and inappropriate nutrition, not intentionally but due to simple ignorance of nutrition. Poor breastfeeding practices and misconceptions about complementary feeding can be addressed through education and awareness. As recommended in Chapter 3, a vigorous education campaign under POSHAN Abhiyan is needed to guide parents on the child's nutrition needs, prioritizing poor-performing districts. The over-emphasis on supplementary nutrition at the anganwadi centres has led to the neglect of parental counselling and guidance. POSHAN Abhiyan, which is the rechristened National Nutrition Mission (NNM), must be further strengthened and expanded to fully implement the positive interventions that were introduced in NNM.

The first of the NNM interventions is the close growth monitoring of the child by regular measurement of children's height and weight. Anganwadi workers must carry out regular checks to detect stunted, wasted, and malnourished children, and closely monitor their progress. Equally, they will need to check for micro-nutrient deficiencies, including anaemia prevalence amongst young children.

The second focus must be on convergence in service delivery through ASHA workers for immunization and institutional delivery, and the Rural Development department for drinking water and sanitation. The third related area for intervention is the improved use of Information Communication and Technology (ICT) for real-time monitoring. The fourth intervention is promoting infant and young child feeding through behaviour change and multimedia campaigns focusing on exclusive breastfeeding, early initiation of breastfeeding, and complementary feeding. Each of these four initiatives of NNM is sorely needed under the newly christened POSHAN Abhiyan scheme. While we recommend strengthening of POSHAN Abhiyan, the programme components need review; for example, some technology monitoring indicators appear to have become burdensome for anganwadi workers.[44] Urban areas, especially in slums and places with a concentration of the socially disadvantaged, need particular focus and greater engagement with municipal governments. Anganwadi and ASHA workers must lead the campaign through frequent and regular home visits to spread nutrition awareness among parents.

Reimagining the ICDS

Child Rights and the Right to Food activists have advocated strengthening the supplementary nutrition component in the ICDS by enhancing the per-child calorie norm and increasing the budgets under this component. However, we have already noted the limited impact of supplementary nutrition at the anganwadi centres, the low coverage of under-threes under ICDS, and the neglect of child nutrition at home. Therefore, the focus must shift to nutrition and healthcare of the child at home. In other words, the ICDS must become a home-based programme, rather than being confined to the anganwadi setting as it is at present. Anganwadi workers must make regular home visits to every household for awareness dissemination and counselling, to ensure protocols are followed, and to monitor each child's physical and cognitive development. Such home visits are essential to reach the 0–3 age group who cannot attend anganwadis. In addition, anganwadi workers must work in close coordination with ASHA workers. Had the ICDS been viewed as a home-based programme, the negative consequences of the closure of anganwadis during the COVID-19 pandemic could have been prevented.

Such sustained counselling and education of both parents are vital for behaviour change. A significant limitation of the ICDS is its mostly 'mother and child' approach with little outreach to fathers. There is a need for gender and socially transformative parenting (Ch5, SYCI). ASHA workers and anganwadi workers will need to educate both parents on basic care principles and on their combined role in creating a supportive learning and caring environment at home. Such behaviour change in fathers will need a change in mindsets and cultural attitudes through measures discussed in Chapter 7.

The multiple responsibilities of anganwadi workers make it imperative that the government treat them as professional full-time childcare workers by substantially enhancing the current remuneration.[45] Higher remuneration could motivate anganwadi workers to give their best. Anganwadi workers must be local recruits, and their residence in the village must be made mandatory.

At present, anganwadi workers receive minimal training. To discharge their duties effectively, they will need comprehensive training on an ongoing basis. Institutions like the National Institute for Public Cooperation and Child Development (NIPCCD) and the state branches in the ICDS are inadequate for this task and are unable to provide quality training. The training framework needs to be re-visualized, and the network of training institutions expanded. The government should also seek the aid of academic institutions and civil society organizations which have the experience and expertise to upgrade the training curriculum. A critical component of the training curriculum must be sensitizing anganwadi workers to ensure that there is no discrimination against the girl child, disadvantaged children, or on caste grounds. The training must also equip anganwadi workers with community outreach skills for interacting with parents and community leaders. The use of online training methods could ensure there is no dilution in training quality. In addition, the supervisory staff, including the child development project officers and supervisors, also need to undergo intensive training and closely engage with anganwadi workers to encourage and guide them.

The ICDS, like most government programmes, faces governance issues. Staffing at anganwadis is inadequate. Vacancies are exceptionally high at the level of supervisors and child development project officers. Recruitment by state governments must take place regularly so that posts do not remain vacant for long. Urban areas, especially slum settlements, need special focus.

The lack of accurate records on each child's performance is another significant governance issue and compromises the effectiveness of the programme outcomes. Though anganwadi workers maintain voluminous records on each child, it is difficult to rely on them. The fundamental problem is that anganwadi workers are judged based on their records. This means that they hesitate to record the actual status of children. The simple solution is that an anganwadi worker's performance assessment must be divorced from the anganwadi records. Simultaneously, the government must conduct regular third-party independent surveys to measure the success of ICDS interventions.

Active government collaboration with NGOs, the local community, and other stakeholders and advice from child sector experts will significantly enhance the effectiveness of ICDS. There are several successful examples of this in the Indian context.[46] In Maharashtra, the Bhavishya Alliance Initiative to improve childcare services was conducted by government agencies in collaboration with corporates and NGOs across multiple sectors. The Kerala government engaged a private technology company to help reduce infant and child mortality rates in pockets that had a high incidence of both. An IT-enabled monitoring tool was used to capture child indicators online via mobile phone and web-based systems. Another pertinent example is that of Karnataka which has rolled out the Mathrapoorna programme in districts with poor maternal health indicators. The programme provides a full-cooked midday meal to pregnant and lactating women. The Odisha government has engaged local women's self-help groups to prepare and supply supplementary nutrition at anganwadis. Such initiatives need to be encouraged by the centre and these success stories should be shared with other states for adoption.

We have primarily discussed health and nutrition interventions to improve the effectiveness of the ICDS. The other crucial ECD components – ECCE and day care – also need to be addressed. Failure to address these two components will seriously compromise the young child's cognitive and emotional development. The next two sections will spell out strategies to improve these two areas.

Making ECCE Meaningful and Effective

The National Education Policy, 2020, has rightly highlighted the importance of ECCE, vital for the young child's early cognitive, social, and emotional development. The absence of quality ECCE cannot be bridged through schooling in later years. However, several educationists and social activists have opined that the new policy should go further and include children below six years in the Right to Education Act (RTE). Making ECCE a fundamental right can accelerate its implementation across the country – mere policy focus cannot have the impact that a legal entitlement would ensure.[47]

Currently, ECCE falls under the purview of both the Women & Child Development and the School Education departments. In both departments, ECCE is a neglected area: in anganwadis, ECCE is virtually non-existent, while not even 10 per cent of government schools have pre-primary sections. The NEP 2020 has recommended a formal two-year ECCE programme across the country. However, if states keep opening pre-primary sections, anganwadis would have hardly any children left.

There are 1.4 million anganwadis in the country. The National Family Health Survey-5 (NFHS-5) finds only 13.6 per cent of children enrolled in pre-primary schools.[48] Some educationists have suggested that owing to the high workload of anganwadi workers, ECCE in anganwadis would remain a non-starter – and, therefore, all government primary schools should open pre-primary sections, with anganwadis limiting themselves to the 0–3 age group. This proposal, however, has multiple logistical challenges and is fiscally unsustainable. It would require a massive outlay to build over a million classrooms with a million nursery teachers and helpers – even a conservative estimate would put the additional annual outlay at over Rs. 30 billion.

Therefore, rather than opening pre-primary sections, a more intelligent strategy would be to implement a comprehensive and full-fledged ECCE programme in anganwadis itself.[49] The government had in March 2022 appointed a Task Force with the author as Chairman to recommend ways to strengthen ECCE in anganwadis.[50] The Task Force in its Report submitted to the central government in August 2022 provides the detailed operational framework for universal ECCE implementation. The recommendations are action- and solution-oriented and specifically provide the framework for the early stimulation and care of the hitherto neglected 0–3 age group, vital for the foundational learning of young children. The Task Force recommendations are in conformity with the vision of NEP 2020 on foundational learning. The Task Force has made key recommendations on home-based learning and community outreach, with a special focus on the 0–3 years age group.[51]

The preschool curriculum recommended by the Task Force builds on the vision of the ECCE Policy, 2013 and considers the local socio-cultural context and is flexible enough to enable children to learn at their own pace, enabling them to transition to primary schools smoothly.[52] The Task Force has also recommended drawing upon the resources of NGOs who have designed good quality localized, activity-based content. Though NGOs serve a tiny fraction of the young population, their role is vital in innovation and creating replicable models for service delivery. Organizations like BODH, Mobile Creches, and Pratham have innovated and experimented with community engagement. These organizations have demonstrated that even among the very poor, families are eager and willing to contribute to preparing local play materials.[53] State governments must make use of their experience to improve the preschool system.[54]

Second, routine tasks of anganwadi workers can be reduced and non-ICDS work, such as surveys, removed altogether to enable to focus on ECCE. Many anganwadi helpers have studied up to matriculation. With training and an additional incentive, helpers can be redesignated as child-care workers and handle routine work. This would provide time for anganwadi workers to handle ECCE. Over time, the minimum qualification of the childcare worker can be set at 10 years of schooling.

Third, as recommended by the Task Force, there is a need to develop and implement an intensive capacity development and training programme for ICDS functionaries on ECCE, including their assessment through group activities and child observation.

Four, anganwadi workers must be re-oriented to closely engage with parents, as they play a crucial role in the cognitive development of young children. Responsive parenting requires both parents to play an active role in ECCE activities at home; therefore, anganwadi workers should be asked to consciously engage with fathers too instead of limiting their interactions with mothers. Much of a child's early learning can and must take place at home.

Apart from the implementation of the Task Force recommendations, the government must make other interventions. One, government policy should mandate that primary schools should enrol children only at six years of age. The existing practice of enrolling children below six years in primary schools must be strongly discouraged. Enrolling young children into primary grades puts them at a learning disadvantage, and this learning gap persists in higher classes.[55] Two, the government must supply age-appropriate activity-based play materials in adequate quantities for children, and anganwadi workers should be encouraged to utilize them; one way of doing this would be to supply ECCE materials regularly without accounting for the previous stock. Third, there is a need for anganwadi infrastructure to be radically upgraded. Currently, many of them do not have toilets and have little space for children to play or engage in preschool activities.

Given the limited ECCE in the government sector, there has been a massive increase in private preschools. However, in both government and private preschools, what is missing is the play component – children's activities are primarily rote and repetitive learning.[56] As noted by Krishna Kumar, the noted educationist, the existing nursery institutions are 'mostly a downward extension of the school' and 'likely to stress further an already embattled childhood'.[57] Therefore, there is also a need to review the system in private pre-schools and suggest an age-appropriate curriculum framework.

Expanding Child Day Care Services

The lack of articulated demand by low-income families has led to government apathy and neglect in child day care services for young children. The government needs to rectify the situation by setting set up crèches and day care services, prioritizing poor households.

First, the government should leverage the vast anganwadi infrastructure in all villages and many urban slums. The massive network of anganwadis provides an immense outreach to young children. The scope of the ICDS must expand to cover day care services by progressively upgrading anganwadis to anganwadis-cum-crèches. The ICDS Mission Statement of 2012 had envisaged converting 10 per cent of anganwadis into anganwadis-cum-crèches, and as noted, several states had also set up a few of them. The government must quickly get back to the drawing board and translate the intent of the Mission Statement onto the ground. Besides extending the anganwadi timings to cover most of the day, each upgraded centre would require one additional trained worker, the requisite helpers, and the paraphernalia necessary for crèche facilities. The additional crèche worker should be well-versed in ECCE to support the anganwadi worker in organizing ECCE activities for children. Ultimately, the focus should be on putting in place a caring and nurturing ecosystem at the centres.

Second, the government must sharply increase National Creche Scheme budgets with liberal and realistic financing terms to encourage more NGOs to come forward to set up crèches. A revised scheme should provide for at least two workers and one helper for each unit of 25 children. Also, the present honorarium for workers and helpers is pitiably low and must be enhanced to meet the minimum wage norms. The current scheme also fails to provide for costs related to renting safe and adequate spaces, purchasing safe cooking fuel, transportation for food, and providing a special diet for underweight children. More importantly, NGOs coming forward to establish crèches must be paid the entire cost as grant-in-aid, rather than the 90 per cent they get in the existing scheme.

Third, the centre must encourage and support state-level initiatives. One such example is the Phulwari day care programme launched in the Sarguja district of Chhattisgarh in 2013, which now covers all 85 tribal blocks of the state. This model focuses on both nutrition and child day care. The centre (Phulwari) is set up in one of the homes in the village and managed collectively by the mothers of the village. The Phulwari receives funding support from the village panchayat to provide three hot-cooked meals to young children and one meal to pregnant and lactating women. Every day, two mothers volunteer to take care of children at the Phulwari for the day while others go to work.[58] This model has the potential, with local modifications, for adoption by other states – Odisha is already piloting a similar model.

A few NGOs such as Mobile Creches and SEWA have also taken initiatives to set up crèches to cater to poor households. Mobile Creches has demonstrated that it is possible to provide quality care to children of vulnerable sections of the population through creative partnerships with different stakeholders with limited infrastructure and resources.[59] Similarly, day care arrangements promoted by SEWA are managed in close collaboration with the local community.[60]

There has also been a rapid growth of day care services in the private sector, though it has been entirely ad hoc, with a wide variety of childcare facilities. Therefore, day care services in the private sector require a regulatory framework. The government should establish an independent body to ensure minimum norms for ECCE and childcare services across private facilities. The government must design the regulatory system and set standards and protocols for these private facilities. The regulatory framework should be designed in consultation with NGOs and other stakeholders to avoid the pitfalls of an 'inspector raj'.[61] For instance, while Karnataka has notified a registration system with minimum norms and standards, it does not have an enforcement mechanism.

Enhancing ECD Budgets

We have identified many glaring gaps in childcare services in the country. The strategies recommended will have to be implemented in their entirety to address these lacunae in the services and ensure the needs and entitlements of young children. To achieve this, budgetary outlays for ECD must be enhanced manyfold. However, as child indicators show wide variance across and within states, central outlays must prioritize states and districts that are the worst-off.[62] Budget enhancements would have to include the additional expenditure towards increased remuneration to anganwadi workers based on full-time roles; allocations for the rollout of the ECCE component in the ICDS; provision for crèches and day care services; enhanced outlays for education and awareness; and training and strengthening of POSHAN Abhiyan.[63]

It needs to be reiterated that the ecosystem around the child requires a multi-sectoral approach. Well-designed and adequately funded health and nutrition strategies, such as those recommended in Chapters 2 and 3, are the foundation of a child-centred approach. We have also noted the vital importance of education and awareness of parents, requiring the universalization of quality school education. Equally, households also need secure livelihoods and jobs to nurture and care for their children. Similarly, there is a need to address gender discrimination against both the girl child and mother. Further, with increased migration and urbanization, the quality of urban life must improve to enable families to have a better environment for their children to grow (Chapters 5–8 discuss these vital areas).

Notes

1 Vinita Bali, "We Need a Nutrition Mission," *The Hindu*, 16 July 2016.
2 "State of the Young Child in India", Mobile Creches, *Routledge*, 2020.
3 Chapter 1, "State of the Young Child in India", Mobile Creches, *Routledge*, 2020.
4 "National Family Health Survey- 5 (NFHS-5)," Fact Sheets Press Information Bureau (PIB), *Government of India*, 12 December 2020 and National Family Health Survey, "NFHS-5 (2019–21) Factsheets," Ministry of Health and Family Welfare, *Government of India*, November 2021., http://rchiips.org/nfhs/; date of

access March 9, 2022. Phase I results released for 22 states in December 2020 showed a worsening in child indicators in several states, while the more recent release shows improvement in the remaining states. There is an increase in proportion of overweight children in almost all states. At the same time there is evidence of falling mortality rates, enormous improvements in sanitation, higher immunization coverage, and better utilization of maternal care facilities.

5 "National Family Health Survey Report (NFHS 4)," Ministry of Health and Family Welfare, *Government of India*.

6 "Children in India, A Statistical Appraisal," Ministry of Statistics and Programme Implementation, *Government of India*, 2018. States with high anaemia prevalence include Bihar, Madhya Pradesh, Uttar Pradesh, Haryana, Chhattisgarh, Andhra Pradesh, Karnataka, and Jharkhand.

7 Murray, J.E. Shaw, J.-C., Tardif, Perez, M. V., and Eskander, A., "Health Effects of Overweight and Obesity in 195 Countries over 25 Countries," Institute for Health Metrics, *NEJM*, 6 July 2017.

8 "Children in India, A Statistical Appraisal," Ministry of Statistics and Programme Implementation, *Government of India*, 2018.

9 "Each Year, 600,000 Newborns Die Within 28 Days in India; Highest in World," *Business Standard*, 20 February 2018.

10 "India's Infant Mortality Down 42% in 11 Years Yet Higher Than Global Average," *IndiaSpend* Retrieved from: https://www.indiaspend.com/indias-infant-mortality-down-42-in-11-years-yet-higher-than-global-average/.; date of access August 5, 2021. Child mortality varies widely, from 78 deaths per 1,000 live births in Uttar Pradesh, to 7 deaths per 1,000 live births in Kerala. Chhattisgarh and Madhya Pradesh in the central region, Assam and Arunachal Pradesh in the northeast, Jharkhand, Orissa, and Bihar in the east and Rajasthan in the north have high levels of infant and child mortality. In contrast, all states in the south and the west have fared much better.

11 Mukherjee S., "Emerging Infectious Diseases: Epidemiological Perspective," *Indian Journal of Dermatology*, 62(5):459–467. NHP 2015, Table 3.1.6, pp 103, 2017.

12 Sharma, Rinku, "Birth Defects in India: Hidden Truth, Need for Urgent Attention," *Indian Journal of Human Genetics*, vol. 19,2, 125-9, 2013. Retrieved from: https://www.ncbi.nlm.nih.gov/pmc/articles/PMC3758715/; date of access August 10, 2021.

13 Shalini Rudra, "Immunisation Coverage: India Far Away from Meeting Targets," *Orfonline*, 15 April 2017.

14 Gaudin, Sylvestre, "Son Preference in Indian Families: Absolute Versus Relative Wealth Effects," *Demography*, 48(1), pp. 343–370, 8 February 2011.

15 "The Young Child in India," Chapter 1, State of the Young Child in India, Mobile Creches, *Routledge*, 2020.

16 "Beti Bachao Beti Padhao Scheme Implementation Guidelines," Ministry of Women & Child Development, *Government of India*, 2019. Retrieved from https://wcd.nic.in/sites/default/files/Guideline.pdf.; date of access April 10, 2020.

17 "Beti Bachao Beti Padhao Scheme," *Save the Children Report*, December, 2018. www.savethechildren.in.

18 "Prioritising the Disadvantaged Child," Chapter 4, State of the Young Child in India, Mobile Creches, *Routledge*, 2020. The number of young children living in the poorest households varies enormously across states. Of the 30 million in the lowest income quintile, an estimated 8 million belong to SC households and another 6 million to ST households. Unequal distribution of income, goods, and services pushes children of SC/ST households into the most disadvantaged category. Children with disabilities (about 2 million), street children (0.27 million),

children living in slums (estimated 8 million), and children in institutions are the most vulnerable to neglect, violence, abuse, and exploitation.

19 "National Family Health Survey 3 (NFHS 3), National Report," Vol. 2. Page 183, Ministry of Health and Family Welfare, *Government of India*.

20 "NFHS-5 (2019–21) Factsheets," Ministry of Health and Family Welfare, *Government of India*, November 2021., http://rchiips.org/nfhs/; date of access March 9, 2022.

21 "UNESCO Institute of Statistics," *UNESCO*, 2017. Retrieved from: https://data.worldbank.org/indicator/SE.PRE.ENRR.FE?end=2017&locations=IN&start=1971&view=chart; date of access: 29 November 2019.

22 "UDISE data," *Government of India*, Retrieved from: http://udise.in/Downloads/Publications/Documents/Flash_Statistics-2015-16_(Elementary).pdf; http://udise.in/Downloads/Elementary-STRC-2015-16/All-India.pdf; date of access: 29 November 2019. Nagaland leads the list with 97 per cent of primary schools having a pre-primary section. It was followed by West Bengal (94 per cent), Meghalaya (82 per cent), Sikkim (81 per cent), Assam (75 per cent), Kerala (69 per cent), Jammu and Kashmir (60 per cent), Haryana (51 per cent) and Delhi (51 per cent).

23 Kaul, Venita, Bhattacharjea, and Suman (Eds), "Early Childhood Education and School Readiness in India: Quality and Diversity", *Springer*, 2019.

24 Sonali Khan, "To Accelerate Learning, Press Play," Early Years, *ASER* 2019. Khan's paper refers to a study conducted by Sesame Workshop in November 2016 with parents of children aged 3–6 years in 4 zones of Delhi, from a mix of migrant and non-migrant low-resource communities, which revealed negative perceptions around play. http://img.asercentre.org/docs/ASER%202019/ASER2019%20report%20/sonalikhan-toacceleratelearningpressplay.pdf; date of access September 5, 2021.

25 Nandita Chaudhary, Shraddha Kapoor and Punya Pillai, "Early Learning and Holistic Development: Challenges, Prospects and Way Forward," Technical Background Paper for Mobile Creches. www.mobilecreches.org.; date of access April 4, 2021.

26 Vikram Jain, Ahmed Irfan, Gauri Kirtane Vanikar, "Program to Improve Private Early Education (PIPE): A Case Study of a Systems Approach for Scaling Quality Early Education Solutions," *Annals of The New York Academy of Sciences*, Volume 1419, Issue 1, 23 May 2018. https://nyaspubs.onlinelibrary.wiley.com/doi/10.1111/nyas.13695; date fo access Sptember 19, 2021. The paper refers to a survey across urban India that showed that 95% of 4407 low-income families send their children to preschools, most of them choosing affordable private preschools, as parents perceive the quality of government schools to be poor.

27 Ashish Dhawan and Krishnan S, "Pre-primary Schooling: An Urgent Priority for India," Early Years, *ASER* 2019. http://img.asercentre.org/docs/ASER%202019/ASER2019%20report%20/ashishdhawanandkrishnans-pre-primaryschooling-anurgentpriorityforindia.pdf; date of access March 2, 2021.

28 "Resilience," Center on the Developing Child, *Harvard University*. Retrieved from https://developingchild.harvard.edu/science/key-concepts/resilience/; date of access April 2, 2021.

29 Moussie, R., "Childcare from the Perspective of Women in the Informal Economy," *UNHLP*, 2016. Retrieved from: https://www.wiego.org/publications/childcare-perspective-women-informal-workers; date of access March 4, 2021.

30 "Reimagining Childcare and Protection for All: Mapping Vulnerabilities of Children of Informal Women Workers in Delhi," *Mobile Creches*, 2019, https://www.mobilecreches.org.; date of access April 10, 2021.

31 The already poor allocations for the National Creche Scheme declined from ₹2 billion in 2017–18 to only ₹0.5 billion in 2019–20.

32 Data given in response to Question in the Rajya Sabha, Unstarred question no. 3797 asked by Mr Nadimul Haq. 7,930 creches were functional in 2019.

33 "Needs Assessment for Creches and Childcare Services," *Forces*, 2013, sourced from Mobile Creches, www.mobilecreches.org.

34 Raj A, McDougal LP and Silverman JG, "Gendered Effects of Siblings on Child malnutrition in South Asia: Cross-sectional Analysis of Demographic and Health Surveys from Bangladesh, India, and Nepal," *Maternity Child Health Journal* 19(1):217–226, 2015.

35 "Tackling Childcare: The Business Case for Employer-supported Childcare," IFC, 2017. Retrieved from: https://www.ifc.org/wps/wcm/connect/topics_ ext_content/ifc_external_corporate_site/gender+at+ifc/priorities/employment/ tackling_childcare_the_business_case_for_employer_supported_childcare; date of access July 10, 2021.

36 "Advancing Physical Well-being." Chapter 2, State of the Young Child in India, Mobile Creches, *Routledge*, 2020.

37 Priyanka Dixit, Amrita Gupta, Laxmikant Dwivedi, Dyuti Coomar, "Impact Evaluation of ICDS in Rural India: Priority Score Matching Analysis," *SAGE Open*, 27 June 2018.

38 Kaul, V., Bhattacharjea, S., Chaudhary, A. B., Ramanujan, P., Banerji, M., and Nanda, M., "The India Early Childhood Education Impact Study," New Delhi: *UNICEF*, 2017.

39 "Advancing Physical Well-being." Chapter 2, State of the Young Child in India, Mobile Creches, *Routledge*, 2020. www.mobilecreches.org.

40 "Children in ASEAN Report," *UNICEF*, November 2019.

41 World Health Organization *(WHO)*, 2017. Retrieved from: https://www.who. int/gho/child_health/mortality/causes/en/; date of access September 10, 2021.

42 Universal Immunisation Programme UIP), Government of India. https://www. nhp.gov.in/universal-immunisation-programme_pg; date of access April 10, 2021.

43 National Health Mission, Ministry of Health and Family Welfare, *Government of India*, website. Under UIP, immunization is provided free of cost against 12 vaccine preventable diseases nationally against 9 diseases – Diphtheria, Pertussis, Tetanus, Polio, Measles, Rubella, severe form of Childhood Tuberculosis, Hepatitis B and Meningitis & Pneumonia caused by Hemophilus Influenza type B. A child is said to be fully immunized if the child receives all the vaccines as per national immunization schedule within the first year after birth.

44 Aarefa Johari, "A New App is Failing India's Fight Against Child Nutrition", *Scroll.in*, Oct. 12, 2021. *https://scroll.in/article/1007521/a-new-app-is-failing-india-s-fight-against-child-malnutrition*; date of access Deecmber 10, 2021.

45 Chapter 6, State of the Young Child in India, Mobile Creches, *Routledge*, 2020. This Report has recommended that the centre should revise the minimum monthly remuneration to at least ₹10,000 per month, from the current national-level average honorarium of ₹4,500.

46 Chapter 2, State of the Young Child in India, Mobile Creches, *Routledge*, 2020.

47 The Right to Free and Compulsory Education (RTE) Act, 2009, applies to the 6–14 age group even though its Section 11 recommends necessary arrangements by the state governments for pre-primary education to prepare children for elementary education.

48 Sanjay Kaul, Uma Mahadevan-Dasgupta, "Anganwadis Should Provide Early Childhood Care and Education", Indian Express, January 29, 2022.

49 Ibid.

50 "Constitution of a Task Force for ECCE", Government Order, GO CD-I-11/4/2017-CD-I, Department of Women and Child Development, *Government of India*, March 10, 2022.
51 Wilima Wadhwa, "The Early Advantage: Learning Levels in Std I," Early Years, ASER 2019. http://img.asercentre.org/docs/ASER%202019/ASER2019%20report%20/dr.wilimawadhwa-theearlyadvantage-learninglevelsinstdi.pdf; date of access June 8, 2021.
52 "National ECCE Curriculum Framework," Ministry of Women and Child Development, *Government of India*, 2014. Retrieved from: https://wcd.nic.in/sites/default/files/national_ecce_curr_framework_final_03022014%20%282%29.pdf; date of access June 10, 2021.
53 "Promoting Early Childhood Learning," Chapter 3, State of the Young Child in India, Mobile Creches, *Routledge*, 2020.
54 Vikram Jain, Ahmed Irfan, Gauri Kirtane Vanikar, "Program to Improve Private Early Education (PIPE): A Case Study of a Systems Approach for Scaling Quality Early Education Solutions," *Annals of The New York Academy of Sciences* Volume 1419, Issue 1, 23 May 2018. https://nyaspubs.onlinelibrary.wiley.com/doi/10.1111/nyas.13695; date of access June 10, 2021. The paper refers to a survey across urban India showed that 95% of 4407 low-income families send their children to preschools, a majority of choosing affordable private preschools (APSs), as parents perceive the quality of government schools to be poor.
55 Kaul, V., Bhattacharjea, S., Chaudhary, A. B., Ramanujan, P., Banerji, M., & Nanda, M., "The India Early Childhood Education Impact Study," New Delhi: UNICEF, 2017.
56 Ibid.
57 Krishna Kumar, "Perils of Prematurely Imparted Literacy," *The Hindu*, 27 August 2020.
58 Team YS, "The Community Run Daycare Centres in Tribal Districts of Chhattisgarh is Helping Tackle Malnutrition," *Your Story*, 25 September 2018. https://yourstory.com.; date of access April 10, 2020.
59 Mobile Creches. Website www.mobilecreches.org. Mobile Creches adopts different models for day care services to suit local conditions. Its programme is holistic with components that can be replicated in other situations with minor refinements. Mobile Creches works with government, civil society organisations, communities, and employers, to provide a comprehensive set of childcare services to young children.
60 SEWA website, www.sewa.org. In the SEWA childcare model there is focus on elements of care and, simultaneous promoting capacity-building of parents for them to be involved in childcare. SEWA was an early starter in recognising the link between women's work, social security entitlements, and quality childcare services, as it provided a flexible, community-led network of crèches to its members. In partnership with the government, SEWA has worked to help policies and programmes better adapted to the specific needs of women workers in the informal sector.
61 "Childcare and the Childcare Worker," Chapter 5, The State of the Young Child in India, Mobile Creches, *Routledge*, 2020.
62 "The Young Child in India," Chapter 1, State of the Young Child in India, Mobile Creches, *Routledge*, 2020. The report presents two child indices, viz., the Young Child Outcomes Index and the Young Child Environment Index. The Mobile Creches report has identified eight states that rank low on the Young

Child Index. Eight states rank poorly in both these indices – UP, Bihar, Odisha, Rajasthan, Assam, Meghalaya, Chhattisgarh, and Madhya Pradesh. These states need additional funding support and special attention; urban slums equally need priority attention.

63 "Fiscal Allocations and Expenditure for Child Development," Chapter 6, State of the Young Child in India, Mobile Creches, *Routledge*, 2020. Based on estimates for each component of the young child eco-system, it has been recommended that the budget should be quadrupled from the present level to ₹1.25 trillion annually (20 per cent of the social sector outlay).

5

ENSURING QUALITY SCHOOLING

Education is the most powerful weapon you can use to change the world.

Nelson Mandela

Education is the premise of progress, in every society, in every family.

Kofi Annan

Issues Plaguing School Education

Education is vital for individuals to develop and grow to their potential and widen their livelihood opportunities. World leaders have acknowledged the vital role of education. Nelson Mandela viewed education as the 'most powerful weapon you can use to change the world' while Kofi Annan noted that 'education is the premise of progress in every society, in every family'.[1] Our discussion on public policy imperatives on health, nutrition, food security, and the young child's well-being has also demonstrated that a critical ingredient to improvement in these sectors is education.

Though the Right of Children to Free and Compulsory Education Act, 2009 (RTE Act), has refocussed attention on school education in recent years, some fundamental problems continue to plague the system. Despite the constitutional and legal obligations of governments, education budgets have remained modest and woefully inadequate to requirements. While there has been a reasonable expansion of coverage and enrolment in schools, the fundamental issue of poor learning outcomes, especially in government schools, has not been addressed. Poor households – both parents and children – remain alienated from the education system. Further, the education policy has not come to grips with the legitimate aspirations of poor households for 'English' education.

The COVID-19 pandemic has been particularly devastating for school children. The vast majority of the country's estimated 260 million school children did not set foot in school for almost 18 months since the beginning

80   DOI: 10.4324/9781003346258-5

of the COVID-19 lockdown. During this period, they only depended instead on various forms of distance education. But this has only aggravated the situation of students, particularly those from low-income households.[2]

This chapter identifies the shortcomings in the school education system and suggests strategies to address them, especially the specific challenges faced by children from low-income families.

Gaps in Enrolment

At India's independence in 1947, literacy was a low 12 per cent, while school enrolment averaged 40 per cent.[3] The country has since witnessed a rapid expansion in the number of schools. Over 85 per cent of villages now have schools, 21 per cent of villages have upper primary schools (classes 6 to 8), and around 11 per cent have high schools.[4] The country has 0.78 million primary schools and 0.44 million upper primary schools that feed into 0.15 million secondary schools.[5]

Along with the growth in the school network, enrolment has also increased at a rapid pace. By 2015, primary school enrolment had gone up to 97 per cent, and attendance was reasonably high, at over 70 per cent.[6] However, enrolment at the secondary level remains low, with the net enrolment rate (NER) remaining below 50 per cent.[7] In addition, the dropout rate in the age group of 6–13 years is as high as 45 per cent.[8] Dropout rates are exceptionally high among socially disadvantaged groups.

The Annual Status of Education Report (ASER), 2019, survey shows that while gross enrolments are high, significant age-specific gaps exist. Within each cohort of the same age, there is an enormous variation in which grade children are enrolled. While the RTE Act mandates that children enter Class 1 at age six, only 60 per cent of children enter Class 1 between five and six years of age. The remaining 40 per cent fail to get enrolled in school at the appropriate age, primarily due to a lack of parental awareness. A perverse gender gap is also apparent, with close to 10 per cent more girls than boys enrolled in government institutions; the reverse is true in private institutions, reflecting a parental preference for boys in providing their children with quality education.[9] These gaps in age-appropriate enrolment and gender inequities are contributory factors to low learning levels and have a long-term adverse impact on girls and children from low-income families.

Our discussion on inequity in school education must go beyond access to schooling for all children. The poorest households send their children to government schools, while children of relatively better-off households attend private schools or better-endowed government schools. In effect, children from the poorest households, the landless, and the most deprived social groups – the SCs and STs – are still alienated from actual schooling, though they may have been enrolled and even attend school.[10]

Children Are Not Learning

As shown by Pratham's ASER survey, a central issue in school education at the primary stage is the low learning levels.[11] While there could be a debate on the methodology adopted by Pratham in assessing learning levels, it is undisputed that despite the recent focus on measuring outcomes, learning continues to show only marginal improvement at best. Policymakers have focused on access but have ignored quality. Children from poor households and those enrolled in anganwadis have far lower cognitive skills and foundational ability than their counterparts in private pre-schools, leading to their inability to accomplish early language and early numeracy tasks. The performance of children is also strongly related to their age. Twenty-five per cent of Class 1 students in government schools is below five years of age, though they should rightly be in anganwadis, with the result that none of them can read a Class 1 level text.[12] Though the performance of Class 1 children in private schools is somewhat better, the higher learning levels may partly be an effect of the fact that these schools have a higher proportion of students of the appropriate age group in each class.

ASER surveys show that, by Class 3, the average Indian child's language and numeracy outcomes are already well behind curriculum expectations in both government and private schools. For example, according to the government's specification of learning outcomes, children are expected to be able to recognize numbers up to 99 in Class 1.[13] But the survey reveals that only 50 per cent of children in Class 3 can read a Class 1 level text. Similarly, only 40 per cent of Class 1 students can recognize double-digit numbers, and even in Class 3, 30 per cent are unable to do so.[14] In respect of Class 5, covered by an earlier 2011 ASER survey, less than 50 per cent could read simple Class 2 level texts, and less than one-third could solve a two-digit subtraction problem. The survey further observed that only one in three children could read a simple story or solve Class 2 level mathematics problems.[15] These ASER survey results also indicate that, though the gap between private and government schools is rising, the learning outcomes continue to be poor even in private schools. Given the significant gaps at the foundational levels, the learning curve remains flat even after several years of schooling. In the absence of any review of learning levels, many children go on to Class 5 and beyond without learning to read or write. The low learning levels continue even as children move up the ladder. By Class 10, only 39 per cent of children have reached the required level.[16]

Social and economic conditions are major factors that influence student achievement. These factors include gender, class/caste, household financial status, and parental education. And as noted before, parents who are better off in terms of their socio-economic status, and are concerned about their children's educational achievement, send their children to private schools, which largely explains why these children perform better.[17]

With learning at such abysmal levels, it is not surprising that children, even after eight years of schooling, are not significantly improved in their ability to face the world as adults, compared to those less lettered. Most children end up being neither functionally literate nor numerate, primarily because of the system's obsessive and misplaced focus on rote learning, and the need to pass exams trumping conceptual understanding.[18]

Unmotivated and Inadequately Trained Teachers

On the other end are the teachers on whom the system depends to provide education. But even here, the situation is highly unsatisfactory. There are several fundamental flaws in the way the government has managed its teachers. First, teachers are only required to complete the prescribed textbook in a fixed number of sessions and are not required to ascertain what their students have learned. Second, most school teachers lack the training to address the challenges of educating first-generation learners and children from impoverished families, who together account for an overwhelming majority of the student population in government schools. Third, teachers lack the skills to deal with the multi-grade situations often present in many rural government schools, which undermines the learning potential. Fourth, often the social distance between teachers and students is vast, with teachers belonging to different cultural and social milieus, and teachers remain unsensitized to the child's environment. Fourth, systemic issues of mismanagement and corruption in the state education departments have vitiated the environment. Further, teachers are engaged in a range of non-teaching tasks that significantly reduce the time available for taking classes; these include routine tasks such as arranging mid-day meals, as well as occasional extra tasks such as census enumeration and election work.

Significant shortcomings in teacher training programmes are also substantial factors that adversely affect the performance of both teachers and students. While there has been a focus on training infrastructure and teacher-trainer qualification, pedagogy and practical training have remained on the backburner. The government has set up an extensive network of training institutions at three levels – the District Institutes of Education and Training (DIETs), Block Resource Centres (BRCs), and Cluster Resource Centres (CRCs). However, the emphasis on training programmes is on numbers and logistics rather than on the content. Further, the faculty at these institutions are primarily drawn from the education administration department and possess no specialized teaching skills or pedagogy training. In addition, most of the administrative faculty perceive a posting to a training institution as a 'punishment', as it does not have the same power and prestige as administrative posts.

The challenge is that the teachers themselves were once students of this flawed system. This means that, at the time of their recruitment, most teachers have weak foundations, especially in science, mathematics, and English.

Many states require only a higher secondary certificate (12 years of schooling) along with a teacher-training diploma, for recruitment as primary and elementary education teachers. Moreover, while teacher-training institutes focus on physical infrastructure and educational qualification, softer but more critical components such as pedagogy, training methods, and practical training remain neglected. Consequently, the teacher-training institutes do not equip the newly recruited young teachers for the challenges they will face in the classroom.[19]

Poor Performance of Government Schools

Four factors influence a school system's performance – inputs (facilities, teacher-pupil ratios, student attendance, mid-day meals), the pedagogical process employed in classrooms, the school system's overall governance, and the home environment. Unfortunately, in India, there are significant gaps in each of these enablers. For one, the school system does not appear to be accountable to anyone, least of all the students or the parents. This stems from the fact that the government seems satisfied with monitoring numbers – students enrolled, teachers appointed, textbooks distributed, mid-day meals supplied, buildings constructed, and toilets built. There is very little motivation for doing anything else.[20] The education system perpetuates, especially in the governmental structure, 'a rigid and hierarchical mode of functioning, with a high degree of employee protection, extreme rigidity in rules and procedures, and unstated patronage and rent-seeking practices'.[21] Children from low-income families, whose parents are mostly uneducated, are particularly disadvantaged as they lack a conducive environment and learning support at home.

Schools vary widely in facilities, with the worst being the village schools for marginalized communities; these schools do not possess even the most rudimentary facilities. The efficacy of the educational system is incorrectly measured by the government in terms of marks and test scores, rendering irrelevant both cognitive development and creative thinking. Both schools and students tend to get trapped in this narrow vision of education. Parental ambitions also reflect society's myopic understanding of educational goals. The parental view of education as a fiercely competitive race for marks thwarts creative thinking. It also leads to a new segmentation in the school system, with the underprivileged being harmed the most. As only the very poor study in government schools, this creates the erroneous perception that children from less privileged backgrounds are unlikely to make good students, and that differences in learning capacity are purely due to genetic factors and socio-economic background.

Compounding this problem is that the number of days that government schools work is hugely deficient in many states. Several states have teacher absentee rates of over 20 per cent. Overall, 50 per cent of government teachers are not taking a class when they should be.[22] In some cases, the

ENSURING QUALITY SCHOOLING

actual time spent in teaching-learning can be as little as 25 minutes a day![23] Further, children from low-income families are also not able to attend school regularly. How, then, are children supposed to learn?

At this point, let us go to Birsa and Rasika's family and see how their daughter Komal fares at school.

> Komal, Birsa and Rasika's oldest child, is enrolled in Class 3 in the village primary school. She is reasonably regular in attending school but, as noted before, often stays at home when required, to look after her younger siblings. She performs poorly at school, and teachers ascribe this to her caste/tribe status. Most of the time, Komal just stares vacantly into space, as she does not comprehend what is being taught, and is seldom helped. She and other so-called 'low caste' children sit away from others because the 'high caste' children have been taught to shun them. Komal's parents do not appear too concerned about how Rasika fares in school; they are not aware in any case about what is supposed to happen in school. It is no surprise that Komal finds little joy in school and does not seem to mind staying home when asked to do so.

There is no shortage of schools; 95 per cent of children have a school within a kilometre of their house. However, child absentee rates are high, varying between 14 and 50 per cent across states. This absenteeism isn't driven only by the fact that students often need to stay at home. As in Komal's case, children themselves are reluctant to go to school, especially those belonging to low-income households such as Birsa and Rasika's.[24]

Flourishing Private Schools and 'English' Education

Because of the poor quality of education in government schools and a burgeoning middle class seeking quality education for their children, India has seen a rapid increase in student enrolment in private schools. In respect of high schools, there is a growing dominance of private schools, which now account for 60 per cent of total enrolment.[25] Recent estimates suggest that over 40 per cent of school enrolment in India is in private schools, with as much as 70 per cent enrolment in private schools in the 20 large cities.[26] A survey conducted by the Azim Premji Foundation reveals that, while parents prefer private schools, they do not always make sound choices for educating their children. The concept of 'school choice' presumes a high level of awareness and understanding of parents; they may only be going by perceptions rather than objective assessment.[27] The learning achievements in private schools are also much below the desired grade-level competency. Thus, by and large, all children in our current education system are learning inadequately, irrespective of the school management type. As the ASER 2018 report notes, the problem

85

is 'not only are we not creating a sufficiently literate population but that most of our population is functionally illiterate'.[28]

One of the primary reasons for the accelerating growth in the number of private schools is that many parents seek an 'English' education for their children. However, though parents send their children to private schools to get them an English-medium education, over half of these private schools, in reality, teach only in Indian languages.[29]

This issue of 'English' education has become compounded by the debate over the three-language formula.[30] The decision to make the local tongue the medium of instruction across government schools has led to the proliferation of private, English-medium schools. Close to 50 per cent of private schools are English medium schools, in which nearly one-third of all rural children are enrolled.

English has emerged as an aspirational language – it is seen as a passport to a lucrative (especially white-collar) job and entry into the country's growing middle class. The 2011 Census showed that English is the mother tongue of only a quarter of a million Indians. However, it is the second language of over 80 million and the third language of close to another 50 million, making English the second most widely spoken language in India, after Hindi.[31] Moreover, the aspiration to learn English now cuts across income classes.

The New Education Policy 2020 (NEP 2020) reinforces the mother-tongue focus, based on the logic that children learn and grasp concepts more quickly in their home language. Both public and private schools are to follow this prescription. Though the central government has clarified that it will not make the language policy mandatory and that the decision to adopt it is up to the states, NEP 2020 has led to uncertainty about the continuance of thousands of English-medium schools across the country. If implemented, the policy would be counterproductive as it could create a problem for students to study English medium subjects in higher classes.[32] Moreover, side-lining English may not go down well with the southern states, the northeast region, and urban areas, where English as a medium of instruction has helped Indians compete in the global market.[33] Moreover, the virtual absence of teaching English in government schools would also widen existing inequalities. The solution, however, does not lie in making English the medium of instruction. However, government schools must change the popular perception that there is inadequate attention to English language teaching. We discuss a few measures that should be taken by the states in the latter section of the chapter.

Modest Education Budgets

Much more challenging than the language issue has been the inadequate budget allocations for school education. Education budgets have remained small since Independence. According to the Constitution, the state was to provide 'free and compulsory education for all children until they complete the age of fourteen within ten years'. Despite this mandate, there was only a very negligible increase in education budgets in the period up to the 1980s – the central government prioritized poverty alleviation and food security rather than the social sector. The mid-1980s ushered in a significant change in the educational policy: for the first time, the government accepted assistance from international donors for primary and elementary education.

Along with budget increases in the 1980s, the central government took several new initiatives in primary education. These included Operation Blackboard, the District Primary Education Project (DPEP), and the Sarva Shiksha Abhiyan (SSA), the SSA being a flagship programme to universalize elementary education.[34] However, the government remained focused on primary education; it was only in 2003 that the programmes expanded to include the entire elementary education cycle. It took another seven years for the government to recognize the criticality of secondary education and launch the Rashtriya Madhyamik Shiksha Abhiyan (National Secondary Education Mission) in 2010.

However, the expectation that the central government would substantially hike school education budgets following the RTE Act enactment has not been met. The RTE Act also faced criticism from private schools because of the 25 per cent reservation for students from low-income households and the no-detention policy. This criticism was laid to rest after the Supreme Court upheld the constitutional validity of the RTE Act, including the provision for reserving 25 per cent of seats for students from low-income families.[35] Well-intentioned NGOs have also criticized RTE for its unrealistic standards for infrastructure and teacher qualification, resulting in the closure of many private schools. Eminent economists such as Abhijit Banerjee have criticized RTE as an input-based approach that does not enable learning; they suggest that the focus should be on 'outcomes' instead.[36]

Some of the criticism against the RTE Act may have merit. However, critics appear to have lost sight of the spirit and essence of the Act. The legislation is pathbreaking and marks the conversion of a directive in the Constitution into a 'right'. Unfortunately, the reservation and the no-detention debates have overshadowed the RTE Act's central focus on ensuring quality standards and improving government schools' performance.

Transformative Strategies

In respect of government schools, policymakers have focussed mainly on the 'supply' side. They feel that once you get the children into a classroom and get a well-trained teacher to deliver classes, the rest will follow. The implicit assumption here is that learning will follow from enrolment. Unfortunately, and surprisingly, even the international Millennium Development Goals do not specify any learning outcomes for children; the requirement is only that they should complete a basic education cycle. On the other hand, those that ascribe failure to problems on the 'demand' side believe that education quality is low because poor parents do not care enough about it and do not see any demonstrable benefits. Whatever be the diagnosis, a civilized society cannot deprive children of the right to a decent education.

School education should widen livelihood opportunities and, at the same time, enable children to learn to live with others and learn to act with autonomy, judgment, and responsibility.[37] Unfortunately, the current education system is alienated from both children and parents and has failed to look at issues from their prism. For example, why are parents not committed and strict in sending their children to school? And when children do attend school, how can we get them to learn? To address these questions and correct the systemic faults in school education, we need transformative strategies. The following sections spell out the required steps to bring our schools on par with the global best. These comprise strategies to improve learning outcomes, address 'demand' side issues, upgrade physical infrastructure, enhance teacher-training quality and teacher motivation, fix accountability, improve governance, resolve the contentious language issue, and explore the benefits of enhancing school budgets.

The 'Mantra' For Improving Learning Outcomes

The starting point for improving the quality of schools is to focus on learning outcomes. This must begin by transforming preschool education and Early Childhood Care and Education (ECCE). Studies across developing countries show that children from low-income families who do not go through pre-school have a higher chance of falling behind their grade level and remaining there.[38] Therefore, a universal and well-planned school readiness programme is vital. We have already discussed (in Chapter 4) the government's neglect of ECCE and the steps required to strengthen anganwadis and pre-schools.

The second strategy would be to work closely with teachers to improve their pedagogic practices and move them away from a rigid curriculum and rote learning methods.[39] Teachers need greater autonomy inside classrooms and should be freed from the limits of curriculum-based timetables to focus only on learning. Evidence suggests that making sure every child learns the basics in school is possible, as long as teachers concentrate on doing that and nothing else. The present abysmal school situation reflects the total disconnect between the child's actual learning and the prescribed learning levels. Teachers must be trained to ensure that learning at the foundation level is not compromised and be enabled to do so. Unless the child has attained basic literacy and numeracy skills at the primary stage, there will be little learning gained even after several years of schooling.

As noted, because of the COVID-19 lockdowns, most government school children went through 18 months of virtually little learning, while many private schools managed to impart at least some learning through the online route.[40] However, only 22 per cent of schools in India had internet facilities, with wide variance across the States. Among government schools, less than 12 per cent have internet facilities. Even in schools that can facilitate a teacher to conduct an online class, the number of children who access the internet through a smartphone or computer is limited. Only 42 per cent of families have a smartphone; in rural India, the number is close to 25 per cent.[41] Consequently, the COVID-19 pandemic has sharpened the divide in the learning levels between children from rich and poor families. Digital education cannot and should not replace interactive study material.[42] As Krishna Kumar, the eminent educationist points out: 'Online teaching had extremely limited reach in most regions and even more limited value for its receivers'. The post-COVID-19 situation for the school education sector is complex, and as Krishna Kumar explains, the 'where we left it' approach will not do for school education.[43] In the short term, learning expectations at the primary school level must be recalibrated and, perhaps, scaled down and brought to a realistic level for government schools.

However, wouldn't lowering expectations further exacerbate the divide between private and government schools, and between children of poor and rich households? This is a legitimate concern. There are also potentially enormous gains to be had by reorganizing the curriculum to allow children at the primary level to learn at their own pace. The stress and isolation of the COVID years would also require the school system to address the learning gaps and focus on fundamentals rather than try and cover the entire curriculum. The curriculum gap can be progressively bridged at higher levels so that children in government schools are broadly on par with their private school counterparts by the time they complete high school.

Third, besides curriculum reform, changes in pedagogic practices will significantly enhance learning outcomes. Paulo Freire, best known for his classic *Pedagogy of the Oppressed*, flipped mainstream pedagogy on its head by pointing out that knowledge and expertise already exist in children, including the poor. Even children from low-income families acquire a lot of learning from observing their environment. Conventional thinking presumes educators are experts while students are empty and passive receptacles in which knowledge can be deposited.

The traditional classroom centres around the teacher's culture; the teacher decides what constitutes appropriate and acceptable knowledge and approaches to learning and understanding. In the present system, rigid curricula and textbooks make the learning environment stifling both for the teacher and the students. There is a need for the curriculum framework to be flexible and to break away from an excessive standardized monolithic system.[44] To quote Paulo Freire, teachers need to be 'liberating educators', 'a situation where the teachers and the students *both* have to be cognitive subjects'.[45] In such a transformative setting, the learners' own culture is central to their learning activities. Then, children build on their own cultural experiences and understanding.[46]

One way to achieve this would be for each school to incorporate a local flavour within a common curriculum; for example, by including the local names of crops, rivers and mountains, surrounding villages, local festivals, harvesting, and sowing seasons. The curriculum design could have two components – a formal one that would provide each child with the basics of numeracy and literacy and a non-formal part designed by each school to cater to its own local community. However, at the high school level, perhaps, a more uniform curriculum may need to be imparted as students approach the centralized board examinations. While the flexible curriculum in the lower classes may not entirely limit the competitive race for marks at the school board level, it would help in building confidence in the child and provide a solid foundation for future learning.

In India, Eklavya, a voluntary organization based in Madhya Pradesh, in collaboration with the District Primary Education Programme (DPEP) in Karnataka, successfully implemented these ideas in government primary schools.[47] Unfortunately, NEP 2020 does not appear to provide much space for innovation and creativity, nor does it present any hope of a more liberating environment in the foreseeable future.

Four, we need to recognize that much formal learning in educated and well-off households occurs at home. On the other extreme, low-income families in which parents are illiterate have a near-total absence of a learning environment at home. Children from poor households are slow learners compared to children of wealthier and educated families, primarily due to the absence of a learning environment. As COVID-19 has further deprived children of low-income families of many months of schooling and learning, bridging these learning deficits is imperative. Continuous remedial instructional support for children falling behind can bridge this learning gap.[48] Failure to do so will leave these children irreparably handicapped in terms of future work potential. NGOs like Pratham and Sewa Mandir have successfully demonstrated the effectiveness of remedial instruction.[49] Pratham showed that it takes relatively little training to be an effective remedial teacher, at least in the lower grades. The experiments of Pratham and Sewa Mandir with educated volunteers and teachers drawn from the community have shown striking results. The government must institutionalize and scale up this volunteer-based remedial 'catch up' programme on a massive scale and make it an ongoing scheme even after the COVID-19 situation returns to normal. To attract the best available local talent, and ensure that volunteer teachers take the work seriously, the government must offer them reasonable remuneration. Along with this, regular assessment of the child's learning through this programme is vital for its success.

Fifth, the government needs good quality teacher-training systems and institutions to enable teachers to improve their knowledge and pedagogic practices. Providing appropriate training is a formidable challenge, given that there are close to 1 million government schools and an estimated 4 million government teachers in India. These are mind-boggling numbers! The government must prioritize addressing the infrastructure problems and inadequacy of budgets that plague training institutions at all levels. In addition, the teacher training division should be a separate cadre of professional faculty, who must be provided specialized content, curricula, and pedagogy skills. Also, there is a dire need to re-conceptualize teacher training institutions to incorporate relevant and modern pedagogic practices. More critically, teacher-trainers need to sensitize practicing teachers to the present shortcomings in the methodology, such as over-emphasis on the curriculum, rote learning methods, and disconnect between the child's understanding and the imparted lesson. Training must emphasize the need to focus on learning outcomes, incorporate in their training modules extensive practical training, and foster a creative environment for teachers.

Governments and civil society organizations have taken several successful initiatives in reforming school education which provides directions for reform. These include innovations to improve the performance of government school teachers by getting them to teach at the child's level, remedial support through volunteers, and programmes for improving outreach to girls (Box 1). There is also much to learn from the education policies and strategies of other countries (Box 2).

Broadly based on the above principles, the District Primary Education Programme (DPEP), Karnataka, between 1996 and 1999, successfully implemented an innovative programme, *Nali Kali*, in over 3,000 schools in several districts. *Nali Kali* introduced an activity-based curriculum, rather than a textbook-based one, in Classes I–IV. Primary school teachers themselves designed these graded activities and took ownership of the curriculum content. The teacher gave each child activities appropriate to their learning level.[51]

**Box 1   Successful Innovations in School
Education in India**

Eklavya was one of the first to introduce innovative experiments in primary education in Madhya Pradesh based on the following principles:

- Every child has an enormous capacity to learn and comes to school with substantial knowledge.
- The best learning takes place through a dynamic interaction between the teacher and children.
- The pace at which children learn varies considerably.
- Mistakes are a crucial part of the learning process.
- Government school teachers can be innovative and creative.[50]

ENSURING QUALITY SCHOOLING

Box 2 International Initiatives in School Education

China is a huge success story in ensuring universalization and quality education. In the past, China had a highly politicized curriculum and communist indoctrination. Deng Xiaoping, soon after taking over in 1978, introduced significant educational reforms. Nine years of schooling were made compulsory. Having achieved its quantitative goals, China turned its focus to curriculum reform. Shanghai was the first province to introduce reforms in teaching methods and curriculum. An effective strategy followed in Shanghai was introducing the reforms in 'key' schools which became the model for other schools. As a result, Shanghai performed exceptionally well when it participated in the PISA exams in 2009. China is now extending these changes to other parts of the country.[56]

In Rajasthan, the Educate Girls Development Impact Bond (DIB) programme exceeded targets in both the enrolment of girls as well as in learning outcomes. UBS Optimus Foundation made upfront investments with disbursal linked to learning outcomes and enrolment. The programme made four interventions – home-based teaching, outreach for girls, activities customized to girls' specific needs, and an increase in teaching sessions.

The state government implemented the Andhra Pradesh Schools Programme for Innovation, Research and Excellence (ASPIRE) in partnership with Ammachi Labs, an NGO, in 40 tribal residential schools. The programme successfully introduced students to experiential learning, computational thinking, life skills, digital literacy, and soft skills.

The STiR Education programme enhances the performance of teachers by motivating them to see themselves as agents of change. The programme relies on teacher-network meetings, supplemented with training and joint coaching programs with government officials to ensure their buy-in and cooperation. STiR has reached around 200,000 teachers in India in 24 districts across several states, impacting 4.7 million children and aiming to reach 40 million children by 2025. Its interventions have shown improved academic performance in government schools, even in comparison to private schools.

The Mindspark programme showed an impact on educational outcomes through computer-based instruction modules. In addition, the study found that weaker students benefited the most from the intervention.[52]

Pratham, an NGO well-known for its ASER learning surveys, has designed an attractive 'Teaching at the Right Level' (TaRL) programme, enabling children to acquire foundational skills. Teaching starts at the child's level and helps children with foundation building blocks – reading, understanding, expression, and arithmetic. TaRL is a low-cost strategy that enables children to catch up in a short period. Pratham's programme is implemented in two ways – directly by its instructors through 'learning camps' or as part of a Pratham-government partnership programme with government teachers. Pratham is partnering with several state governments to implement TaRL.[53]

A micro-initiative by ABC, an NGO based in Bengaluru, uses CSR funding and comprises volunteers who teach in government schools. Like Anupama Harish and Jayashree Narayanan, some informal volunteers work with the One Billion Literates Foundation (OBLF).[54]

A once-moribund network of state-run social welfare schools in Telangana catering to marginalized communities is now well-run and sought after. Praveen Kumar, himself an SC officer, as head of these institutions, led this transformation by empowering students to excel in a range of extracurricular activities. Many seats used to remain vacant in the past, but now the schools have ten applicants for each seat. Seeing the success of these initiatives, the state government provided additional funding to these schools and gave Kumar an extended tenure.[55]

Finland's education system is one of the world's best, primarily due to the quality of its teachers and government focus on accountability, curriculum, instruction, and school management. To ensure that the system continually adapts to changing needs, the government prepares a development plan for education and research every four years.

Hong Kong is a world educational leader and scores high on the Program for International Student Assessment (PISA), a widely recognized educational assessment ranking system, partly because it retained a large part of the education system developed before it became part of China. Though education became nearly universal by the 1980s, and higher education expanded significantly, the curriculum was focused on memorization. Recognizing the shortcomings, the government launched a new curriculum. It moved from rote learning to curriculum and teaching designed to encourage conceptual understanding and active teacher-student interaction, which provided schools with the flexibility to adapt. While implementing the reforms, the government engaged with stakeholders at all levels.

Taiwan is among the best in student performance. While initial reforms focused on access to a high-quality education, recent reforms develop teacher capacity. Responding to the criticism that the education system is too heavily focused on exams and rote memorization, the government is now focusing on application-based knowledge.

South Korea's education system has undergone rapid changes and ranks among the top in PISA assessments. South Korea has built a strong, highly qualified teaching force. Today, teaching is a popular career choice among young South Koreans, with high social status, job stability, and high pay. In addition to exam reforms, South Korea has remade its curriculum to focus on creativity, character building, and competency across all subject areas. The country has dramatically expanded ECCE, increased support for needy students, developed leadership paths, expanded training for teachers, and restructured vocational education to meet labour market needs. It has also made efforts to address the high level of private spending on tutoring to ensure equity and reduce stress levels among students.

Japan has attempted to relieve student pressure without decreasing student performance and has consistently performed high on PISA. While demanding the absorption of large amounts of information, the Japanese curriculum requires a good deal of problem-solving and concept mastery. The system is highly egalitarian, where access to opportunity is a function of merit, determined by school achievement. All students are funded equitably and have the same curriculum. Students in Japanese schools do not jump grades, nor are they held back. These policies have provided students from low-income backgrounds with equal educational opportunities. Japan's policy focus is on five major areas: development of emotional intelligence and physical health in addition to academic abilities; preparing students to participate and innovate in the global economy; promoting lifelong learning; creating 'safety nets' such as free access to ECCE; and ensuring universal access to classroom technology.

Addressing the Demand Side

The recommendations made in pedagogy, reorganization of the curriculum, local content, and remedial instruction may remedy the 'supply' side of schooling and reduce the disconnect between the school and the child to a large extent. However, these measures may not fully address the 'demand' side. As Komal's story suggests, there are multiple reasons why children do not attend school regularly. Access is not a significant reason; in a survey, it was found that only 7 per cent of rural female children and less than 2 per cent of rural male children cited school being far away as the main reason for not attending. The most common reason cited was 'not interested in studies'.[57] Along with indifference, apathy, and limited bandwidth, the perception of parents is that education in government schools does not offer much benefit. At the same time, except for girls when they approach puberty, there is no evidence of parents coming in the way of children going to school. As we saw in Komal's case, many children from poor households get alienated over time; in a way, the system 'pushes' them out of school.

Like China, where nine years of schooling is compulsory, many countries give parents no choice about sending their children to school. While serving as Commissioner of Schools in the 1990s, I had accompanied a high-level delegation from China to rural schools in Karnataka. I pointed out girl children tending to goats along the route. I asked the visitors how China had ensured that all girls attended school regularly. They were puzzled by my query; their straightforward response was that all children must attend school. China had mandated that all children attend school – the system provided no choice in the matter.

In the Indian context, a 'compulsory' approach may not be feasible as it would penalize impoverished families. Instead, we must find ways to get children actively and meaningfully engaged in school to ensure their regular participation. The present perception amongst parents about government schools – that it is not worthwhile to send children there – also needs to be changed. And there is no societal action to put pressure on the government to improve the performance of its schools, as educated and well-off parents now send their children to private schools. Raising the awareness of parents will compel governments to improve education quality.[58]

The physical environment and available facilities impact demand. Several state governments have provided sizeable budgets in recent years to enhance the physical facilities of schools and build thousands of new classrooms. Many government schools now have fully functional toilets and drinking water facilities. However, notwithstanding these improvements, it is widely believed that private schools have a far superior infrastructure. This perception can be quickly changed, as demonstrated by the AAP government in Delhi, where government schools now, on average, are better equipped than private schools and have also shown better performance in exams.[59] Prioritizing school education was a major factor in the AAP government getting re-elected with a thumping majority. The right priorities can also make for good politics.

An attractive physical school environment may not be adequate. Children will attend school if, alongside the regular curriculum, it offers activities that children enjoy; then children will have reasons to attend school. Thus, even at the cost of reducing the time allocated to formal classroom teaching, it would be worthwhile to organize school periods where at least one hour is devoted to activities outside the formal curriculum. For example, games and art enhance learning. Schools could include a games period after school hours, instead of physical training (PT) periods in between; one could have a local sportsperson taking on the games teacher's role for that.

Similarly, if there are local musicians or dancers available, they could be engaged. Empowering headmasters of schools to organize such activities would also bring them closer to the local community. Unfortunately, providing remuneration for organizing activities outside the curriculum, such as remedial instruction or games and music lessons, is not included in current budget provisions. This reflects systemic restrictions in the organization of government school budgets.

If the changes suggested are implemented, will parents prefer government schools over private schools? There is no clear answer, though there are a few favourable signs. For example, many parents would prefer to send their children to Kendriya Vidyalayas ('Central Schools'). However, such schools are limited, and admission is not open to all. Many non-poor parents now prefer government schools in Delhi, especially those that are better funded, such as the 'Model' and 'Navodaya' schools. Kerala is another state where a good number of children from the middle class attend government schools. These examples show that a significant section of parents prefer government schools when quality schooling is available. There is evidence from across the world that public schools can deliver high-quality education. As the AAP initiative has shown, the perception of government schooling improves, when the government visibly revisits its priorities.

Putting a Brake on New Government Schools

As noted, a central focus since the 1950s had been on expanding coverage and enrolment. Hence, there was a race to start new primary schools. During my years as Commissioner of Schools in Karnataka, we added over 2000 new primary schools each year without bothering about the budgets for concomitant infrastructure or teachers! As we noted in the context of hospitals, governments of the day like to announce 'new' institutions. Even the original AAP manifesto had announced the setting up of hundreds of new schools.[60] The tussle between the AAP government and the central government resulted in the centre not allotting land for new schools, which came as a blessing in disguise. Had the land been allotted for new schools, the state government's focus may never have shifted to improving existing schools.

Changing demographics and the rapid expansion of private schools indicate that the government may not need many more schools. Also, with the drop in fertility, the school-age-group population has declined. The next two decades (2020–40) will likely see a further fall of 18 per cent in the child population. Thus, the number of schools per capita will rise significantly.[61] There is now a need to consolidate/merge elementary schools in many states to keep them viable. Other economies witnessing a decline in elementary school-going population – such as Japan, China, South Korea, Singapore, and Canada – have also implemented policies to merge or close down schools.

There may continue to be a few gaps in the country in respect of high schools. The overriding priority given to primary and elementary schools has led to the neglect of government secondary schools. For example, while primary schools are near-universal in villages, only 15 per cent of villages have a government high school. As a result, a significant proportion of students leave the education system before reaching higher levels. While elementary education provides students with basic literacy and numeracy, secondary schooling is critical to reading and writing with comprehension, retaining literacy skills, and widening livelihood opportunities. Therefore, it is necessary to ensure universal enrolment and participation up to the secondary level. As we have noted, with schooling limited to eight years at best, compounded by low learning levels, the vast majority of the country's children of low-income families relapse into illiteracy as adults – a colossal waste of human capital. It is quite another matter that official literacy rates continue to show an increase. Because there is no benchmark, even persons who are only able to write their names are pronounced literate.[62]

However, the deficit in high schools does not mean that the government should open many stand-alone high schools. Access to a high school is no longer a problem in most areas since the road network has improved vastly, and private schools have mostly met the gaps. Instead, the government must prioritize and focus on enhancing the quality of existing schools. There is merit in selectively upgrading elementary schools with high enrolment levels to high schools, where there is no nearby secondary school. Such composite secondary schools perform better and retain more students.[63]

Secondary education budgets remain small. The NEP 2020 recommends universalization of school education until 18 years, without making it a legal right. Many educationists advocate that RTE must extend from preschool (as recommended in Chapter 3) and go up to high school. A disturbing feature of the NEP 2020 is the recommendation that vocational training should begin from class 6; this move is likely to perpetuate the divide between the rich and the poor. There is a genuine apprehension that children of poor households, who may be relatively poor performers, could be made to shift to vocational education at an early stage. Depriving such children of secondary education would eventually condemn them to the low-value-chain labour market. Therefore, it would be best to introduce vocational education and skilling after all students have gone through 10 years of formal schooling.

Improving Teacher Motivation, Accountability, and Governance

A vital component of the strategy to improve school quality is to address teacher motivation and accountability. Without this, reforms in teacher training, curriculum, and pedagogic practices may not significantly enhance performance. If you speak with government school teachers across states, they will tell you that a significant pain point is the manner of their posting to schools. Guidelines on posting and transfers in many states are not teacher-friendly. Teachers commonly need to use political influence or resort to bribes to be assigned to schools of their choice. To the extent possible, the education department should post teachers to schools convenient to them. Several states have impractical guidelines for the posting of teachers. These relate to the maximum duration of stay, denial of posting to their native places, and posting fresh recruits to remote areas. At the core of these poorly conceptualized guidelines and practices are fixed mindsets – it is presumed that teachers assigned to their native regions and for prolonged periods develop vested interests. The reality, based on my own experience, is just the opposite. Teachers posted to their 'native' villages are more likely to be regular in school, remain in the villages, and also perform better because their community is watching. They are unlikely to perform well in inconvenient distant locations because almost their entire bandwidth is expended on finding ways of getting a transfer to a preferred location. There is a gender issue as well. At the primary school level, the percentage of women teachers is rising; in several states, including in the southern states, over 80 per cent of primary school teachers are women. Ensuring their safety and their posting to locations convenient for them should be prioritized.

During my first year as Commissioner of Schools, Karnataka, transfer requests swamped our office and many with recommendations from elected representatives and ministers (obtained at a 'cost'). During the 'transfer' season teaching naturally took a back seat. We solved this issue through a simple district-wise IT-based transparent 'counselling' protocol. This system involved three steps: The first was to decentralize all transfers to the district education officers. Second, teachers seeking a change of their schools were assigned fixed days to attend the counselling session based on a priority list drawn up in advance; for example, physically disadvantaged, women, and SC/ST teachers were prioritized and received earlier counselling dates. The third step was to enable teachers, during their appointed counselling session, to choose any available school where there were vacancies and obtain posting orders on the same day. Following each selection by the teacher at the counselling, the post from which the teacher was transferred became vacant and, along with other existing vacancies, became available to the next teacher on the priority list, and so on. This meant that no teacher could ask for a school that had no vacancies by pushing out another teacher. Those happy in their locations could remain there as long as they wished.

The government of Karnataka addressed nepotism in the recruitment and posting of new teachers, on similar lines to the system adopted for transfers of teachers. The earlier interview-based system that led to corruption was done away with and replaced with an online test. The test performance, the teacher qualifying examination, and the 12th standard examination results became the basis for generating the merit list. While drawing up the merit list, the reservation of posts for SC/ST and other categories such as women and the physically handicapped was kept in mind. Successful candidates were scheduled for 'counselling' based on their merit. Then, on their appointed date, the selected teachers opted for their choice from any of the available schools that had a vacancy and were issued appointment orders on the spot. The system is similar to that being adopted for filling up seats in engineering and medical colleges. The system has worked well and has, by and large, survived political and administrative changes over the last three decades; a fairly transparent system continues even at present. Several states have since adopted this transparent and open recruitment and posting system, in its entirety or partially.[64]

As in recruitment and postings, IT systems can track and monitor teacher attendance in schools through GPS-enabled apps on which teachers can enter their arrival and departure times. This type of tracking has been very successfully employed in the private sector and is an excellent monitoring tool.[65] Of course, a teacher's presence in the school does not necessarily mean that they are in class and teaching. However, even ensuring teacher presence represents a significant step forward.

The suggested reforms to improve teacher performance and accountability will need support at supervisory levels. Most observers agree that the vast majority of people at senior positions at both the state and district levels in the education system have an inadequate understanding of pedagogy and have low motivation levels. Many of them also have questionable integrity; corruption is widespread. Apart from matters relating to recruitment, transfers, and postings, most education officials and senior officers are occupied with supply chain management – organizing mid-day meals, distributing textbooks and uniforms, and the procurement and supply of laboratory and other materials. Decisions regarding new schools, coordination with the district administration for construction and repair, supporting census, survey, and election work, occupy the remainder of the time of these education officers. Inspection and school supervision are more about filling forms, entering data, filing reports, checking enrolment records, and checking materials supplies. Academic management and supervision, and performance assessment of teachers and schools, get the lowest priority.

So, where should governance reform begin? Perhaps the best way forward would be to separate administration and supply chain processes from academic management and supervision. The division tasked with mid-day meals, the supply of uniforms, school infrastructure, and information collection, should be separated from educational administration. Academic supervisors should fully devote their time to overseeing and guiding teachers and monitoring the academic performance of schools and nothing else. Until the 1970s, frequent visits by subject inspectors impelled teachers to complete the syllabus and pay attention to teaching methods. Things have since changed; inspectors now visit merely to collect data and look at registers.[66] The government should mandate that academic supervisors should report to the heads of the training division and not to the education officers, as at present. They should *not* judge teachers' performance as this would create a substantial vested interest in fudging data. Teachers and supervisors would tend to work together to create fictitious data on enrolment, attendance, and learning levels if judged on this basis. The academic division (including the training institutes) should work with teachers and support them in improving performance and outcomes without being judgmental. This change would require an expanded role of teacher-training institutions to include supervision of all field-level academic staff. Education officers would continue to be responsible for supply chain management, organization control, and administrative matters, including ensuring that teachers take classes regularly.

Fixing the Vexed Language Issue

Governments must resolve the present confusion and ambivalence on the language front. The past hostility of states to English is quickly dissipating, but significant concerns remain. English education creates a vast divide between the rich and the poor, and between students of public and private schools. Children who do not acquire basic English language skills at the school stage find it difficult to get jobs. Children in government schools face multiple challenges in developing English language competency.[67]

While working as Commissioner of Schools, I observed that most elementary school teachers do not possess even a rudimentary knowledge of English. Thus, they are ill-equipped to teach the language, let alone teach other subjects in the English medium. English is as alien to the teachers as to the students! Until recently, Karnataka and several states did not require any special qualifications to teach English. So, you could qualify as an elementary school teacher, even after having fared poorly in English in high school. There was fierce resistance when as Commissioner of Schools, Karnataka in 1998, I had sought to create separate cadres for science and English, as teachers were apprehensive that this would affect their promotional avenues. It took over a decade in Karnataka to create separate posts for English and Science teachers at the elementary stage.

The first step in ensuring that English language teaching takes place is to have a dedicated cadre of English teachers with extensive English language skills. It is only when an adequate number of well-trained English language teachers join schools that it would become possible for the government to claim that it teaches English in elementary schools. This should be supported by an imaginative curriculum that focuses on oral communication and basic comprehension and writing skills.

There is strong evidence that we learn best in the language we speak most fluently.[68] English is a foreign language for most families and must be taught as a subject, not a medium of instruction.

Along with the local language as the medium of instruction in the early years, the curriculum should include narratives in the local dialect, which would allow children to smoothly transition from the native dialect language to the language of instruction.[69] Till a full-fledged cadre of teachers proficient in English is in place, introducing English only at the upper primary stage makes better sense. Students can choose to opt for the English medium at the high school stage. Students opting for science would need it, as English alone is the medium in most universities across the country for engineering, science, and medical courses.[70]

The Way Forward for Private Schools

Given the dismal quality of education delivered in public schools, should parents spend their hard-earned money to put their children into private schools? Would that be the way forward?

Private schools do appear to perform better than government schools. According to a study, in the same village, teachers at a private school are eight percentage points more likely to be in school on a given day than teachers at a public school. Children who go to private schools perform better, but as noted earlier, this may be because families who decide to send their children to private schools are usually better educated. However, parental education does not explain the vast gulf in performance: the difference is close to ten times between the children from the highest and lowest socio-economic categories. There is also a sizable gap in learning between children enrolled in public and those enrolled in private schools from the same family.[71] It is no surprise then, that most parents would prefer private schools.

In India, the percentage of children studying in private schools is significantly higher than in many developed countries, including those in the US and Europe. This is not to say that there are no constraints on setting up private schools, due to a rigid interpretation of the RTE Act and red tape at the state government level. One reason that private schools do not perform as well as they should is that 'learning outcomes are under-regulated, whereas entry and operations are heavily regulated'.[72] Private schools need autonomy and space to function with flexibility in the fixation of tuition fees and teacher salaries. For example, there is no need to enforce rigid and high salary scales across all schools, which only pushes up tuition fees: several private schools cater to poorer households and cannot match government scales if tuition fees are low. Of course, unjustified fee hikes or unreasonably low salaries need checks. There are hundreds of credible organizations willing to establish and run schools for children from economically weaker families if offered per-child compensation by the government of a similar magnitude as the current spending per child by government schools; such institutions should be encouraged.

While Delhi's AAP government has done much to improve government schools, it has been rather harsh on private schools. It has not permitted private schools to enhance fees even on bonafide grounds. In 2019, of over 2,000 private schools, only 49 were permitted to increase fees. The example below illustrates the position of most private schools, not only in Delhi but across the country:

A private girls' school in south Delhi promoted by a credible minority institution has earned a reputation for academic excellence over the years.[73] However, its fee structure is less than half of what Delhi's elite schools charge. The school's annual revenue in 2019–20 was ₹117 million, against which it spent ₹128 million. Its teaching staff's salary bill was ₹75 million, leaving the school with just about ₹25 million for meeting all its other expenses, including administration and salaries of its non-teaching staff. Given a choice, the school would have spent more on academic support activities and improved its infrastructure, services, and labs, and reduced the student-teacher ratio, which would mean adding more teachers. The RTE Act requires all private schools to reserve 25 per cent of their fresh enrolments every year for students from economically weaker sections from whom they cannot charge any fees. However, the government reimburses less than 23 per cent of the school's expenses to these students. Despite these financial constraints, the Delhi government has not granted permission to the school to raise fees for the past three years.[74]

What should be the structure of tuition fees charged by private, unaided schools to make them viable?[75] First, schools should be permitted to fix the fee structure, to leave them a modest surplus of about 10 per cent. Second, the schools and parents should mutually decide the fee hikes and none other; of course, the government and the courts should intervene if there is profiteering or dispute. Third, the overall government approach needs to be facilitative and supportive; this will require a change in bureaucratic mindsets. Finally, apart from the rigid enforcement of teachers' pay scales that many schools cannot afford to implement, other restrictions relating to space for innovation, promotion of arts and sports, and rigidity on the curriculum to be followed need to be relaxed. Such conditions have deterred the entry of philanthropic organizations from coming forward to establish schools.

On the other hand, learning levels in private schools leave much to be desired. Over half of all private schools do not extend up to a board exam level, making it difficult for parents to assess quality. Such schools may spend on observable things like computer labs and may claim to teach in English, but they are less likely to invest in learning-focused improvements such as teacher training. The NEP 2020 has proposed a central regulator for school education, which may lead to over-centralization and even morph into a new 'Inspector Raj' while limiting the scope for innovation by states. Instead, each state should have an independent regulator who should only facilitate setting up, monitoring, and disseminating learning markers. The state regulators should create a school accreditation ecosystem and mandate information disclosure to enable parents to make more informed choices.[76] The regulators should permit flexibility in input standards like land, infrastructure, and salaries while remaining firmly against institutions that see school education as a business.

Enhancing and Re-prioritizing Education Budgets

While promoting credible private schools, the government must accord the highest priority to improving the performance of government schools, which cater to children of low-income households. We have noted that school education is chronically underfunded.[77] A study of the educational budgets of two states, Andhra Pradesh and Rajasthan, revealed three critical findings. First, salaries and allowances of teachers and other staff allowances account for over 90 per cent of the elementary school budget. Second, education is financed mainly out of state budgets; the centre's share is only 10 per cent. Third, household expenditure on education is significant, at between 25 and 30 per cent.[78] At present, the education budgets of the centre and the states have four main heads: teacher salaries; infrastructure for new schools and new classrooms; mid-day meals; and, to a lesser extent, teacher training. As noted in Chapter 4, massive budget enhancements must begin with a universal and effective school readiness programme in ICDS and other government pre-school sections. Other critical areas that need enhanced budgets at the central and state levels are teaching-learning, remedial support, and improving existing school infrastructure. The school education system must move from coverage, enrolment, and rote learning and ensure every child has access to quality education. The strategies we have recommended in this chapter are workable, fiscally prudent, and sustainable. They will empower persons to enhance their well-being, access improved livelihood opportunities, and build the foundation for a lifetime of continuous learning.

Notes

1 Nelson Mandela made this statement at a speech in Madison Park High School, Boston on 23 June 1990 (www.oxfordreference.com) while Kofi Annan made his statement at an address to the World Bank conference on June 22, 1997, *UN Press Release SG/SM/6268*, June 23, 1997 (www.un.org/press).
2 Sanjay Kaul, Uma Mahadevan-Dasgupta, "The Lessons That Count", *Indian Express*, March 7, 2022.
3 Anders Kjelsrud and Rohini Somanathan, "Poverty Targeting Through Public Goods," Chapter 18, Poverty and Income Distribution in India, *Juggernaut Books*, 2019. The data in the paper is drawn from the Census Village Directories and shows that by 1991 itself the fraction of villages with primary schools had increased to 75 per cent.
4 Ridhu Tewari, "More Than 14 Percent Villages In India Don't Have Any School, Says Government Data," *The Print*, 31 December 2018. https://theprint.in/india/governance/over-14-per-cent-villages-in-india-dont-have-schools-says-latest-data/170440/; date of access March, 12, 2021.
5 "Unified District Information System For Education Plus (UDISE+), 2019–20," *Government of India*. https://www.education.gov.in/sites/upload_files/mhrd/files/statistics-new/udise_201920.pdf; date of access June 5, 2021.
6 Vimala Ramachandran, "Inside Indian Schools", *Social Science Press*, 2018. While the gross enrolment ratio (GER) at the secondary level is 78.5 per cent, the net enrolment ratio (NER) is still low at 48.5 per cent. In 2010–11, GER at the primary level is 116 with no gender gap, but at the upper primary level, it drops to 85. It drops even further to 65 in classes IX and X and to 39 in classes XI and XII and at the higher education level, GER is only 16 per cent, far below the global average of 27 per cent. The situation in 2015 did not show significant improvement. Thus, access remains limited at the higher stages.
7 Ibid.
8 "SDG India Index, Baseline Report," NITI Aayog, *Government of India*, 2018.

9 "Early Years," Annual Status of Education Report (ASER) Report, *Pratham*, 2019. http://img.asercentre.org/docs/ASER%202019/ASER2019%20report%20/aserreport2019earlyyearsfinal.pdf; date of access July 20, 2020. Overall, only 46 per cent of children in Class 1 are of the RTE mandated age of 6, 36 per cent are 7 or 8 years of age, and 22 per cent are 4 or 5; 30 per cent of children at age 6 are still at anganwadis.
10 Vimala Ramachandran, Chapter 7, "Systemic Issues Framing Equity," The Elementary Education System in India, *Routledge*, 2009.
11 "Early Years," Annual Status of Education Report (ASER) Report, *Pratham*, 2019.
12 Ibid.
13 V Santhakumar, "The Need to Strengthen Government Schools in India," *Azim Premji University*, 2016. https://practiceconnect.azimpremjiuniversity.edu.in/the-need-to-strengthen-government-schools-in-india/#easy-footnote-bottom-1-480; date of access August 2, 2021.
14 Vimala Ramachandran, "How to Improve Learning Outcomes," *Hindustan Times*, 21 October 2020. The survey referred to is the National Assessment Survey 2017, conducted by NCERT.
15 "Annual Status of Education Report (ASER) Report," *Pratham*, 2011.
16 Karthik Muralidharan, "Reforming the Indian School Education System in India," What the Economy Needs Now, *Juggernaut Books*, 2019.
17 Rashmi Sharma, Chapter 5, "The Internal Dynamic," The Elementary Education System in India, *Routledge*, 2009.
18 Vimala Ramachandran, Chapter 7, "Systemic Issues Framing Equity," The Elementary Education System in India, *Routledge*, 2009.
19 The creation of a separate cadre for English was proposed in Karnataka during my tenure as Commissioner School, Karnataka. Besides English, most teachers had no science instruction beyond the elementary stage; thus, teaching of science or maths was difficult for many teachers. And, when they were posted to schools, they were expected to impart the teaching of English, science, and maths. There was fierce resistance when I sought to create separate cadres for science and English, as teachers were apprehensive that this would affect their promotional avenues. It took over a decade in Karnataka to create separate posts of English and Science teachers at the elementary stage. There is a need to create a separate cadre of Science and English teachers in all states.
20 Vimala Ramachandran, Chapter 7, "Systemic Issues Framing Equity", The Elementary Education System in India, *Routledge*, 2009.
21 Rashmi Sharma, Chapter 5, "The Internal Dynamic", The Elementary Education System in India, *Routledge*, 2009.
22 Nazmul Chaudhury, Jeffery Hammer, Michael Kremer, Karthik Muralidharan, and Halsey Rogers, "Missing in Action: Teacher and Health Worker Absence in Developing Countries," *Journal of Economic Perspectives*, 91–116, Winter 2006.
23 Vimala Ramachandran, Chapter 7, Systemic Issues Framing Equity", The Elementary Education System in India, *Routledge*, 2009.
24 Abhijit Banerjee and Esther Duflo, Poor Economics, *Juggernaut*, 2011. The authors have quoted the probe team's report on this; Public Report on Basic Education in India, *Oxford University Press*, 1999.
25 Vimala Ramachandran, Inside Indian Schools, *Social Science Press*, 2018. 37 per cent of schools at the secondary level are run by government, 8.5 per cent are managed by local bodies, with the balance being private schools.
26 Karthik Muralidharan, "Reforming the Indian School Education System," What the Economy Needs Now, *Juggernaut Books*, 2019.
27 Shreya Roy Chowdhury, "Huge Mismatch Between What Indian Parents Seek From Private Schools and What they Get, Finds Study," *Scroll*, 2019.

ENSURING QUALITY SCHOOLING

28 "Early Years," Annual Status of Education Report (ASER), *Pratham*, 2018.

29 Roshan Kishore and Abhishek Jha, "Mapping Education Inequalities," *Hindustan Times*, 1 August 2020. Overall, access to English medium schools varies massively across states. According to the recently released National Statistical Office (NSO) survey conducted in 2017–18, just 6 per cent of students were in English medium education in Bihar. The number is 63 per cent in Telangana and as much as 95 per cent in Jammu & Kashmir.

30 Nandan Nilekani, "The Phoenix Tongue," Imagining India, *Penguin*, 2008. As explained by Nilekani, in the initial colonial period, English was viewed by some as a tool of imperialism while the elite associated English with cultural prestige. English teaching also received support from Indian social reformers such as Raja Ram Mohan Roy; they saw English as a language for spreading literacy and education. English thus represented repression to some, and emancipation and social freedom to others. As India neared Independence, leaders such as Gandhi expressed strong views against teaching the language in schools. However, other leaders like Rajagopalachari viewed English as "Saraswati's gift to India". By 1950, English had become the lingua franca of India's central government and educational institutions. This change came about as the proposal to adopt Hindi as the official language, favoured by many of the Hindi speaking leaders, met with strong resistance from the Southern States, especially Tamil Nadu, who denounced this as language imperialism. The language also gained support from the Dalit community as Hindi texts had references to caste and untouchability, while English was perceived as liberating. Initially, English was permitted only as a transitory arrangement, and Hindi was to be the only official language by 1965. This decision again saw protests across the southern states, and the Language Act was amended in 1967, specifying both English and Hindi as official languages. The 1968 National Policy for Education had to accommodate the demands from the proponents of Hindi, advocates of English as the link language, and those in favour of using local languages. Hence the three-language formula was developed, where people from non-Hindi-speaking areas were to study their regional language and Hindi and English. Hindi speakers could learn Hindi, English, and a third language.

31 Rukmini S. "In India, Who Speaks in English, and Where?" *Mint*, 2019. https://www.livemint.com/news/india/in-india-who-speaks-in-english-and-where-1557814101428.html; date of access June 5, 2021.

32 PTI, "NEP 2020 Makes Studies in English Compulsory in Regional Languages up to Class 5, School Principals Think English is Important," *India Today*, 31 July 2020.

33 Amandeep Shukla, "New Education Policy Lays Emphasis on Learning in Mother Tongue," *Hindustan Times*, 2020. https://www.hindustantimes.com/india-news/education-policy-lays-emphasis-on-learning-in-mother-tongue/story-7yRtLx7AmFJrqyd1MbrB5K.html. ii) Also see, Pratham, 2005, Final edition, available at http;/scripts.mit.edu/-varun_ag/readinggroup/images1/14/ASER.pdf.

34 Vimala Ramachandran, Chapter 7, "Systemic Issues Framing Equity," The Elementary Education System in India, *Routledge*, 2009.

35 J. Venkatesh, "Supreme Court Upholds RTE Act, *The Hindu*, 12 April 2012.

36 Abhijit Banerjee, What the Economy Needs Now, *Juggernaut Books*, 2019.

37 Ibid

38 Jacques Delors, Delors Commission Report, *European Commission*, 1998.

39 Vimala Ramachandran, "How to Improve Learning Outcomes," *Hindustan Times*, 25 October 2020.

40 Sanjay Kaul, Uma Mahadevan-Dasgupta, "The Lessons That Count", *Indian Express*, March 7, 2022.

ENSURING QUALITY SCHOOLING

41 "In Academic Year 2019–20, only 22% Schools had Internet," *The Hindu*, 2 July 2021. The government UDISE+ data shows that there was a stark digital divide between government and private schools and across states. In many Union Territories and Kerala, over 90 per cent of schools had access to working computers. In contrast, in states such as Assam, Madhya Pradesh, Bihar, West Bengal, Tripura and Uttar Pradesh, less than 20 per cent of schools had working computers. Overall, only 37 per cent of schools had functional computers. The connectivity divide is even starker. Only 3 states have internet facilities in more than half their schools.

42 Kaushik Deka, "Online Transition," *India Today*, 1 June 2020.

43 Krishna Kumar, "Returning to School 17 Months Later," *The Hindu*, 14 September 2021.

44 Manabi Majumdar and Jos Mooji, The Marks Race: School Education, Pluralism and Marginality, *Orient BlackSwan*, 2012.

45 Ira Shor and Paulo Friere, "How Can Teachers become Liberating Educators," A Pedagogy for Liberation, page 33, *Bergin & Garvey Publishers*, 1987.

46 Russell Bishop, "A Culturally Responsive Pedagogy of Relations", School Education, Pluralism and Marginality, *Orient BlackSwan*, 2012.

47 Prashika, "Eklavya's Innovative Experiment in Primary Education", *Ratna Sagar*, 1994. Anita Kaul while she worked as Project Director, District Primary Education Programme, Karnataka drew on the same principles but used teachers to themselves create activities so that children could learn at their own pace. The activity-based curriculum has stood the test of time and has been adopted by several states.

48 Karthik Muralidharan, "Reforming the Indian School Education System", *What the Economy Needs Now*, Juggernaut, 2019.

49 Abhijit Banerjee, Raghuram Rajan, and Gita Gopinath, Chapter 9, Good Economics for Hard Times, *Juggernaut Books*, 2019.

50 Prashika, "Eklavya's Innovative Experiment in Primary Education", *Ratna Sagar*, 1994.

51 The Nali Kali initiative was taken by Anita Kaul while she worked as Project Director, District Primary Education Programme, Karnataka.

52 "Enhancing Quality of Education in India by 2030 – A F.I.T. approach," *KPMG*, 2019. https://assets.kpmg/content/dam/kpmg/in/pdf/2019/11/enhancing-quality-of-education-in-india-by-2030.pdf; date of access June 15, 2021.

53 "Learning at the Right Level," *Pratham*. https://www.pratham.org/about/teaching-at-the-right-level/; date of access June 21, 2021.

54 Navya P. K., "How Volunteer Teachers are Making a difference in Bengaluru's Govt Schools," *Citizen Matters*, 15 November 2018. https://bengaluru.citizenmatters. in/bangalore-volunteering-in-government-schools-aims-for-better-quality-education-29007; date of access My 20, 2021.

55 Indulekha Aravind, "Operation Classroom," *The Economic Times*, 11–17 October 2020.

56 "The World's Best Performing Education Systems and What Sets Them Apart," *National Center on Education and the Economy (NCEE)*. https://ncee.org/what-we-do/center-on-international-education-benchmarking/top-performing-countries/; date of access My 21, 2021.

57 Karthik Muralidharan, "Reforming the Indian School Education System," What the Economy Needs Now, *Juggernaut Books*, 2019.

58 V Santhakumar, "The Need to Strengthen Government Schools in India," *Azim Premji University*. https://practiceconnect.azimpremjiuniversity.edu.in/the-need-to-strengthen-government-schools-in-india/#easy-footnote-bottom-1-480; date of access April 10, 2021.

59 Manish Sisodia, "Shiksha", *Penguin Books*, 2019.

ENSURING QUALITY SCHOOLING

60 "AAP's Delhi Budget: 236 New Schools to be Opened," *DNA*, 25 June 2015.

61 *Economic Survey*, Chapter 7, 2018–19, Ministry of Finance, *Government of India*.

62 The estimated literacy rate (age 15 and above) is 70.3 per cent – NSS 71st round, 2014 (cited in *KPMG* 2019 report).

63 Vimala Ramachandran, "How to Improve Learning Outcomes," *Hindustan Times*, 25 October 2020.

64 "Introducing Transparency, Merit and Rationalisation in the Recruitment and Deployment of Elementary Education Teachers," Education Department, *Government of Karnataka*, July 1999. The Karnataka reform was introduced in 1998 while I worked as Commissioner of Schools, documented, and circulated to other states for adoption. This was also used by IIM Bangalore as a successful case study on administrative reforms.

65 For example, NCML, the company that I had been associated with, has been using the 'Point of Presence' App for all its employees and is no longer perceived as a harsh policing measure.

66 Vimala Ramachandran, The Elementary Education System in India, *Routledge*, 2009.

67 Gunjan Jain, "English Language Competency: Need & Challenge for Enhancing Employability in Indian Graduates," *Social Values and Society*, 2019. https://www.researchgate.net/publication/333996775_ENGLISH_ LANGUAGE_COMPETENCY_NEED_CHALLENGE_FOR_ENHANCING_ EMPLOYABILITY_IN_INDIAN_GRADUATES; date of access August 10, 2021.

68 Michel DeGraff, *Linguistics*, MIT, 2015.

69 Saktibrata Sen and Simmi Sikka, "Importance of Literature to Literacy," Early Years, *ASER*, 2019. http://img.asercentre.org/docs/ASER%202019/ASER2019% 20report%20/saktibratasenandsimmisikka-importanceofliteraturetoliteracy. pdf; date of access May 20, 2021.

70 PTI, "NEP 2020 Makes Studies Compulsory in Regional Language up to Class 5, School Principals Think English is Important," *India Today*, 2020. https://www. indiatoday.in/education-today/news/story/nep-2020-makes-studies-compulsory- in-regional-language-upto-class-5-school-principals-think-english-is-important- 1706442-2020-07-31; date of access January 10, 2021.

71 Sonalde Desai, Amaresh Dubey, Reeve Vanneman and Rukmini Banerji, "Private Schooling in India: A New Educational Landscape," *Indian Human Development Survey*, Working Paper No. 11, 2010.

72 "Private Schools in India, State of the Sector Report," *Central Square Foundation*, 2019. https://centralsquarefoundation.org/State-of-the-Sector-Report-on-Private- Schools-in-India.pdf; date of access February 5, 2021.

73 The school has not been named as the management was wary on making its accounts public.

74 The expenditure details have been taken from the audited accounts of the school.

75 The Supreme Court, in a landmark judgment in "Islamic Academy of Education v. State of Karnataka" held that "Each institute must have the freedom to fix its fee structure, taking into consideration the need to generate funds to run the institute and to provide facilities necessary for the students. They must also be able to generate a surplus which must be used for the betterment and growth of that educational institution." In a very recent case, "Unaided Private Schools of Delhi v. Director of Education" the Supreme Court observed that "private unaided institutions are permitted to have a profit but not permitted to profi- teer…." A recent Delhi High Court judgment pronounced on 15 March 2019 has attempted to clear the air on private schools' regulation. It has held that

regulatory measures cannot be permitted to trespass on the unaided schools' autonomy in the matter of fixation of fee or even the appropriation of financial resources. Further, it has stated that regulation cannot trespass into the arena of administration of unaided schools. So long as the fee charged does not amount to commercialization there is a guaranteed 'hands off' by the government in fee fixation.

76 Shah and Kelkar, "Private Schools in India, State of the Sector Report," *Central Square Foundation*, 2019. https://centralsquarefoundation.org/State-of-the-Sector-Report-on-Private-Schools-in-India.pdf; date of access January 10, 2021.

77 Budget documents, Ministry of Finance, *Government of India*, 1 February 2021. Despite the fanfare surrounding the announcement of the New Education Policy, the education budget for FY 2020–21 has a Budget Estimate (BE) down by 6 per cent from ₹9,931 billion to ₹932 billion.

78 Vimala Ramachandran, Inside Indian Schools, *Social Science Press*, 2018.

6

IMPROVING LIVELIHOODS, CREATING JOBS

There is nothing as degrading as the constant anxiety about one's means of livelihood.[1]

W. Somerset Maugham, British playwright and novelist

Overreliance on the Market

Despite economic liberalization since 1991, livelihood opportunities in India have remained limited. Jobs have been mainly available to the more educated men and those possessing skills; women have been kept out of the labour market for the most part. As economic reforms did away with the 'license raj' of the 1960s and 1970s, many new enterprises flourished, though large corporates benefited disproportionately. However, since 2016, many small and tiny firms have run aground due to the compounded effects of demonetization, the goods and services tax (GST), and COVID-19. Poverty and unemployment levels are at a record high. The COVID-19 pandemic has put further strain on the already fragile economy and has been especially devastating for the poor. The agriculture sector, the mainstay of 65 per cent of households, has stalled and offers little scope for improving rural livelihoods.

The fundamental problem is that government strategies since liberalization have placed reliance on market forces and have not directly addressed the livelihood and jobs crisis, nor have they significantly alleviated poverty. There has been no coherent strategy to create the millions of jobs required to improve the lives of the millions mired in poverty.

The strategies recommended in the chapters on health, nutrition and food security, school education, and the young child would significantly enhance physical well-being and widen opportunities for people. However, there would be a limited economic benefit to the average household without an enabling policy environment. Moreover, the COVID-19 pandemic has led to unprecedented levels of unemployment and poverty. The country and its people can wait no longer. Therefore, targeted and well-designed strategies focused on improving livelihoods and job creation are imperative.

DOI: 10.4324/9781003346258-6

We outline a comprehensive set of policies that complement each other, prioritize job creation, enhance millions of livelihoods, and provide the foundation for sustainable economic growth. The delineated strategies focus on each significant socio-economic group, including the most impoverished households, agricultural households, women, people engaged in traditional livelihoods, migrant labour, the self-employed, and educated unemployed youth. A vital element of the proposal is its urban-centric approach to promoting a vast number of labour-intensive enterprises in urban clusters to potentially create millions of jobs.

Poverty and Unemployment

In Chapter 1, we alluded to the likelihood that poverty levels in the country may have gone up beyond the last government estimate of 21.92 per cent in 2011.[2] An independent assessment showed a poverty percentage of 27.9 per cent for 2016–17, while another computation for 2017–18 puts poverty even higher at 35.1 per cent.[3] Irrespective of the exact figure, the fact remains that a huge proportion of rural agricultural labour households is impoverished and caught in perpetual debt. To better understand the situation of such families, we return to Birsa and Rasika's story.

Birsa and Rasika have not seen any improvement in their lives for as long as they can remember. They remain in perpetual debt that keeps mounting, and they cannot better their lives or acquire any productive assets. They are forced to continuously borrow money as they lurch from one crisis to the next. At the beginning of their story, we saw that Birsa had to borrow because his cash reserves had run out once the planting season had ended. When PDS supplies got disrupted, he again needed to borrow, to procure rice from the open market. A year ago, following the birth of their youngest child, Shibu, Rasika had to be hospitalized as her platelet count had fallen precipitously; Birsa had been forced to borrow from the village moneylender once again. And he had to borrow before that to repair the damaged roof of their house after heavy rains lashed their village. Just a couple of months ago, Bindu, their second child, had fallen ill, and he had to borrow to spend on her treatment.

The local moneylender has been the primary source for Birsa to borrow money. However, last year, Rasika joined the local self-help group (SHG), through which she has taken small loans, though the interest rate has remained high. Intermittently, Rasika earns some extra money when government employment guarantee work is taken up in the village, but that only helps in debt repayment. Birsa has a 'Jan Dhan' account with the local bank but has not deposited money into it, caught as he is in this perpetual debt cycle.

IMPROVING LIVELIHOODS, CREATING JOBS

Birsa and Rasika are reconciled to remaining agricultural labourers and do not reflect on a better life or vastly improved livelihoods. Higher wages come with education and skills, both of which they lack. In any case, alternate employment opportunities are virtually non-existent in their village. Birsa has, on a few occasions, thought about breaking out of this vicious cycle of poverty by migrating to Ranchi to try his luck as a labourer. A few people from the village have migrated to Ranchi and now earn much more than his casual agricultural labour earnings. But he is aware that those who left had some skills and could get employment at construction sites. And, he wonders, where would he live in a new city with his wife and three small children?

The situation of Birsa and Rasika's family holds a mirror to the vicious poverty trap in which most landless agricultural households and many migrant labour urban households are caught. What is even more worrisome is that more and more families are falling into the poverty trap. A significant contributor to this ever-increasing poverty has been the declining levels of employment. Equally worrying are the low wages, employment uncertainty, and poor conditions of work. The full-time employment growth rate steadily decelerated throughout the 1999–2018 period to even lower than 1 per cent. Growth in part-time jobs also declined throughout this period.[4] The deceleration was shockingly high for six years during 2011–17 when the country even witnessed 'jobless growth'.[5] Surprisingly, this decline in employment took place during high and unprecedented economic growth in India. The unemployment situation has worsened in the period following the COVID-19 pandemic.

The non-student working population in 2018 was an estimated 841 million, and those employed were an estimated 458 million, translating to an employment rate of 54.5 per cent, against 65 per cent in 1999.[6] The Periodic Labour Force Survey (PLFS) for 2018–19, released in June 2020, estimates that 25 million were unemployed (PLFS Annual Report 2018–19).[7] The unemployment rate stood at 5.7 per cent while the Labour Force Participation rate was a low 36.9 per cent.[8] The COVID-19 pandemic has further exacerbated the unemployment situation – the unemployment rate had risen to 6 per cent in January 2021.[9]

Even more alarming is that only about 90 million people are in regular employment; the manufacturing sector employs 60 million, a meagre 12.8 per cent of the country's total workforce. Of this, the organized manufacturing sector employs only 15 million workers. This means that 75 per cent of manufacturing workers are in the unorganized sector.[10]

Most labour-intensive manufacturing industries – apparel, tobacco products, textile, non-metallic mineral products, food products, and beverages – have witnessed either stagnation or decline in employment.[11] Youth face the biggest challenge. Between 2012 and 2018, youth unemployment tripled

111

from 6 to 18 per cent, while graduate unemployment rose from 19 to 36 per cent. The number of self-employed youths has declined from 81 to 49 million between 2005 and 2018.[12]

Women's low work participation contributes significantly to the low labour force participation rate (LFPR) in the country. Despite rapid economic growth, educational gains, and fertility decline, India's women have remained conspicuously absent from the labour force. In contrast to the rest of the world, where almost half of the female population is part of the workforce, only 32.6 per cent of India's half a billion adult females report being part of the labour force. National Sample Surveys show that the LFPR for married Indian women declined from 35 per cent to 24 per cent from 1983 to 2011. While male rural employment has stayed around 55 per cent for the past two decades, female rural LFPR has remained much lower, at 30 per cent; urban female employment is even lower at 15 per cent.[13] *However, in interpreting this data, it should not be understood to mean that a large proportion of women are not engaged in productive work. On the contrary, the low LFPR is also a reflection of the understatement of women's work in official data and low formal employment.*

Looking at groups within the population, scheduled caste women are most likely to be working, while higher castes and married women post the lowest work participation rates. In terms of sectors, agriculture has the highest number of women – 55 million – working as casual labour, followed by textile, food, food products, and construction. Outside agriculture, most women are self-employed or work as domestic workers, primary school teachers, and health workers. The government's employment guarantee works require no skills and are accessible to unskilled women.[14] Overall, women's employment in low-paid, unskilled jobs reflects a regressive form of feminization.[15] At the higher end of the value chain, women's participation in the workplace is limited.

The vast gender wage disparity compounds the problem of low LFPR. According to an International Labour Organization report of 2018–19, India's gender wage gap is the highest among 73 countries studied, with women's hourly wages being 34 per cent less than for men. In manufacturing, the wage disparity is starker – women's wages are only half of the men's wages.[16] A low wage reflects the undervaluation of women's work – we saw this in the context of the poor remuneration paid to ASHA and anganwadi workers. Apart from gender discrimination, which is deeply rooted in cultural beliefs and the prevailing patriarchal structure, other contributory factors for low LFPR among women are limited access to assets and resources, with concomitant deficits in educational level and skills.[17]

Jobless growth in sectors that employ more women or are friendlier to women has only exacerbated the situation. Only 20 per cent of new jobs created in finance, construction, and business services in the last two decades went to women.[18] The sharpest drop in women's employment has been among married women, and this decline appears to be a long-term trend. The vast majority of those outside the labour force but willing to work are women, though most seek part-time work and work locations closer to home. Ironically, over 90 per cent of poor, young women wish to work, yet nearly 70 per cent of them are unemployed.[19]

Indian households – traditionally patriarchal – require that women prioritize housework, and many even explicitly constrain married women from working. The societal expectation that women function only as caregivers and caretakers of the home often means that women who seek work encounter opposition from their peers and families. Even in the absence of such overt constraints, women often internalize these views and suppress labour supply. These norms are typically more binding among wealthier, upper-caste households, suggesting that economic growth may not change patriarchal influence. Indian women are also still subject to laws governing when and in which industries they can work. For example, female participation in export-oriented manufacturing jobs fell due to legal constraints placed on women's working hours through the factory laws. Even if these laws change, employers may be less likely to hire a woman over an equally qualified man.

Government policies have focused on female education but not their entry into the workplace.[20] However, even education has not helped. The experience of India, and even developed economies like Japan, shows that most women with the requisite education and job skills remain outside the job market.[21] More young women are enrolled in higher education than ever before and are now more successful in clearing board exams than young men. However, they are either marrying early or not finding (or not looking for) jobs.

An increase in the female student ratio should lead to higher female work participation, but the reverse has taken place. While the enrolment of young girls in higher education rose from 39 to 46 per cent between 2007 and 2014, female LFPR fell from 34 to 27 per cent in the five years ending in 2014.[22] This paradox of higher enrolment paired with a decline in India's female LFPR is disturbing and indicates that traditional patriarchal norms run extremely deep. There is a U-shaped relationship between education and female employment, as well as income. The U-shape effect in income is most evident for urban women. Women with only secondary level education have the lowest work participation levels, while those with high levels of education post higher employment rates. As household incomes rise, women, even with school education, initially opt out of the labour force. However, highly educated women opt back into the labour force as the opportunity cost of remaining out of it increases.[23] (We discuss strategies to address these cultural barriers to women's employment in Chapter 7.)

Limited Opportunities in Agriculture

A significant reason for high poverty and unemployment levels in India is that the share of agriculture in GDP has steadily declined from 42 per cent in 1967 to 16 per cent in 2019. The government has, not unexpectedly, failed to meet its over-ambitious goal set in 2016 of doubling farmer incomes by 2022; the harsh reality is that farmer livelihoods have not improved at all during this period.

Of course, there is an enormous potential for enhancing agricultural productivity. Agricultural yields in India are way below global averages. Focusing on improving productivity in poorly performing states could result in significant gains. Currently, crop yields show considerable divergence within the country, even in similar soil and climatic conditions. The balanced use of fertilizer alone would improve productivity; the present pricing regime over-subsidizes urea at the cost of other nutrients. The seed industry is crying itself hoarse, seeking clarity on using genetically modified crops that could hugely raise yields. Even proven technologies to enhance productivity do not get adopted, as there is no governmental outreach to the farming community. Further, as noted in our discussion on food policy in Chapter 3, the MSP regime has resulted in considerable distortions in cropping patterns.

Some allied areas show excellent prospects for growth. Livestock production has grown at a compound annual growth rate of 8 per cent, fisheries by 7 per cent, while the food processing sector has grown at 5 per cent. Though India has been a net exporter of agricultural products since the 1990s, its share in global agricultural trade is only 2 per cent; there is enormous potential to do better.[24] Facilitation of investment by the private sector in agriculture could enhance both productivity and exports. Public investment in irrigation projects has been minimal and has resulted in the irrigation potential not being realized; state budgets are tight, and there is no major central scheme for irrigation.

A major structural bottleneck in Indian agriculture is the wide divide between the government-notified Minimum Support Prices (MSP) and the market prices in respect of food grains, which has led to cropping distortions and an unsustainable food grains market. As indicated in Chapter 3, this appears to have been the underlying logic for notifying three major farm laws focused on marketing reforms. It was expected that these laws would, through opening up the market, encourage greater private sector participation, and thereby reduce the need for government to procure higher and higher quantities each year. The first law sought to free a host of farm commodities from the Essential Commodities Act. The second sought to open agricultural markets to the private sector, while the third provides a framework for buyers to enter into contracts with farmers directly. However, as noted in Chapter 3, several farmer groups had vociferously opposed these legislations. In their view, the new laws would only have paved the way for a few select large corporates to dominate the market and squeeze them. On the other hand, the government had attempted to argue that the three legislations would expand the choices for farmers and make transactions more open and transparent. The underlying logic of the government appeared to have been that agricultural markets, because of their opaqueness and high levels of intermediation, are highly inefficient and that farm gate prices would automatically become much higher once the markets become 'freer'. This assumption may not hold. The reality is that farm gate prices for many agricultural commodities, even in crops where there are no notified minimum support prices (MSP), are already higher than globally traded prices, principally due to high production costs and low yields. The assumption of high marketing costs or inefficiencies may not be the principal reason that farmers do not get remunerative prices. Therefore, the laws by themselves would not have led to efficiencies on the production front and would not fundamentally have altered farm incomes.[25]

The bottom line is that, even with improved farm practices, higher public investments, and marketing reforms, agriculture's growth prospects are not bright and will improve only marginally at best. Indian agriculture continues to be vulnerable to the vagaries of weather, and climate change has the potential to expose this vulnerability further. Studies indicate that crop yields in India could decline by 4.5–9 per cent by 2039 and by a whopping 20–25 per cent in the long run by 2070–99 in the absence of adaptation by farmers. Consequently, an estimate suggests that farm incomes could fall by 15–18 per cent on average in irrigated lands and by 20–25 per cent in unirrigated areas.[26] Adaptation by farmers to climate change could mitigate the impact while the strategies recommended in the previous chapters for improving health, nutrition, and education could boost the productivity of farming households. Even with these measures, based on past trends, the best-case estimates indicate an annual increase of 5 per cent in agricultural GDP. It is thus clear that agricultural GDP as a proportion of total GDP would continue to decline; this reflects the experience across nations.

Agricultural households in India have supplemented their incomes through non-farm activities, and as much as two-thirds of rural income now comes from such activities.[27] While non-farm income growth has been impressive, a NITI Aayog study highlights that this has neither brought significant employment gains nor enhanced worker productivity.[28] Growth in non-farm employment has primarily been in the services, transport, communication, and construction sectors. However, it is mainly educated males in the 18–26-year age group who have benefited from non-farm wage employment; women are only slowly moving into the non-farm employment sector. There is evidence that both pull and push factors are responsible for non-farm jobs. These factors vary widely across regions. For instance, in Uttar Pradesh, the lack of employment opportunities in agriculture has pushed the rural workforce to non-farm activities; in contrast, in Kerala, greater literacy and higher levels of social development caused this shift of workers.[29] This shift to non-agricultural occupations has mainly been in the informal sectors of the economy. Employment in these sectors is insecure and does not lead to much income enhancement.

The growth in non-farm employment has not kept pace with the growth in the labour force. With agriculture unable to sustain the livelihoods of the burgeoning rural population, the government needs to formulate policies that will accelerate the shift of workers away from agriculture into meaningful livelihoods. It needs to jettison the notion that agriculture is the primary source of food security and livelihoods and that households must rely on their produce to meet their food requirement. Many agricultural families already access food from the market, and 88 per cent of farming households rely on some form of non-farm income to sustain their livelihoods.[30]

In the four decades since 1980, Indian rural output has increased seven times – from ₹3,199 billion to ₹21,107 billion – but the share of agriculture in rural income has dropped from 72.4 to a low of 39.2 per cent, showing its reduced dependence.[31] Moreover, an estimate suggests that a whopping 84 million agricultural workers must move from agriculture to the non-farm sectors to absorb the labour force productively. In any case, the next generation of youth, especially youth who have received high school education and above, are no longer inclined to remain in agriculture.[32]

Steep Decline in Traditional Livelihoods

Outside agriculture, traditional livelihoods – handicrafts and handlooms – have been in decline. These have been part of our rich cultural heritage. Handicrafts of various states reflect the influence of different empires. India boasts of a wide range of handicrafts: metal crafts such Bidriware and Dhokra; bamboo, jute and silk products; paintings such as in the Madhubani style; needlework; and the world-famous hand-woven carpets of Kashmir, among many other smaller ones. This cottage industry employs 7 million artisans, and the annual value of handicraft products is an estimated ₹300–350 billion, with export earnings of over ₹100 billion. Close to 80 per cent of handicraft production is in rural areas, with over 40 per cent of artisans working from their own homes. The number of artisans has steadily declined, as the younger generation does not find this profession attractive.[33]

Most traditional artisans have low education levels and have failed to adopt modern technology to upgrade their skills. Quality control and standardization of products are lacking, while innovation and design improvements have not kept pace with market needs. There has been stiff competition from machine-made craft products from other countries, such as China, which has emerged as the market leader. India has over 67,000 handicraft export enterprises; they are spread across the country and find it challenging to adhere to the complex export requirements. Most of them operate on

IMPROVING LIVELIHOODS, CREATING JOBS

a small scale and find it difficult to cater to bulk orders. There is little wonder that India's share in the global exports of handicrafts is a mere 1.2 per cent.[34]

After agriculture, the textile sector has been the largest traditional means of livelihood, with over 45 million people employed directly and another 60 million people in allied sectors. Women account for more than 77 per cent of the overall employment in the industry. India is among the largest manufacturers and exporters of textiles and clothing in the world, second only to China. The share of textile and clothing in India's total exports stands at a significant 12 per cent, though the country's share of global trade is only 5 per cent. Traditional sectors like handloom and small-scale power-loom units account for over 75 per cent of India's textiles production.[35]

The Vital Importance of Migrant Labour

A key barrier to India's growth story has been that, while agriculture and traditional sources of livelihood have been in decline, there has been an inadequate migration of people to alternative jobs. The shift to other sectors in India has been very slow, in sharp contrast to China, where the movement out of agriculture was very rapid. Rural enterprises and self-employment in rural areas have not improved livelihoods. Rural firms are more capital-intensive than urban manufacturing and do not create adequate jobs.[36]

Most jobs that pay better than agriculture are found only in a few large cities. Therefore, migration to these places has been the first step to changing the poor household's economic trajectory. Though migration has not been as rapid as in China, the migrant labour force has been a significant proportion of India's urban workforce. It contributes an estimated 8–10 per cent of GDP. India has an estimated 65 million migrants, of whom one-third are workers. Add to them street vendors, whose numbers the data does not capture, and you have a possible increase of 12–18 million. However, a large proportion of migrants are not permanent settlers. Many are circular migrants, who come to the cities only in the non-agricultural season for work and return to the villages during the agricultural season. According to the government's Economic Survey, 9 million people move between states every year.[37] Migrant labourers often lack identity and domicile documents and thus remain invisible. They mostly leave their families behind, often because cities have little planned housing for the very poor. The result is that most migrants live in deplorable conditions in urban areas – on a few occasions even being forced to live near drains or garbage dumps.

Despite their sizeable contribution to the economy, the government has failed to provide even basic living facilities for migrant households (Chapter 8 will suggest possible policy interventions). State governments must revisit their misplaced mindset against migrants who are often classified as 'outsiders', which leads to policies for job reservation for locals, as in Haryana and Maharashtra in recent months. Neither evidence nor logic

117

supports such a mindset. As economists Banerjee and Duflo point out, we tend to overlook the beneficial impact. Yes, the influx of outside workers does increase competition in the labour market. However, because they also spend money on goods and services that push consumer demand, it neutralizes the adverse effect. Outsiders are typically willing to take up jobs the locals are not willing to do; hence there may, in effect, not be any job loss for locals.[38] Global evidence shows that countries that have encouraged immigration have prospered; this is equally true for migration within Indian states.

The Vicious Circle of Poverty and Indebtedness

Before we turn to strategies that can transform the dismal livelihood scenario, there is a need to understand better the underlying causative factors that lead poor households into perpetual debt. Debt by itself is not bad. In fact, as in Birsa and Rasika's case, access to credit on easy terms could be a vital tool for providing sustainable livelihoods for rural households. Most low-income families borrow and borrow heavily. The major problem is that this credit is costly because it is mostly taken from the informal market. The share of bank credit drawn by poor households is small, but it is not that there is a lack of physical access to a bank. Hence the question is: why is this so?

Banks are required to lend 40 per cent of their portfolios to the priority sectors. The National Bank for Agriculture and Rural Development (NABARD) oversees and supervises rural credit at the country level, with many regional rural banks dedicated to rural lending. And yet, credit is inadequate, seldom available when required, and mostly does not reach small and marginal farmers. Private commercial banks focused on profitability are reluctant to lend to rural households even when mandated by the government. On the other hand, public sector banks have high repayment defaults in rural loans and are unable to expand. The cooperative credit structure is under-capitalized, mired in poor governance, suffers from political interference, and lacks skilled staff. Though lending rates are relatively low, high default rates have eroded their profitability.[39]

Given the limited credit outreach of banks and credit cooperatives, private money lenders and Micro Finance Institutions (MFIs) have tried to fill the vacuum. The standard explanation that the poor have to pay exorbitant interest rates as they tend to default is erroneous. The default rate on loans given by money lenders and MFIs is low. However, these low default rates are anything but automatic; they require hard work on the lenders' part. Banks are not equipped to do the necessary due diligence and, of course, cannot threaten borrowers as money lenders do.[40]

MFIs have emerged as an essential vehicle for providing credit to low-income families. The typical MFI contract involves loans to a group of borrowers, mostly a women's self-help group (SHG) such as the one Rasika has joined, liable for each other's loans and ensuring the others repay. MFIs insist on weekly repayment and have a weekly monitoring system. Like moneylenders, MFIs too use intimidatory tactics on defaulters to recover their dues. The shame attached to default also pushes borrowers to repay. Unlike moneylenders, MFIs have rigid, standard protocols, though they too charge between 18 and 20 per cent interest.

Since 1976, when Mohammed Yunus pioneered microfinance in Bangladesh, micro-credit has taken deep roots in India and has 150–200 million customers. But does microfinance help families? Microfinance is mainly drawn to smooth consumption troubles – to tide over a crisis or to meet non-business expenses such as a wedding or a funeral. A few borrowers do use it for their business, but they operate on a tiny scale that makes very little money and rarely generates jobs for others.

As noted by Vijay Mahajan, the present micro-credit system has four 'fatal' assumptions and does not promote growth: first, that credit is the leading financial service needed for the poor; second, that it can automatically translate into successful micro-enterprises; third, that the poorest all wish to be self-employed, in which micro-credit helps; and four, that those above the poverty line do not need micro-credit and providing it to them amounts to mistargeting. The reality is that only about 100 of over 10,000 MFIs worldwide are financially self-sufficient. It also appears that micro-credit works less well for the poorer clients – the poorer they were to start with, the lower the impact of the loan.

At the same time, the women's mobilization through micro-credit organized through SHGs presents a great opportunity as it provides women the space to meet and discuss their issues outside the home. Unfortunately, there is substantial evidence to show that micro-credit through SHGs does not increase household income. A study by BASIX, the MFI promoted by Vijay Mahajan, found that only half of their borrowers reported an increase in income, while a quarter reported a decline.[41]

Multiple Building Blocks Needed

Let us now turn to possible programme and policy changes needed to tackle the livelihoods and job crisis. As explicated in the preceding paragraphs of this chapter, the crisis in livelihoods and job creation makes a new comprehensive approach urgent and imperative – not only for families such as Birsa and Rasika's but to even those that have education and skills. Simply tweaking existing schemes will not work. Of course, the post-1991 economic reforms did give an impetus to private investments in several sectors. However, their impact on livelihoods, especially on the rural poor and the uneducated, has been negligible. Therefore, the government must put in place actions that will make a material improvement in people's lives.

IMPROVING LIVELIHOODS, CREATING JOBS

The comprehensive set of strategies that we will set out encompasses the following aspects:

(i) supporting impoverished families,
(ii) improving migrant labour conditions,
(iii) widening agricultural insurance coverage,
(iv) enabling women's work,
(v) aiding tiny and small businesses,
(vi) supporting urban labour-intensive enterprises, and
(vii) job creation by the government.

Supporting Impoverished Households

The most impoverished households comprise the bottom consumption decile. Most SC/ST households and landless agricultural labour fall under this category. They are malnourished, have poor health, are the least educated, and lack job skills. As with Birsa and Rasika's family, these households face day-to-day struggles for basic survival. In this situation, they have neither the bandwidth nor the cash reserves to take advantage of government programmes. Providing such families credit may only increase their indebtedness. My own experience in the 1980s in the districts with the Integrated Rural Development Program (IRDP), which subsidized loans to poor households to acquire assets or start tiny businesses, bears this out. The default rates on such loans were so high that the government had to abandon the programme. If targeted at educated households at the upper end of the poverty scale, income generation schemes have a better chance of success.

The most impoverished families need income protection until they reach the minimum economic threshold level needed to benefit from income enhancement schemes. Such households should be encouraged to save and build up some cash reserves to use on a rainy day rather than being caught in a perpetual debt cycle. To enable this, the implementation of a basic income scheme is very critical.

The central government's existing PM Kisan Samman Nidhi income transfer scheme only covers landowning families and excludes landless agricultural labour households, such as Birsa and Rasika's. States have already identified the most impoverished households under the Antyodya scheme, which currently provides only subsidized cereals. Therefore, as recommended in Chapter 3, there is considerable merit in reforming the TPDS and deploying the savings in food subsidy by extending income support to all Antyodaya households on the lines of the PM Kisan Samman Nidhi scheme. Such income support to the poorest families would be cost-effective and give multiplier benefits to the economy.[42]

The centre and the states have between 300 and 400 social protection cash transfer schemes. The vast majority of these have minuscule budgets but take up sizeable bureaucratic capacity. It would be ideal to merge all of them under the proposed income transfer scheme covering the neediest households. One valid concern regarding basic income transfer schemes is that, over time, the amount diminishes in value with inflation. The erosion in value can be prevented by indexing the quantum of cash transfer to inflation.

Improving Conditions for Migrant Labour

One way for impoverished households to break the vicious circle of poverty is to migrate to towns and cities that offer them better livelihood opportunities. Most workers in the informal sector in urban areas are migrants, and they too have no social security and need safety nets. The numbers of urban migrants have exploded, and the COVID-19 pandemic, which forced so many of them to undertake arduous journeys back home on foot, has opened our eyes to their plight. The Interstate Migrant Workmen Act, 1979, provides minimum wages, journey and displacement allowance, residential accommodation, medical facilities, and protective clothing. Similarly, the Building and Construction Workers Welfare Fund aims to give a range of benefits to construction workers, mostly migrants. However, there is neither enforcement of the provisions under the Act nor effective utilization of the Fund. The centre has introduced a new social security code in 2020 that would enable the registration of migrant workers and make them eligible for social security and health coverage under the Employees State Insurance Corporation (ESIC). The code also incorporates the recommendation made in 2017 by the government's Working Group on Migration, to build an IT architecture to provide portability to all social welfare schemes to enable registered migrants to access benefits in whichever state they are working.

Labour laws can play a critical role in ensuring job security for migrants and casual labour. However, the current legislation needs review to be made flexible. The law should not be so stringent that it deters businesses from hiring, as has happened in the case of women workers. Further, minimum wages should be proportionately lower in small towns, cities, and emerging settlements where housing, transport, and food expenses are lower. Rather than putting the burden of job security, health coverage, and housing on employers, the government should ensure affordable housing, employment guarantee, and health coverage for migrant and casual labour.

Widening Agricultural Insurance Coverage

Agricultural households face enormous risks and uncertainty because farm gate prices and agricultural production are highly volatile. Many farmers die by suicide because of their inability to repay the debt when prices crash due to bumper harvests, or when produce is wiped out because of natural calamities. Apart from price support through minimum support prices and income support through PM Kisan, agricultural insurance is the only instrument available for farmers to mitigate these risks. Agricultural insurance schemes have been in place for several decades, and successive governments have tweaked them over time. Since its inception in 1985, which saw the Comprehensive Crop Insurance Scheme launch, programmes have been re-christened and launched.[43] Prime Minister Fasal Bima Yojana (PMFBY) is the principal scheme under implementation, while the Weather Based Crop Insurance Scheme (WBCIS) is also in operation in a few states. In PMFBY, yields and the resultant crop loss are the basis for insurance pay-outs, while WBCIS relies wholly on weather parameters, such as rainfall. The centre and the states bear most of the premium in both schemes. Despite this, the PMFBY has had limited coverage and success with less than 15 per cent of farmers opting for it. Those enrolled have been mostly loanee farmers who were required to do opt-in by the lending institutions. The coverage is likely to decline further, as the government has now made the scheme optional. Contributory factors for low enrolment are perceived high premium, previous bad experience, non-updating of land records, and payment delays due to tedious procedures in calculating crop loss. The PMFBY also does not cover tenant farmers because they lack formal leases and cannot establish their cultivator status. Private insurance companies are opting out of the scheme as the loss ratios have been close to 100 per cent, and agriculture production and yield data of the government is opaque.

In contrast, the WBCIS has an advantage, even though its coverage is much lower than the PMFBY because it eliminates the need for yield estimation; its IT architecture enables the weather data to be immediately uploaded and is not subject to manipulation.

As in health insurance, agriculture insurance schemes are too rigid and are poorly designed. Instead of the central government designing the scheme, insurance companies should have the flexibility and autonomy to design their schemes. The role of the government should be limited to determining a uniform subsidy on the premium across different schemes – this would enable a level playing field for private insurance companies and the Agricultural Insurance Corporation, the public sector entity. The objective should be to give farmers a wide choice and develop a competitive agricultural insurance market.

Enabling Women's Work

Improving women's livelihood and increasing their work participation is vital to improving not just their situation and their entire family's well-being. A World Bank report shows that gender parity in the workplace would lead to an annual increase of 1.5 per cent in the GDP in India.[44] Individual companies also stand to gain as there is a strong business case for gender diversity. Moreover, there is an added urgency; there is evidence that women's jobs may have been disproportionately affected during the COVID-19 pandemic.[45]

We suggest five strategies to improve women's livelihoods and access to jobs: promoting savings by women, livelihood finance, legislative provisions, job reservations, and skilling. But, of course, these strategies will only succeed if firmly entrenched in gendered mindsets on women's position and role change. (Chapter 7 discusses the ways to achieve this.)

The first critical step is to help poor households escape the vicious poverty trap by reducing their indebtedness. A substantial portion of a low-income family's earnings goes towards repaying high-cost debt rather than meeting household expenses. If households build saving reserves, they would be able to tide over difficult times and not have to borrow. However, this is easier said than done as families living on the margin fail to save even when they get additional income. They value the present much more than the future.[46] We recall that Birsa and Rasika spent the extra money they earned on a mobile phone and sweets.

There is evidence from the experience of SHGs that poor women can save. SEWA has been able to get poor women to put a small portion of their hard-earned money into savings. SEWA achieved this success by educating its members on the benefits of saving and fostering confidence and trust in its SEWA Bank. Similarly, the government can promote savings among poor households through sustained awareness campaigns. In addition, the government can encourage women to save by providing women-only savings accounts which give a higher interest rate and by making it mandatory for all Jan Dhan savings accounts to be in the joint names of women and men.

The second strategy would be to leverage women's vast mobilization through SHGs by shifting microcredit to livelihood finance instead of the current system that only meets consumption needs. There are pointers on how to achieve this. For example, based on its experience, BASIX reworked its strategy and now offers microcredit along with an integrated suite of products and services that covers insurance, agro and business development services, and market linkages.[47] Like BASIX, SEWA also provides microcredit along with financial guidance on savings, insurance, social security, and pensions. The government can encourage such initiatives by subsidizing these additional services, classifying such credit as priority sector lending, and providing a loan default guarantee for a portion of the credit.

The third strategy for the government would be to pass into law the numerous constitutional provisions that already exist to prevent gender discrimination: Article 15 prohibits discrimination against women, with Article 15(3) explicitly providing for framing specific laws to benefit women; Article 39(a) mandates equal rights to livelihood, and Article 39(d) lays down equal wages for both men and women; Article 42 stipulates that there should be just and humane conditions of work, including maternity relief.

Unfortunately, legal provisions to promote women's work participation have been few and far between. The Maternity Benefit Act, 1961, is one of few legal provisions that can benefit women workers. The government made several amendments to the Act in 2017; the most highlighted was the extension of the paid maternity leave from 12 to 26 weeks. However, only 70 per cent of women work outside the home, of which only 16 per cent work in the organized sector, while 84 per cent work in the unorganized sector, where the law does not apply. Consequently, estimates suggest that only a meagre 1 per cent of women in the labour force would benefit from this Act. Moreover, lack of awareness causes a further obstacle to women in asserting their rights under the law. For example, even when daily wage women employees are eligible for certain benefits under the law, employers successfully mislead them into believing they are not entitled to it.[48]

The extension of maternity leave to 26 weeks under the Maternity Benefit Act may even have led to more significant discrimination against hiring women. A survey showed that two-thirds of women respondents felt that the maternity benefit law had lowered their chances of getting hired.[49] Therefore, the government must make further amendments to the Maternity Benefit Act to overcome the existing lacunae. First, the law must mandate paternity leave in private and public sector organizations; 15 days of paternity leave already exists for central government employees. Second, it should prohibit employers from filling positions of women on maternity leave. Finally, the law should stipulate that the government would reimburse the salary during the maternity leave period. (We discuss the non-legislative measures required to reduce gender discrimination in hiring women in companies in Chapter 7.)

The fourth strategy to enhance women's work participation is reservation in government jobs. Fifty per cent reservation of teacher posts under the centre's Operation Black Board scheme led to a vast increase in the recruitment of women primary school teachers. Government must also increase the representation of women in public administration, the judiciary, and the police. Some states have experimented with gender quotas in government employment across sectors. For example, Rajasthan introduced a 30 per cent reservation for women in government jobs a decade back. Gujarat has a 33 per cent reservation for women in police. Women in the police make women feel safe and secure.

The fifth strategy to improve women's employment is to design and impart skilling programmes for women. Though young women are enrolling in large numbers in educational institutions, they cannot get jobs they would like as they lack the necessary skills. In addition to general skilling, programmes should specifically target women wishing to re-enter or join the workforce after marriage or after their children enter school.[50] Skill enhancement, in the case of rural women is especially critical to transit into the non-farm sector. The government must support NGOs, like SEWA, that impart such training to women.

Aiding Tiny and Small Businesses

A large percentage of poor households depend on self-employment and tiny businesses for their livelihoods. Launched in April 2015, the central government's Mudra scheme offers collateral-free loans of up to ₹1 million to tiny enterprises. By the end of 2019, 192 million loans had been extended under the scheme, amounting to ₹9450 billion. However, NPAs have also jumped to ₹173 billion during this period.

There are three major pitfalls in the Mudra loan scheme. The first is that it is a purely digital product, with no physical interface with the borrower; a poor choice for any kind of loan. The resultant poor underwriting due to inadequate diligence is a significant reason for high NPAs, made worse by unrealistic targets.[51] The second fundamental flaw is that the scheme presumes entrepreneurs need only credit. The fact is that they equally need equity support as their capital base is tiny.

The third and most significant weakness of the Mudra loan scheme is that, in its implementation, it has left out entrepreneurs who wish to set up enterprises that need a scale for commercial viability. Mudra loans have been provided only to micro-enterprises at the village level with no potential for growth and employment. A study shows that Mudra loans are insufficient to employ even one person for one year – the bulk of the loan accounts was extremely tiny, with an average loan size of a mere ₹52,739![52] These are akin to the loans given to women in SHGs, which have only been reclassified as Mudra loans and do not amount to additional credit or lead to new job creation. A government survey puts the cost of each job under the Mudra scheme as high as ₹0.5 million.[53] Most Mudra loans were merely for expanding existing businesses; a study shows that over half of the beneficiaries were self-employed or ran the business with the help of unpaid family members.[54]

With such tiny loans, borrowers obviously cannot hire professional talent, compete with organized players, ensure standardization and quality, and employ skilled workers. Reaching targets and monitoring hundreds of tiny loans fully occupies the bandwidth of lenders. Such mindless obsession with numbers must stop. Tiny businesses hold little potential for sustained income growth of households; to flourish and grow, enterprises require a minimum scale. Therefore, it makes better sense to ensure adequacy in the loan quantum and to target educated households at the upper end of the poverty margin who can work with greater assuredness, rather than continue with business loans to those in abject poverty. Of course, there should be a provision for providing equity support even for such loans.

Supporting Labour Intensive Enterprises in Urban Centres

Every person cannot be self-employed, and most people find it easier to make a living by working for someone else. Thus, the best route out of poverty is a job and a regular salary. Because much of the potential for setting up new businesses and creating jobs is in cities and towns, the government must adopt an urban-centric approach. So far, urban plans have not considered the requirement of enterprises, and cities have grown in an unplanned, ad-hoc, and reactive manner that do not support businesses.

What is required is a holistic and integrated approach that brings in all the elements necessary for businesses to grow and thrive. The first step would entail identifying urban areas with considerable expansion prospects and are best suited to locate businesses. A key consideration in this identification process would be the suitability to host a cluster of companies in specific industries.[55] The next step would be drawing up plans for supportive infrastructure, services, and facilities within the clusters and in the identified urban agglomerations. The third step would be to plan and establish the entire ecosystem required to support such clusters.

The industrial cluster approach gathers a critical mass of interconnected companies and institutions and a concentration of workers with specialized skills. Individual firms do not need end-end production capacity, as everyone adds what they can and leaves it to others to put the pieces together. Once successfully established, the cluster acts as a magnet for more businesses. The presence of other firms in the supply chain ensures quality control as the firm marketing the final product stands to lose its reputation if any intermediary falls short on quality. Although there is intense competition among firms, there is often also a high degree of cooperation among them.[56]

The concept of industrial cluster development is certainly not altogether new for India. However, the multi-pronged approach suggested here is radically different from existing government policy. First, industrial clusters and the urban areas they are located in are to be viewed as a composite whole. Second, each cluster would be well-planned and well-funded. Currently, there are as many as 1,350 modern industry clusters and an additional 4,000 traditional product manufacturing clusters with grossly inadequate budgets, which results in resources being spread very thinly.[57] In contrast, we recommend developing a manageable number of clusters, along with supporting urban infrastructure, facilities, and services. The creation of urban clusters with high potential that can generate the maximum jobs must be undertaken after detailed scrutiny of alternate industries and location options.

A cost-effective and optimal strategy would be to identify 1,000 cities and towns with an average of two clusters each dedicated to a specific industry. Of course, the large cities would be an essential part of the list as they have already proved that they offer enough livelihood for both locals and migrants in search of jobs.[58] At present, the Ministry of Industrial Development identifies manufacturing clusters of Industrial Development. At the same time, the Ministry of Urban Affairs identifies towns and cities under the Atal Mission for Rejuvenation and Urban Transformation (AMRUT) without much consultation with the Ministry of Industrial Development. This silo approach has resulted in a lack of cohesion. Instead, the identification process must be undertaken jointly by the two Ministries.[59]

126

As far as manufacturing sectors are concerned, the government has already identified 10 manufacturing sectors with potential: electrical, pharmaceuticals, electronics, heavy engineering, solar equipment, food processing, chemicals, and textiles.[60] Other potential sectors include livestock and dairy, leather and footwear, wood manufacture, and the traditional sectors of handicraft and handlooms.[61]

In the handicraft clusters, the government must promote large production enterprises that can standardize products, hire designers, deploy state-of-the-art design software, and implement strict quality protocols. In addition, the government should step in to arrange for equity and credit and provide artisans with intensive theoretical and practical training in using software and modern equipment.

In respect of handlooms, the government implements the Comprehensive Handloom Cluster Development Scheme in eight clusters. However, budgets are meagre – these clusters received only ₹284 million in 2017–18.[62] As a result, Indian garment exports lag behind even much smaller countries like Bangladesh. A key reason for this is that, in India, garment exports take place through many dispersed locations; in Bangladesh, exports occur through two major clusters, Dhaka and Chittagong. Other factors for poor performance are weak domestic value chains, skill mismatch, fragmented manufacturing, low research and development, and poor infrastructure.[63] In addition, over 50 per cent of the country's apparel exports comprise cotton garments. India needs to diversify its fibre base, as man-made fibre now commands a much larger market share than cotton.[64] The government must take concerted action to plug these lacunae, and identify selected handloom and textile clusters to help boost the industry. The selected handloom and textile clusters need enhanced budgets, including financing for the latest technologies and processes that are more efficient than traditional ones.[65]

For the identified clusters to become engines for growth, they must attract businesses and new enterprises.[66] These will need institutional structures for planning, handholding, skill development, identifying potential entrepreneurs, and ensuring equity support and credit. The government can draw inspiration from China's experience in promoting modern manufacturing enterprises in identified clusters across the country (see Box 1: Learning from China). As in China, the Indian government will have to strengthen the capabilities of its domestic arms, assist small entrepreneurs, help develop indigenous technological capabilities, and, above all, assist in creating a large domestic market.[67]

The government must establish a central agency to support and facilitate investments into new enterprises in these clusters. The Small Industries Development Bank of India (SIDBI) is an institution that could be re-structured to provide equity support to potential enterprises. But given the lack of expertise within SIDBI, it may make better sense for it to partner with private equity firms investing in the enterprises.[68] Following the initial investments, over time, other multiple avenues for small businesses, services, and technology companies would spring up, leading to further job creation.[69] At the local district level, the existing District Industries Centres (DICs) need to become professionalized. They are currently largely dysfunctional, engaged in the routine processing of capital subsidy applications or merely acting as a post office to grant regulatory approvals.

At the central level, other policy reforms are essential. The existing Atmanirbhar, or 'Make in India', plans have not had a noticeable impact. The share of manufacturing in India's GDP has remained static at around 15 per cent between 2014 and 2020.[70] The Atmanirbhar campaign should not shut out technology and critical components; otherwise, the policy could degenerate into protectionism and make our economy insular. In this context, there is a need to reiterate the promotion of technology adoption by enterprises. Unfortunately, only 7 per cent of enterprises recently surveyed reported technology adoption, and a staggering 70 per cent cited lack of knowledge, guidance, skilled workforce, and high costs as impediments to technology adoption.[71] In addition, stringent rules for local content discourage foreign companies from forging contractual relationships for technology transfer, and there is a need to establish organizations that serve as links between foreign and local firms.

Along with revamping the manufacturing sector through focused cluster development, the government must ensure that trade and manufacturing policies complement each other. Otherwise, the two may work at cross purposes and undermine each other's objectives. Export-led growth strategies, as adopted by China and other East Asian economies, are not easy to replicate. It is not just about low prices. Indian enterprises will have to create a reputation and brand.[72] The perception that Indian firms do not adhere to quality must change. One way of doing this would be for the central government to frame domestic standards at par with its trading partners.[73] Our trade policy must get re-oriented towards labour-intensive product lines and increase its participation in global value chains.[74]

Several sectors have immense export potential. Transport equipment comprises 35 per cent of exports, and India has performed well in the sector. Though India ranks sixth globally in auto components, it remains a small player with an aggregate level of a mere $8 billion. The largest segment in the tiny sector is the gems and jewellery trade which employs close to 5 million workers; India is already a global hub because of its low costs and highly skilled labour. Yet another sector with vast potential is the handmade carpet industry. These industries require dedicated production clusters with quality urban infrastructure and a surrounding market ambience for potential international buyers.[75]

The government must put in place skilling programmes to equip youth to handle the new jobs.[76] Currently, the centre's skilling programmes have inadequate budgets and are of so short a duration that they do not effectively impart the required skills. The modern economy requires specialized skills that need high-quality trainers, proper infrastructure, and a combination of teaching and hands-on training for a sufficiently long duration.

The identified towns and cities and their industrial clusters will need visionary and innovative planning and new governance structures to attract private sector investments. A critical weakness of existing clusters is the minuscule private sector contribution.[77] Ways and means to enhance private sector investment must be found, viz., through debt instruments like bonds and tax incentives so that clusters get adequate capital. The government should avoid getting into spaces where private capital is willing to step in. If executed well, the development of the urban clusters would by itself create many jobs – urban planners, engineers, supervisors, draftsmen, and, as the town grows, jobs to manage water supply, electricity, sewerage and waste management, and health and education infrastructure. (We discuss the strategies for planned development and financing needs of the identified towns and cities in Chapter 8.)

Box 1   Learning from China

China's record in reducing rural poverty has been nothing short of spectacular.[78] China sharply reduced its poverty incidence from a high of 32.9 per cent in 1978 to just 3 per cent by the turn of the century. Non-farm activities, mainly through the township and village enterprises, absorbed a large quantity of surplus rural labour.[79] China followed the more typical example of the First-World countries (though at a much faster pace) of a rapid rise in urbanization and the fast growth of the manufacturing sector.

China's growth was, to a significant extent, fuelled by industrial clusters. Three noteworthy features of these clusters are small products but big markets; small enterprises but large-scale cooperation; and small clusters but large scale. The cluster economy reflects the concept of 'one town, one product' or 'one town, one industry', as exemplified by provinces like Jiangsu, Zhejiang, and Guangdong. The product concentration of certain products in these areas has given rise to phrases such as Shengze textiles, Hengshan sewing machines, Ningbo costumes, Wenzhou shoes, Shaoxing synthetic textiles, Haining leather coats, Yiwu small commodities, and Yongkang hardware. Local government units provide an enabling environment through appropriate policies and regulations and vital infrastructure essential for business.[80]

The government also played a critical supportive role in promoting investment and innovation. State-owned enterprises in China contribute between 23 and 28 per cent of the GDP. The Chinese economy is now rapidly transforming from being an exporter of cheap goods to a focus on domestic consumption and innovation. Despite the rise in wage costs, China continues to be the nucleus of the global and East Asian production networks.[81]

Job Creation by the Government

Most youth now have high school education and do not wish to remain farm hands or engage in unskilled labour. Implementing strategies to promote tiny businesses and labour-intensive enterprises in urban settlements will provide millions of educated youth with employment opportunities. However, the most common dream of the poor is that their children become government workers.

Till the 1980s, over 70 per cent of jobs in the organized sector were in the public sector. However, since liberalization, it is the private sector that is creating most jobs. Along with policies for job promotion by the private sector, the government has to get rid of the mindset that has crept in since the 1991 reforms that it should not be in the business of direct job creation. India must increase government employment manyfold. According to the ILO, India is amongst the poorest performers in government employment, with only 3.8 per cent of the workforce in the public sector. Most First-World countries have over 10 per cent of their workforce in government. Singapore and China have 32 per cent and 50 per cent, respectively; even Bangladesh has 8 per cent of its workforce in the public sector.[82]

The justification for increasing government jobs is not to match international standards but to enhance vital services. The conventional argument against government jobs is that many posts in the government, especially in the government secretariat and its departments, are non-productive and wasteful and lead to needless layers in government decision-making. Therefore, the argument is that the government should shun such posts and continue to pursue administrative reforms for speedier decision-making with lean and high-quality teams. At the same time, the government must prioritize job creation that improves human capital quality and has a multiplier impact on livelihoods.

We have seen in Chapters 2, 3, and 4 the potential for vast returns to society by professionalizing and expanding the cadres of anganwadi workers, ASHA workers, and crèche workers, and by engaging tutors for remedial instruction in schools on a large scale. The country needs upwards of 5 million workers in these sectors, and over 90 per cent of them would be women.

However, even with the suggested measures, millions of young people may not get employment throughout the year. In this context, the Mahatma Gandhi National Rural Employment Guarantee Act (MGNREGA) needs to expand its scope. MGNREGA currently provides 100 days of guaranteed unskilled wage employment every year in rural areas. The ambit of the Act must be expanded to include youth with school education and skills. Unemployed educated youth can provide services under the Act as field workers needed at the village level. They can be engaged productively as health and nutrition extension workers, part-time schoolteachers and tutors, ASHA and anganwadi workers, and village-level assistants in panchayats as agricultural extension workers.

As noted, with agriculture opportunities remaining limited, most new jobs and improved livelihood opportunities will be generated in urban areas and emerging settlements. Therefore, in all towns and cities, and especially in those identified for industrial cluster development, the focus of MGNREGA needs to shift from rural development works to building urban infrastructures such as intra-village road networks, pedestrian paths, and drainage. These areas also require other services to be taken up, such as waste collection and disposal, which should become permitted activities under MGNREGA. There is also merit in extending MGNREGA to urban towns and cities since there is no urban counterpart to the rural employment guarantee Act. For example, in Bihar and UP, the two largest backward states with vast numbers of emerging urban agglomerations, there could be an enormous benefit in creating urban infrastructure through MGNREGA.[83]

While expanding the scope and scale of MGNREGA, its systemic flaws need to be corrected. For example, assessments indicate that, as the programme has focused on labour employment, infrastructure creation may have taken a back seat.[84] The other significant problem is that implementation structures are weak and technical personnel and trained supervisors are highly inadequate. There is a need to fill these governance gaps. Further, to improve the quality of the works MGNREGA needs to introduce third-party assessments, as in the Prime Minister Gram Sadak Yojana, the road construction programme, where strict norms and standards have led to the creation of quality road assets.

The important lesson is that government policy must go beyond liberalization reforms. Leaving matters to the market will only exacerbate inequities and make only a slight difference in livelihoods and jobs. India and its people have waited long enough – they do not have the luxury to live in hope of election promises. Instead, the government must have a multi-layered approach with complementary building blocks, prioritizing livelihoods and job creation.

Notes

1 Somerset Maugham, Chapter 15, Of Human Bondage, 1915.
2 Seema Gaur & N Srinivasa Rao, "Poverty Measurement in India – A Status Update," Working Paper No. 1/2020, Ministry of Rural Development, *Government of India*, September 2020.
3 A. Subramanian, "What is Happening to Rural Welfare, Poverty, and Inequality in India?" *The India Forum*, 6 December 2019. Oxford University researchers Sabina Alkire and James Foster used a multi-dimensional poverty index (MPI) computation that showed a poverty percentage of 27.9 per cent for 2016–17. The estimate by Subramanian, using leaked consumption expenditure data, reveals that the incidence of poverty in India had risen to 35.1 per cent in 2017–18. https://www.theindiaforum.in/sites/default/files/pdf/2019/12/06/what-is-happening-to-rural-welfare-poverty-and-inequality-in-india.pdf; date of access April 5, 2020.

IMPROVING LIVELIHOODS, CREATING JOBS

4 Ajit K. Ghose and Abhishek Kumar, "India's Deepening Employment Crisis in the Time of Rapid Economic Growth," *IHD Working Paper Series*, IHD, WP 01/202.1 Ghose and Kumar have computed employment estimates since 1999 based on the latest available official data. Full-time employment growth decelerated throughout the 1999–2018 period from 1.9 per cent during 1999–2004 to 1.1 per cent during 2004–2011 and further to 0.7 per cent during 2011–2018. Surprisingly, this decline in employment took place during high and unprecedented economic growth in India.

5 K.P. Kannan, and G. Raveendran, "Jobless to Job-loss Growth," *Economic and Political Weekly*, Vol. LIV No. 44, 9 November 2019.

6 Santosh Mehrotra and Mahesh Vyas, "How Can Employment Be Put at the Centre of the Indian Policymaker's Agenda?" *The Wire*, 5 December 2020. https://thewire.in/economy/how-can-employment-be-put-at-the-centre-of-the-indian-policymakers-agenda; date of access February 5, 2021.

7 "PLFS Annual Report 2018–19," NSSO, MOSPI, *Government of India*. https://pib.gov.in/PressReleaseIframePage.aspx?PRID=1629366); date of access May 10, 2020.

8 Yogima Seth Sharma, "India's Unemployment Rate Fell Before Covid-19 Hit," *Economic Times*, 5 June 2020.

9 Statista Research Department, *Statista*, 19 March 2021.

10 Jayan Jose Thomas, "Misses in Manufacturing," *Frontline*, 13 March 2020.

11 Ramesh Chand, S. K Srivastava and Jaspal Singh, "Changing Structure of Rural Economy of India Implications for Employment and Growth," NITI Aayog, *Government of India*, November 2017.

12 Santosh Mehrotra and Mahesh Vyas, *The Wire*, December 2020.

13 Erin K. Fletcher, Rohini Pande, Charity Toyer Moore, "Women and Work in India: Descriptive Evidence and a Review of Potential Policies," Faculty Research Working Paper Series, *Harvard Kennedy School*, January 2018.

14 Rohini Pande, Jennifer Johnson, & Eric Dodge, "How to Get India's Women Working? First, Let Them out of the House," *IndiaSpend*, 9 April 2016.

15 "Women and Men in India," Central Statistical Office, *Government of India*, 2014.

16 Farzana Afridi, Taryn Dinkelman, Kanika Mahajan, "Why are Fewer Married Women Joining the Work Force in India: A Decomposition Analysis over Two Decades," *Journal of Population Economics*, vol. 39, issue 3, no. 4, pp. 783–818, 2018.

17 Nisha Srivastava, Ravi Srivastava, "Women, Work and Employment Outcomes in Rural India," *Economic and Political Weekly*, Vol. 45, No. 28, pp. 49–63, 10–16 July 2010.

18 Rohini Pande, "What the Economy Needs Now", *Juggernaut Books*, 2019.

19 Farzana Afridi, Taryn Dinkelman, Kanika Mahajan, *Journal of Population Economics*, 2018.

20 See for example the NDA government campaign, 'Beti Bachao, Beti Padhao', Ministry of Women & Child Welfare, Government of India.

21 "Still a Struggle for Working Women," *Japan Times*, 8 April 2016. Even 30 years after the equal employment opportunity law took effect, a large percentage of Japanese women are employed only in part time work. https://www.japantimes.co.jp/opinion/2016/04/08/editorials/still-a-struggle-for-working-women/; data of access June 5, 2020.

22 Prachi Salve, "Wide Gender Gap for Similarly Qualified Indian Women and Men," *IndiaSpend*, 5 June 2018.

23 Rohini Pande, Jennifer Johnson, & Eric Dodge, *IndiaSpend*, 9 April 2016.

24 Economic Survey, Government of India, *Agriculture and Food Management*, Vol. II, 2019–20, January 2020.

132

IMPROVING LIVELIHOODS, CREATING JOBS

25 Sanjay Kaul, "Farm Laws: Unlikely to Bring Transformative Change," *Ideas for India*, 14 October 2020. https://www.ideasforindia.in/topics/agriculture/farm-bills-unlikely-to-bring-transformative-change.html.

26 Siddharth Hari, Parth Hare, Arvind Subramanian, "Climate Change and Indian Agriculture", *Ideas for India*, 16 August 2018. https://www.ideasforindia.in/topics/agriculture/climate-change-and-indian-agriculture.html; date of access April 2, 2020.

27 Misra, SB. "Growth of Rural Non-Farm Employment in India: Pre and Post Reform Trends and Patterns," *Journal of Land and Rural Studies*, 1(2):99–112, 2013.

28 Ramesh Chand, S. K Srivastava and Jaspal Singh, NITI Aayog, *Government of India*, November 2017.

29 Misra, Journal of Land and Rural Studies, 2013.

30 Prabhu Pingali, Anaka Aiyar, Mathew Abraham, and Andaleeb Rehman, "Transforming Food Systems for a Rising India," Chapter 3, *Palgrave Macmillan*, 2019.

31 Ibid.

32 Ramesh Chand, S. K Srivastava and Jaspal Singh, NITI Aayog, *Government of India*, November 2017.

33 Shreya Jadhav, "Indian Handicrafts: Growing or Depleting?" *IOSR Journal of Business and Management*, 2014.

34 Manavi Kapur, "India Needs to Focus on the Domestic Market not Exports, to Save its Artisans," *Quartz India*, 1 November 2019. There is little wonder that India's share in the global exports of handicrafts is a mere 1.2 per cent. There is no option but to introduce machines and technology in a big way by treading the Chinese path. A study by Ernst & Young showed that Chinese craft products are machine-made, with 80 per cent of the product made by machines and only the remaining being completed and finished by hand, unlike in India, where it is entirely handmade. With millions of livelihoods on the line, we cannot remain stuck in the past.

35 Shreya Jadhav, IOSR Journal of Business and Management, 2014.

36 Ramesh Chand, S. K Srivastava and Jaspal Singh, NITI Aayog, *Government of India*, November 2017.

37 Kaushik Deka, "The Migrant Mess," *India Today*, 8 June 2020.

38 Abhijit Banerjee and Esther Duflo, "The Pains from Trade," Good Economics for Hard Times, *Juggernaut Books*, 2019.

39 Sunildro L.S. Akoijam, "Rural Credit: A Source of Sustainable Livelihood of Rural India," *International Journal of Social Economics*, Vol. 40, No. 1, pp. 83–97, 2013.

40 Abhijit Banerjee and Esther Duflo, Poor Economics, *Random House*, 2011.

41 Vijay Mahajan, "From Micro-credit to Livelihood Finance," *Economic & Political Weekly*, Vol. 40, issue no. 48, 8 October 2005.

42 "Banerjee Slams Theory of Limited Govt Intervention to Uplift the Poor," PTI, *Mint*, 11 April 2021.

43 "Precious Livelihoods: How the State Fails to Insure its Farmers," E EPW Engage, *Economic & Political Weekly*, 13 February 2020.

44 Erin K. Fletcher, Rohini Pande, Charity Toyer Moore, "Women and Work in India: Descriptive Evidence and a Review of Potential Policies," Faculty Research Working Paper Series, *Harvard Kennedy School*, January 2018.

45 Kanika Datta, "Where Will All the Women Work?" *Indian Journal of Gender Studies* 27(3) 471–473, 2020. https://journals.sagepub.com/doi/abs/10.1177/0971521520939281?journalCode=ijgb; date of access October 2021.

46 Samuel M. McClure, David I. Laibson, George Loewenstein, and Jonatha D. Cohen, "Separate Neural Systems Value Immediate and Delayed Monetary Rewards," *Science*, Vol. 306(5695) pp. 421–423, 2004.
47 "BASIX Resource Book on Economic Activity Profiles," *Basix*, March 2010. The resource book identifies many illustrative livelihoods such as footwear manufacturing, cloth item making, handloom weaving, agarbatti making, bamboo items, blacksmith, leaf plate making, snacks making, grocery store, etc. Investment requirements are less than ₹1 lakh with surpluses of ₹10,000 per month at best.
48 Saumya Uma, Aditya Kamath, "Game Changer or a Trojan Horse," *Economic & Political Weekly*, 16 May 2020.
49 Ibid.
50 Anita Kumar, "What it Would Take to Achieve Gender Parity in India," *Y S Journal*, 09 October 2018.
51 Prabhash K Dutta, "Curious case of Mudra loan failure and Disconnect of BJP's Election Winning Machine," *India Today*, 5 September 2019. https://www.indiatoday.in/news-analysis/story/curious-case-of-mudra-loan-failure-and-disconnect-of-bjp-s-election-winning-machine-1595815-2019-09-05; date of access October 10, 2021.
52 Ila Patnaik, "Mudra Scheme: What the Modi Government Failed to do for Small Businesses," *The Print*, 16 January 2019. https://theprint.in/ilanomics/mudra-scheme-what-the-government-failed-to-do-for-small-businesses/178165/; date of access September 2, 2021.
53 Prabhash K Dutta, *India Today*, 5 September 2019.
54 The Wire Staff, "Only 20% of Mudra Loan Beneficiaries Started New Businesses, Govt Survey Shows," *The Wire*, 04 September 2019. https://thewire.in/labour/only-20-of-mudra-loan-beneficiaries-started-new-businesses-govt-survey-shows; date of access April 6, 2021.
55 K. Choe and A. Laquian, "City Cluster Development: Toward an Urban-led Development Strategy for Asia," *Asian Development Bank*, 2008. https://www.adb.org/sites/default/files/publication/27555/city-cluster-development.pdf; date of access May 2, 2021.
56 Shikha Jha, Sangeetha Raghuram, and Siddhant Awasthi, "Exploring Strategies for Planned Urban Cluster Development in South Asia," *ADB South Asia Working Paper Series*, No. 64, ADB, April 2019.
57 Santosh Mehrotra, "Six Steps to Job Creation," *The Hindu*, 14 October 2017. https://www.thehindu.com/opinion/lead/six-steps-to-job-creation/article 19856022.ece; date of access July 4, 2021.
58 Arup Mitra and Jitendra Singh, "COVID-19 Pandemic and Livelihood Loss: Variations in Unemployment Outcomes and Lessons for Future," *IEG*, 2020. http://iegindia.org/upload/profile_publication/doc-190820_153936wp405.pdf; date of access October 5, 2021.
59 Santosh Mehrotra, "Six Steps to Job Creation," *The Hindu*, 14 October 2017. https://www.thehindu.com/opinion/lead/six-steps-to-job-creation/article 19856022.ece; date of access July 4, 2021.
60 Sesa Sen, "DPIIT to Market Brand India via 10 Mega Clusters," *Express News Service*, 21 May 2020.
61 "RBI has Just Outlined Opportunity in Post Covid World," *Economic Times*, https://economictimes.indiatimes.com/markets/stocks/news/rbi-has-just-outlined-indias-opportunity-in-post-covid-world/articleshow/77738092.cms; date of access August 2021.
62 "Indian Handloom Industry – Position Paper, 2019," *Thought Arbitrage Research Institute* (TARI) for FICCI Ladies Organisation (FLO) http://www.ficciflo.com/wp-content/uploads/2019/03/Indian-Handloom-Industry-Final.pdf.; date of access Augus 10, 2020. Though India has over 67,000 handicraft

export enterprises, they are spread across the country and find it challenging to adhere to the export requirement or cater to bulk orders.

63 Yerragola Prakash, B. Charwak and P. Vijaya Kumar, "Textile Industry in New India: Challenges and Opportunities," *International Journal of Indian Culture and Business Management*, Vol. 21, No. 4, 2020.

64 "11 Issues that are Holding Back Apparel manufacturing in India," *Stitchdiary*, 2018, https://medium.com/@stitchdiary/11-key-issues-that-are-holding-back-apparel-manufacturing-in-india-115ac16f6722; date of access March 5, 2020.

65 Ajay Shankar, "Creating Jobs Through Garment Exports," *Hindu Business Line*, 19 May 2019. https://www.thehindubusinessline.com/opinion/creating-jobs-through-garment-exports/article27178739.ece

66 Neha Arora & Rishika Nayyar, *Modern Diplomacy*, 1 November 2020.

67 Jayan Jose Thomas, Frontline, 13 March 2020.

68 "Report of the Expert Committee on Micro, Small and Medium Enterprises," *RBI*, June 2019. https://m.rbi.org.in//Scripts/PublicationReportDetails.aspx?UrlPage=&ID=924#EXE.

69 Shikha Jha, Sangeetha Raghuram, and Siddhant Awasthi, "Exploring Strategies for Planned Urban Cluster Development in South Asia," ADB South Asia Working Paper Series, No. 64, *ADB*, April 2019.

70 Manavendra Prasad, "Skilled Response: Skilling Can be a Way Out of the Current Economic Crisis," *Financial Express*, 20 June 2020. https://www.financialexpress.com/opinion/skilled-response-skilling-can-be-a-way-out-of-the-current-economic-crisis/1997499/; date of access 21 June 2020.

71 Neha Arora & Rishika Nayyar, *Modern Diplomacy*, 1 November 2020.

72 Abhijit Banerjee and Esther Duflo, "The Pains from Trade," Good Economics for Hard Times, *Juggernaut Books*, 2019.

73 T. C. A. Ranganathan and T.C. A. Srinivasan, "International Trade," All the Wrong Turns, *Westland Publications*, 2019.

74 Yingqi Wei and V. N. Balasubramanyam, "A Comparative Analysis of China and India's Manufacturing Sectors," Economics Working Paper Series, 2015/003, *Lancaster University Management School.*

75 T. C. A. Ranganathan and T.C. A. Srinivasan, "All the Wrong Turns", *Westland Publications*, 2019.

76 Ankush Sharma, "How Can Technology Help Eliminate the Job Crisis in Rural India?" Microsoft: *People Matters*, 25 October 2020.

77 "Report of the Expert Committee on Micro, Small and Medium Enterprises," *RBI*, June 2019.

78 Alain de Janury, Elisabeth Sadou, Nong Zhu, "The Role of non-farm Incomes in Reducing Rural Poverty and Inequality: India, and China," Department of Agricultural and Resource Economics and Policy, *University of California, Berkeley*, March 2005.

79 Sukhdeo Thorat and Shengann Fan, "Public Investment and Poverty Reduction: Lessons from China and India," *Economic & Political Weekly*, Vol. 42 no. 8, pp. 704–20, February 24 – March 2007.

80 "Report of the Expert Committee on Micro, Small and Medium Enterprises," *RBI*, June 2019.

81 Jayan Jose Thomas, *Frontline*, 13 March 2020.

82 Santosh Mehrotra and Mahesh Vyas, "What Should be an Acceptable Employment Rate for India?" *The Wire*, 4 December 2020.

83 Arindam Jana and Archita S., "India's Missing Middle", *IndiaSpend*, 23 January 2019.

84 Ajay Chibber, Salman Anees Soz, Chapter 2, "Unshackling India", *Harper Collins*, 2021.

7

UNSHACKLING GENDERED MINDSETS

Gender equality is more than a goal in itself. It is a precondition for meeting the challenge of reducing poverty, promoting sustainable development, and building good governance.[1]

Kofi Annan

I raise my voice – not so that I can shout, but so that those without a voice can be heard…We cannot all succeed when half of us are held back.[2]

Malala Yousafzai

All-pervasive Gender Discrimination

The strategies on health, nutrition, education, and livelihoods recommended in the previous chapters would significantly improve women's well-being but may not materially give them autonomy and freedom. Gender discrimination is deeply rooted in cultural beliefs, social practices, and a rigid patriarchal ordering. Patriarchy is embedded everywhere, in the family, across institutions and organizations, and in policymaking bodies. The patriarchal mindset limits women's autonomy, mobility, decision-making, and life choices. Gender inequities in health, nutrition, and livelihoods are rampant and stark in poor and well-off households. For example, women shoulder almost all the household responsibilities. However, the national accounting system does not recognize this unpaid work, nor has its social and economic worth been accorded the value and dignity it warrants. A most telling and extreme indicator of gender discrimination is the adverse sex ratio.[3]

Gendered deprivation and inequality persisted down generations in an unending chain.[4] A significant contributory factor to the entrenched patriarchal mentality is the parental influence in shaping children's attitudes.[5] Vital issues such as the practice of dowry, women's right to inheritance, patrilocality, and violence against women are particularly resistant to attitudinal change and prevalent even in the more literate regions.[6]

Discrimination against women cuts across sectors in the workplace in blatant disregard of the constitutional guarantee for equal rights for all

136   DOI: 10.4324/9781003346258-7

genders. The societal expectation of women's role as caregivers and caretakers of the household means that women who wish to work outside the home encounter opposition from their peers and families. These views are frequently internalized by women and lead to lower women's work participation. As noted in Chapter 6, these norms are typically more prevalent among well-off, educated households.

Ancient religious codes and edicts have perpetuated these patriarchal attitudes. For instance, traditional Hindu philosophy portrays the ideal woman as a Sati Savitri (the epitome of purity) or Pativrata (slave to her husband). In some Islamic cultures, the Quran and Sharia law are incorrectly interpreted to perpetuate gender discrimination and permit polygamy. In Christianity, the vows of the bride include obeying the husband. The historical preference for son progeny and the vulnerability of women in these cultural settings reinforces this patriarchal attitude. Women are perceived to be subordinate, weak, and in need of control and protection. Often women internalize this perception even to the extent of silently enduring abuse, both mental and physical, thereby legitimizing it. A survey showed that most women think it is usual for a husband to beat his wife if she leaves home without informing him.[7] Further, the NFHS notes that 30 per cent of women face sexual violence.[8] It is pertinent to note that according to some reports, domestic violence increased significantly during the COVID-19 lockdowns.[9]

Unfortunately, women themselves are unlikely to assert their rights and seek justice. There is evidence that the differences between men and women in their gender attitudes are surprisingly small. For example, a study showed that tolerance for gender-based violence is 37 per cent among women and 33 per cent among men. Similarly, when asked about their ideal sex composition of children, 20 per cent of women and 19 per cent of men wanted more sons than daughters.[10] In other cases, women do have more progressive gender attitudes than men, but not by a wide margin.

Therefore, it is imperative to set out enablers and public policies, to transform the existing situation, and ensure women an equal place in society. In discussing gender discrimination, I include all the LGBTQIA+ (lesbian, gay, bisexual, transgender, queer, inquiring, asexual+) groups that face social discrimination because of their gender identity or sexual orientation.

Female Work Participation and Well-being

In Chapter 6 we focussed on measures to improve female work participation rates. However, even when women get work, they continue to shoulder most household responsibilities. As a result, work participation does not automatically result in a higher level of welfare for women. On the contrary, a woman's employment under impoverished circumstances could only increase her drudgery. For example, a study carried out in Rajasthan showed that when women take up work due to poverty, it is less likely to get them more freedom, improve their well-being, or reduce spousal violence.[11] However, such employment becomes meaningful from a welfare viewpoint when accompanied by higher education capabilities and higher income.[12] In this context, let us go back to the family of Birsa and Rasika and look at what is happening in Rasika's life.

> Rasika has worked outside the home as a wage labourer all her adult life. She has barely taken time off, despite having to care for young children. The family is so impoverished that Birsa, her husband, is not bound by any cultural beliefs about the traditional role of women solely as caregivers. At the same time, he retains the patriarchal mindset that household chores and nurturing of children are a woman's domain. This triple role of being wage labour, housewife, and mother is stressful and has adversely impacted Rasika's health and well-being. She views her multiple roles and the punishing routine of her daily life as her fate as a woman. She considers herself better off than many others in her community, as Birsa is faithful and does not beat her – though he has abused her on a few occasions, mostly when he has returned drunk from the arrack shop. She knows other women in her community, but her social interactions are infrequent. She looks forward to the self-help group (SHG) meetings and community festivals. Conversations with Birsa are limited to day-to-day livelihood issues. In any case, with their bandwidth fully stretched, neither has time for much else.

As in Rasika's case, women working on low wages and at the same time fulfilling the responsibilities of housewife and mother remain stressed and anxious – more so if the family is not supportive. Moreover, the burden of chores, especially for working women with young children from poor households, adversely erodes their psychological and physical well-being.

However, when educated women of better-off households get jobs at the higher end of the value chain, they view their employment positively. Such work raises their status and sense of self-worth and improves their psychological well-being despite their household duties. It also increases the possibility of a more egalitarian relationship in marriage. However, there is a caveat – marital strains could arise if the job does not meet the husband's approval. A study based on quality-of-life indicators reveals that working women had better psychological well-being than non-working women.[13] However, homemakers scored higher in the social quality of life. Respondents from nuclear families had a better quality of life than joint families, and graduates fared better than women who had studied only up to school. Overall, employment at the higher end of the value chain mitigates the disadvantages and frustrations resulting from having to bear almost the entire burden of domestic and childcare responsibilities.

Even with women in well-paid jobs, family circumstances often take a heavy toll on women. Let us see the story of Preethi. The mother of a nine-month-old child, Preethi landed a job at a high-end watch brand store. Unfortunately, her mother-in-law fell ill soon after she started working. With no other support system in place, Preethi was forced to leave her job so she could take care of her child and mother-in-law. When Preethi asked her husband when she could resume work, his only response was, 'Who will take care of our baby?' Preethi's story is the story of most married Indian women today – and unfortunately, this hardly raises an eyebrow.[14] Unmarried girls, too, are subject to family pressures regarding education and employment. Most parents continue to view it as their primary duty to get their daughter married off and decide from this perspective. For both married and unmarried women, going against the family is an insurmountable hurdle.

Gender Discrimination Is a Worldwide Malaise

Global experience suggests that political, social, and economic equality eludes most women, even those educated and with secure professional jobs. In China, for example, even though women have made significant progress in the workplace, patriarchal attitudes have remained (see Box 1: The Chinese Path). The Chinese experience could have relevance for India as it shows that high women's work participation rates do not preclude gender discrimination.[15]

Box 1   The Chinese Path

Chinese society adheres to a patriarchal and patrilineal family system. In Confucian thought, a woman's conduct is conceived in the framework of three types of obedience – first to her father, then to her husband, and finally to her son. Usha Chandran traces transformations in gender equity in China since the country gained independence.[16] Women first began entering public life following their mobilization for the cause of the proletariat revolution. Soon after independence in 1949, China enacted several laws to improve women's status and prevent gender discrimination. Policies provided equal access to education and employment. The women's wing of the Communist Party encouraged women to come out of their homes which contributed to changing the stereotypical image of Chinese women in many ways. Simultaneously, there was a strong emphasis on taking care of women's reproductive health and their role as mothers. The government introduced maternity leave with medical facilities and allowance and set up crèches near the workplace. Initially, women entered the service sectors and light industries. During the Great Leap years (1958–1964), urban women also got employed in manufacturing. Rural women took over the responsibility of tending to agriculture as men moved to set up and participate in large-scale irrigation, mining, and industrial projects.

The traditional patriarchal thinking was altered in some ways but continued along other dimensions. China followed an unusual policy of equality of gender 'sameness', focusing only on women's health and reproductive functions. Even women's attire in the workplace was stark and similar to their men co-workers. Although women discarded their traditional roles, there was no growing consciousness of gender equality and gender difference. State policy also entered women's private lives through the infamous 'one-child family' policy.

In 1978 China entered a phase of economic development with a focus on reform and liberalization. As a result, many welfare policies were discontinued, which had severe consequences for women's employment and welfare. As a result, many women lost their jobs – others were physically overworked.

However, since the 1980s, there have been positive developments. Under Western influence, women have begun seeking a desire for womanhood and femininity in contrast to their earlier projection as asexual workers. The fashion industry is now the third-largest after automobile and tourism. Despite these developments, Chinese women continue to face both covert and overt discrimination. They continue to suffer from employment insecurity due to fewer jobs available to them and wage disparities that have grown recently. Women are often still economically dependent on men, who remain the primary decision-makers. Roles within the family, society, and public life remain firmly gendered. From a demographic point of view, China faces a huge challenge. Discrimination against the girl child and preference for sons has created a shortage of women. This adverse and declining sex ratio may further discriminate against women – now a minority in China.[17]

Role of Women's Groups and Media

Global experience shows that the implementation of public policy regarding gender discrimination and women's rights has taken place only under the pressure of sustained and mass women's movements and civil society as policymakers and elected representatives themselves have gendered mindsets. Fortunately, India has several organizations working for women's empowerment, women workers' rights, gender justice, challenging abuse, and oppressive norms, and fighting for the rights of landless women labourers and destitute women, including prisoners and sex workers. There are also active frontal women's organizations of political parties.[18] These provide the building blocks for seeding and providing the impetus for mindset changes, complementing and influencing public policies and judicial actions.

The central government, on its part, has established the National and State Commissions for Women under the National Commission of Women Act, 1990 (NCW Act), to promote women's rights. The principal objective of the NCW Act is laudatory and provides a statutory platform to protect women's rights and a voice for their issues and concerns. However, in practice, neither the National nor the State Commissions of Women have made any meaningful impact. On the contrary, they often remain mute spectators, even when grave gender injustice and serious crimes against women occur. The main challenge is to ensure the independence and autonomy of these institutions through the appointment of those who have a stellar record of working for women's rights and are themselves ideologically committed. In addition, to be effective, the Commissions must work in close partnership with women's organizations and civil society groups. Needless to add, the government must make adequate fund allocation and support the Commissions proactively.

Television, films, and other visual media can be strong allies in fostering behavioural and attitudinal change.[19] Producers can make a meaningful impact on mindsets via programmes that portray women in non-stereotypical and progressive roles. Scripts could show the female protagonist as the family's primary breadwinner, supporting old parents or conducting funeral rites of her parents or siblings.[20] It is equally vital to portray men in atypical roles – as homemakers doing household chores, nurturing children, and playing a supportive role in the spouse's business or profession as an IAS officer or senior corporate executive. Such imaginative film and TV scripts and features would influence men to share the household and childcare responsibilities at home, reduce son preference, encourage women to exercise more autonomy and freedom, and play an equal role in decision-making.

Focused Public Policy Actions Are Imperative

The overwhelming scale and complexity of gender inequity warrants the government to have wide-ranging and large-scale radical policies and programmes. Current government policy responses have been highly inadequate as they have relied mainly on ineffectual schemes. Simply marking a particular day as National Girl Child Day or haphazardly putting up billboards at prominent intersections telling us to 'Love the Girl Child', 'Beti Bachao', and 'Stop Killing Girls' will not make a dent in societal mindsets. From time to time, the government has implemented cash transfer schemes to counter son preference such as Dhan Lakshmi, Ladli, Beti Hai Anmol, and Kanyadan; but these have largely been non-starters. Ironically, the names of the schemes themselves reflect deeply entrenched patriarchal mentalities. In any case, such programmes offer small amounts at maturity, have complex requirements, and are limited to only BPL families, even though adverse sex selection is rampant across income categories.[21]

The existing approach, which relies on women's education and economic growth on the premise that this will automatically reduce gender inequity over time, is misplaced. Cultural practices and patriarchal attitudes persist over generations and even in educated families. Getting governments and policymakers, who have deep gender biases, to move the needle towards gender equity is a huge challenge. Therefore, civil society and women's groups must launch mass mobilization campaigns and other initiatives to push the government to take transformative actions that address the root causes of gender discrimination.

Focus on women's health and nutrition is vital but impacts only physical well-being and is not an indicator of gender equity (see Chapters 2 and 3). A focused public-policy plan delineated under the following five heads would make a significant difference on the ground:

1 imaginative and massive communication and awareness campaigns;
2 education as a key element in women's well-being;
3 establishing a supportive childcare system;
4 improving women's mobility and safety in the workplace; and
5 asset and cash transfers favouring women.

Of course, a gender equity roadmap must include actions, including legislation, favouring the LGBTQIA+ community. Needless to add, policy actions must be backed by adequate budgets and spread across all government ministries, rather than being limited to the Ministry of Women and Child Welfare.

Imaginative and Massive Communication and Awareness Campaigns

In framing gender policies, the government must prioritize actions directed to patriarchal attitudes that restrict economic freedom and autonomy, even of educated women. These practices include the tradition of the woman joining her husband's family, expecting her to owe allegiance only to her in-laws, and the iniquitous intestate succession.[22] Breaking such gender stereotypes calls for bold and sustained country-wide communication campaigns by the government, including sharing evidence of the positive contribution of women. The content of communication messages must go beyond billboard exhortations on the value of the girl child and move on to issues relating to adult women.[23]

The media campaigns must aim to change the stereotyped perception of what jobs and roles are suitable for men and women. The campaigns must be complemented by well-designed gender sensitization workshops and open sessions, including at the village panchayat level, both for men and women. Such sensitization programmes must be specifically directed against the highly retrogressive and perverted views of several formal and non-formal organizations, such as 'Khap Panchayats' (comprising village elders), that reinforce and perpetuate patriarchal practices, and even justify crimes against women. The government must step in and unequivocally and unambiguously denounce such regressive statements. While abolishing the age-old informal Khap Panchayats may not be easy, the government must engage with them and sensitize them to the issue of gender equity. At the same time, we need to recognize that to expect that getting the government to unequivocally decry the regressive views of elected representatives and religious leaders is not easy – often, prominent political leaders themselves hold such negative perceptions of women. (See Box 2: Shocking Sexist Statements by Political Leaders).

Sexual abuse of women at the household level, workplace, and elsewhere is rampant and often unreported both because the police itself is insensitive and because victims themselves do not come forward to report sexual crimes and abuse due to societal conditioning and fear of consequences. Even serious complaints of rape are often brushed under the carpet. Police personnel need special sensitizing, and, as noted in Chapter 6, there should be reservation of jobs for women in the police force. The reduction of crimes and abuse against women must become the police force's top priority. The police must be made accountable and First Information Reports (FIRs) must be lodged promptly and followed up by speedy investigations, preferably by women officers. Equally, the courts need gender sensitization as judicial officers also often have deeply gendered biases.

Box 2 Shocking Sexist Statements by Political Leaders

Political leaders of various hues have made sexist remarks and sanctified and justified the actions of Khap Panchayats. The Chief Minister of Haryana, Manohar Lal Khattar, had this to say on Khap Panchayats: 'They are like parents minding their children and take swift decisions on matters in which courts are silent. Khap Panchayats comprise experienced members of the society and make sensible decisions'. Along the same lines, the former Congress Chief Minister Bhupinder Hooda stated that 'Khap Panchayats are like NGOs.... they are part of our culture'.

Even when rape takes place, sexist remarks are made by prominent political leaders. In 2014, in Uttar Pradesh, Samajwadi Party chief Mulayam Singh Yadav opposed harsh punishment for rape, saying, 'ladke ladke hain, galti ho jati hain (boys will be boys, mistakes take place)'. Surendra Singh, BJP MLA, had this to say: 'If you are raped, it means you lack good values, the onus lies on women to protect their vagina'. Not to be outdone, Botsa Satyanarayana, Congress chief from Andhra Pradesh, in the aftermath of the Delhi 2012 gang rape in a moving bus, advocated keeping women indoors to prevent the rape of women. 'The woman should have thought twice before boarding the bus that night'.

How deeply ingrained gender prejudices are can be gauged from the fact that even the Prime Minister has held misogynistic views. In 2014 while addressing a rally in Varanasi, he said, 'If we kill the girl child in the woman's womb, then what will happen to the world? If only 800 girls are born against 1,000 boys, then 200 boys would remain unmarried'. Though the Prime Minister's intention may have been noble, his words convey the impression that the only reason to give birth to females is to enable marriage.[24]

In 2012, the former Chief Minister of Haryana Om Prakash Chautala proposed that to prevent sexual assault on women, they should be married off early. Yusuf Bhatt, a Congress leader from Jammu & Kashmir, had this to say: 'Unmarried daughters are a liability to their fathers. My daughters are a liability to me. They are studying now and need to be married off. They are a burden on me!'[25]

Two other critical areas for gender sensitization are equal parenting and sharing of household duties. As noted in Chapter 4, engendered parenting practices make a massive difference in reducing a woman's burden and enabling her to access the workplace equally with her partner. Therefore, communication messages must address both male and female members and emphasize that household and parental responsibilities are not a woman's alone.

The communication strategy must also aim at a change in the perception of household members by highlighting new role models for women. Due to centuries-old conditioning, work and public arenas are variously identified as feminine or masculine domains. However, this perception can quickly change. The pathbreaking 73rd and 74th Constitutional Amendments in 1993, which resulted in the election of over 1.5 million women to village panchayats and town municipalities, secured the entry of women into the public sphere and in decision-making roles. There is also evidence that this increased presence of local women leaders has strongly influenced young women, in terms of their career aspirations and educational preference.[26] Further, as chairpersons of village panchayats, women have positively impacted the village economy in other ways; for example, they invest more in public goods critical to the household, such as drinking water facilities.[27]

Highlighting successful women role models is an effective way to encourage women to make atypical choices. There are numerous examples of women in diverse spheres who can be inspiring role models.[28] 'Seeing is believing': women's groups, media, and the government must highlight the stories of women who have opted for careers that have broken gender stereotypes. When women see other women in non-traditional roles, they find it easier to imagine themselves in those roles. Ordinary women may be more effective as role models to inspire other women to also break the glass ceiling; take, for example, women achievers such as Harshini Kanhekar, the country's first firefighter, Priya Jhingran, the first woman in the Indian army, and Surekha, the first woman train driver.[29]

Along with celebrity role models and highlighting atypical careers that women have taken up, we need to look at unusual role models also. For example, women sitting in the chilly winter in Delhi's Shaheen Bagh dominated the anti-Citizenship Amendment Act (CAA) protests of 2019–20. Bilkis Dadi, an 82-year-old woman with her wrinkled face and lean frame, became the face of these protests nationwide and was included in *The Times* list of the World's Most Influential People. Similarly, the protests against the farm laws saw the active participation of many women and showed that women too can break the traditional barriers which kept them in pre-defined women's areas.

It would be some time before sufficient role models amongst women emerge from impoverished households and communities. However, the vital role played by ASHA workers who come from low-income families can be highlighted. ASHA workers played a critical role in managing the COVID-19 pandemic. Unfortunately, as noted in Chapter 2, their remuneration is meagre at present. However, if they are made full-time frontline health workers with the requisite training and commensurate pay, their self-respect and respect in the local community would get enhanced. Similarly, anganwadi workers can also better influence the local community as professional full-time childcare workers.

Even women in educated families are not the primary decision-makers when they wish to work. Changing men's attitudes is a challenge here as well, as attitudes are only slowly changing. Communication campaigns need to target the way men perceive their roles. Many men in middle-class families pitched in with household chores during the COVID-19 pandemic lockdowns. The challenge is to make this normal behaviour. Communication campaigns must highlight male role models who take on home responsibilities. And, of course, it is not adequate for men to allow their spouses to work – women must control their earnings.

Education Is a Key Element in Women's Well-being

Though education is a powerful transformative force for achieving gender equality, it does not necessarily guarantee it. As noted in Chapter 6, women's well-being improves well-being only when higher education attainment is associated with higher incomes. The communication strategy of the government must, therefore, not only focus on achieving gender parity beyond the secondary school stage, but also encourage women to make non-stereotypical education choices.

Secondly, there is a need to address gender bias in education from the primary school stage. Teachers must ensure that girls recognize themselves as equal and resist discrimination. To address patriarchal attitudes, boys must learn to deconstruct a patriarchal conception of masculinity and construct egalitarian beliefs.[30] Raising a feminist consciousness among boys means they are made to examine the current social system critically and recognize it as unjust.[31] Gender equality must become a vital objective of the school curriculum. Gender education and sensitization modules must be introduced at kindergarten and continued into college education. Teachers must become promoters of gender equality, organize quality teaching-learning processes, and create platforms that address the underlying social norms, attitudes, and behaviour.[32]

Textbooks are pivotal sources of knowledge and must be gender inclusive. While there has been some progress in a few states to remove the more obvious portrayal of gender bias, equality has often been dealt with in a narrow sense by merely increasing the visual representation of girls and women or by their token inclusion in biographies. Even when the text is on women achievers, the effect often gets diluted by referring to them as 'wife of' or 'daughter of'. Women involved in combat, such as Rani Laxmibai, are spoken of as possessing masculine traits. Women are depicted mostly in traditional roles as teachers, nurses, or social reformers, unlike men in various professions. Textbooks describe boys as active participants and engaged in physical activities while girls predominate in traditional or festival contexts. The government needs to review each textbook from the gender lens as it excises gender stereotyping. Showing men in non-stereotypical roles, such as a man feeding a baby while the woman works at a factory, could significantly impact male attitudes.

Another area for government intervention is in influencing the educational preference of girls. Historically, the perception is that studies in STEM (Science, Technology, Engineering, and Maths) are more appropriate for men. Consequently, very few women take to the science and engineering streams in college. Studies have demonstrated the effectiveness of female role models to influence girls' preference for STEM studies.[33] Girls begin choosing different career options once they find others opting for them. Another way of encouraging girls to opt for non-conventional disciplines is through reservation. For example, the legal profession has traditionally been male-dominated.[34] The National Law Schools set aside a 30 per cent quota for women from the academic year 2008–09. By 2020, the enrolment of women in these law schools had gone up close to 40 per cent.[35] The government could reserve 30 per cent in all STEM courses as well.

Establishing a Supportive Childcare System

The lack of a suitable support system for childcare is a huge barrier for women who wish to go out to work. Burdened with most household and childcare responsibilities, it is not easy for a woman to take up a regular, full-time job outside the house while coping with children's school curricula at home and part-time work.[36] We have noted in Chapter 4 the vital importance of child day care services in the context of child development, particularly for poor households. These services are equally critical to enabling women to access the workplace. Unfortunately, the few better-managed crèches set up by the private sector cater primarily to the well-off.

One of the significant aspects of the amendments made in 2017 to the Maternity Benefit Act, 1961, is mandating the provision of a crèche facility for any establishment with over 50 employees. Further, under the Factories Act, 1948, any factory with over 30 women workers is required to have a crèche. However, as pointed out in Chapter 4, only a handful of companies have set up crèches. Therefore, the government needs to ensure stricter enforcement of these legislations and provide financial support to companies to set up crèche facilities.[37] Crèches and day care services should be looked upon as support for the entire family and not for women alone.

As far as the unorganized sector is concerned, the government must prioritize setting up crèches through three measures detailed in Chapter 4: enhanced and liberalized funding under the National Crèche Scheme, progressive conversion of anganwadis into anganwadi-cum-crèches, and the promotion of and financial support to community-led crèches.

Improving Mobility and Safety in the Workplace

The lack of safe and adequate arrangements for commuting to the workplace is one of the key challenges for women. Improvement in the road network and public transportation systems have not translated into substantive gains in women's mobility to work. Apart from the issue of mobility, women are not encouraged to take up jobs outside the home, especially if the workplace is at a distance.

A study found that 80 per cent of women were not even allowed to visit a health centre without permission from their husbands or other family members.[38] The farther from home the job opportunity, the less likely women are to take it up. Given that India's future economic growth will take place in urban areas, the current situation on mobility suggests that most women will remain excluded from this urban boom. (We discuss strategies to improve urban mobility, with a specific focus on women's mobility and safety, in Chapter 8.) The government must also work with companies to ensure that women are safe in the workplace and while commuting to work and back.[39]

Even when women are willing to work night shifts, discriminatory legislation, such as the Factories Act prohibits women from doing so. The government needs to review its labour laws and the Factories Act to ensure gender-friendly policies across sectors and at all times of the day. The actions by some industries such as the IT industry and nursing services for arranging transport for women employees to the workplace and back home also need encouragement and support.

Promoting Actions by Companies

Gender discrimination in the workplace is prevalent worldwide. The experience of China, the US, and other First-World countries shows that it takes a long time for progress to take place. In such countries, even though women have fought relentlessly for recognition on equal terms, gender inequality persists in the workplace (see Box 3: Gender Inequality Persists in the US and Elsewhere). It is, therefore, imperative for the government to take proactive steps, intervene and encourage companies to take decisive action to ensure gender equity and diversity.

Box 3 Gender Inequality Persists in the United States and Elsewhere

Since the 1980s, women have made great strides in the workplace in the US, but inequality persists. The issue of equal pay is still a hot-button topic. Women earn 80 per cent of what men get paid, even though in the US and many First-World countries, women surpass men in educational achievement. The problem arises when young adults try to balance work and family, and women carry nearly all the caregiving responsibilities. It is unrealistic to expect gender equality if workplaces demand women to be available all the time.

In Japan, women take up education to pursue a career. But within the home, gender equality is not on par with workforce equality. As a result, women end up doing a 'second shift' of housework and childcare when they return home from work. Alternatively, women are waiting longer to get into a partnership. They are choosing, instead, to focus on their career. And when they do get married, they have fewer children, leading to a drop in Japan's population. The reduced

---

148

UNSHACKLING GENDERED MINDSETS

> number of young, home-grown workers entering the workforce and paying into the pension systems could undermine Japan's economy.
>
> Gender stereotypes are hard to break. In both Japan and the US, increasing gender equality is an integral part of public policy for the workplace and the home. Yet, many people still hold on to their practices. Companies state that they are highly committed to gender diversity, but that does not translate into meaningful progress. The proportion of women at every level in corporate America has hardly changed. A 2018 study drawing on data from 279 companies revealed that progress isn't just slow but stalled.[46] In the US, women are under-represented at every level – women of colour are the most under-represented, lagging behind white men, men of colour, and white women. Women are less likely to be hired into entry-level jobs. At the step up to manager and beyond, the disparity widens further.
>
> Many factors contribute to this lack of gender diversity, including everyday discrimination, sexual harassment, and the experience of being the only woman in the room. Sexism and racism are both subtle and explicit. For almost two-thirds of women, such micro-aggressions are a workplace reality. Most commonly, women require more evidence of their competence than men and have their judgment questioned in their area of expertise.
>
> Thirty-five per cent of women in corporate America experience sexual harassment at some point in their careers, from hearing sexist jokes to being touched sexually. Many women think their companies are falling short of putting policies into practice. One in five women say they are often the only woman or one of the only women in the room at work – they are 'Onlys'. Women who are 'Onlys' have a significantly worse experience than women who work with other women.

In India, three important legislations are already in place. The first is the Sexual Harassment of Women at Workplace (Prevention, Prohibition and Redressal) Act, 2013, to protect against sexual harassment. However, there is low awareness and poor enforcement of the Act.[40] The second legislation is the requirement under the Companies Act, 2013, for every listed company and those with a turnover exceeding ₹3 billion to have at least one woman on their Board of Directors.[41] A study carried out in 2020 revealed that 55 per cent of the listed companies surveyed had fulfilled this mandate.[42] The third legislation is the amended mandate in the Maternity Benefit Act, 1961, which provides for 26 weeks of maternity leave.[43] However, as noted in the previous chapter, the provision may have become counterproductive as many companies are tending to reduce their recruitment of women because they perceive the new obligations as not practicable.

The Ministry of Corporate Affairs needs to make gender equity a key element in regulating and overseeing companies. While doing so, it should be mindful of the fact that mandates which companies perceive as hurting business will be counterproductive. The approach needs to be supportive and facilitative. The first imperative would be for the government and civil society to collate and widely share evidence from companies that have increased their share of women and seen their businesses grow. The IT/BPO sector was among the first in the country to realize the potential of the female workforce and now has 60 per cent women at senior levels.[44] Several other companies have also taken the initiative.

To take another example, Tata's Starbucks has an organizational mandate on gender diversity and introduced effective interventions favouring women. These include interactions with family and friends at the workplace, flexible working hours for young mothers, and structured career paths for part-timers. Within a year of these interventions, Starbucks saw a significant jump in the number of women on the rolls, and a lowering of attrition rates. There was also clear evidence that stores with higher gender diversity had higher footfalls and higher revenue as well.

The second step would be for the government to ensure that companies have gender-inclusive policies. While companies should be left free to formulate their gender action plans, the government must monitor their progress. Limited women in an organization make it difficult for them to feel comfortable. A critical element of the policy would be to ask companies to set a minimum number of women employees so that the 'Only' experience becomes rare (see Box 3: Gender Inequality Persists in the United States and Elsewhere). The government must encourage companies to offer employees flexibility in their work schedules and work locations. Most organizations that offered this flexibility to their employees during the COVID-19 pandemic found that productivity did not suffer.

For undertaking the above steps, the government must work in close collaboration with progressive employers. Focusing on diversity in the workplace may require companies to provide investments towards training, sensitization, and support services. For example, in service sectors, the store manager must stay back after hours to tally the accounts and the inventory. This requirement forces women to reconsider their choices and resign themselves to junior positions or less strenuous jobs to deliver their household responsibilities and avoid disturbing the family dynamics. To enable women to perform roles that require additional work hours, companies will need to provide extra support to handle their responsibilities at home (e.g., childcare beyond regular hours). It would also require flexible shifts and additional security during late hours. Women-friendly policies in the private sector need to be supported by the government, but legislating that they will need to pay to provide childcare support and maternity leave may discourage companies from employing women. Therefore, the government needs to bear the cost of such supportive activities, including maternity leave, at least until private firms start recognizing the benefits of gender diversity.[45]

To ensure that employment contracts are fair, the government must intervene in the event of a violation. Women working in the unorganized sector, such as domestic workers, also need formalized contracts that provide them social protection and a fair wage. Similarly, sex workers also have the right to health protection and institutional arrangements to prevent exploitation.

Asset and Cash Transfers Favouring Women

Asset transfers to female members instead of the male members of the household could have a positive and empowering effect. Women with land rights exert greater authority, are less likely to experience domestic violence, have healthier children, and farm agricultural land more efficiently, resulting in higher household income.[47] Several states have enacted laws granting women rights to ancestral land in India and yet women constitute barely 14 per cent of landowners and own merely 11 per cent of land in landowning households across the country.[48] Moreover, women are more likely to inherit land as widows than as daughters. This highlights the continued denial of daughters' rights while recognizing the social legitimacy being accorded to widows' claims. This is due to the perception that daughters are no longer part of the parental family once they get married.

Land and property are state subjects, but there are no mechanisms to monitor and enforce legislation. The most effective way would be to legislate that all land and house titles are automatically passed on to the male and female heirs equally on the demise of a household member. Such legislation should include amending the Hindu Succession Act to make land title changes automatic.

Another efficacious policy would be financial incentives for parents to invest in the education of daughters in school and college. While many states in India offer incentives to families to send their daughters to school and college, the existing schemes are too small to make a meaningful impact. Opportunities for girls improve when women control a large share of the household income because women have a less pro-boy bias than men. A transformative step by the central government would be to ensure that all direct-benefit cash transfers, especially under the PM Kisan scheme and MGNREGA, are to the woman members of the household.

The above five policy interventions, complemented by the measures to enhance women's livelihoods spelt out in Chapter 6, would make for a more equal society between men and women.

Changing Perceptions About the LGBTQIA+ Community

Conventional discourse on gender issues limits discussion to women. However, the lesbian, gay, bisexual, transgender, queer, intersex, and asexual (LGBTQIA+) community faces even greater stigmatization and social discrimination because of their gender identity and sexual orientation. India has made progress on these issues over the last decade; however, there is still a long way to go for full LGBTQIA+ equality, even in law.

Transgender and intersex Indians have more legal protections than lesbian, gay, or bisexual people but experience intense discrimination and stigmatization. Eunuchs (or Hijras as referred to in India) are members of a community of intersex, transgender, and gender non-conforming persons, who have historically had a specific cultural role in India. However, it was only in 2014 that the government legally recognized the 'third gender'. Parliament has passed several laws protecting Hijras from discrimination; for example, transgender people can legally change their legal gender after a sex assignment surgery. However, despite the legal protections, public attitudes remain negative.

In 2018, the Indian Supreme Court struck down laws criminalizing same-sex relations, which has improved the tolerance and acceptance of the LGBTQIA+ community. The Supreme Court has held that sexual orientation is natural and inherent in an individual; an individual has little or no control. Furthermore, it has been pointed out that any discrimination due to a person's sexual orientation would violate the fundamental right of freedom of expression. This judgement has to some extent alleviated the fear of legal repercussions for the LGBTQIA+ community. However, there is no protection against discrimination due to sexual orientation, nor is there any legal recognition of same-sex couples.[49]

To counter the discrimination, violence, and social rejection of the LGBTQIA+ community, a vital step would be to enact laws that reflect the Supreme Court's decision. Legislation must allow same-sex marriage, provide same-sex couples the right to adopt children, and recognize their inheritance rights. In addition, the law must include provisions to ensure that there is no discrimination against LGBTQIA+ persons, both in government and in the private sector, in job recruitment, or at the time of promotions. The International Commission of Jurists in 2019 has recommended a comprehensive set of laws to prevent discrimination against the LGBTQ community emanating from housing and the home environment, the workplace and employment environment, and public spaces or spaces generally open to the public.[50] This report can become the foundation of the legislative road map for the government; there is evidence that legal reforms can improve societal attitudes.[51]

Till the enactment of new laws, it is incumbent on the central government to unequivocally and unambiguously recognize the rights of the LGBTQIA+ community prominently in policy statements. The second step would be to run massive and sustained campaigns on the positive role of LGBTQIA+ persons and project as role models prominent LGBTQIA+ persons who have shed their inhibitions and publicly announced their transgender or gender orientation. The government must also broadcast that homosexuality is not a criminal offence, create public awareness, eliminate the stigma that members of the community face, and give the police force periodic training to sensitize them about the issue. Sensitization of the people to gender diversity in society must begin from the school-going stage.

Central to public policy on supporting the community is for the government to recognize its limitation to reach out directly to LGBTQIA+ individuals. Therefore, the government must work closely with groups, including NGOs, working with the LGBTQIA+ community. The government must gain the community's confidence and trust so that they come forward to report cases of injustice, discrimination, and abuse. The government must institutionalize immediate investigation and speedy justice in such cases. Credible NGOs working in this area could be provided funding support from the government through a well-designed grant-in-aid scheme.

To ensure there is no discrimination against the LGBTQIA+ community in the workplace will require the Equal Remuneration Act, 1976, and the Maternity Act, 2013, to be suitably revised to include LGBTQIA+ persons in their ambit.[52]

Gender Budgeting

The Women and Child Development department's budget for women's schemes is meagre – a mere ₹39 billion in the 2020–21 budget.[53] The Union Budget Statement since 2005–06 also includes a Gender Budget Statement, which reports the proposed allocations earmarked for women in respect of all ministries. This statement is in two parts. The first gives the budgets of schemes exclusively for women (₹286 billion in 2020–21), while the second gives expenditures that have over 30 per cent earmarked for women (₹1149 billion in 2020–21).[54] Several ministries either report nil expenditure or a flat 30–50 per cent of the provision for the scheme without indicating the assumptions made, making the entire exercise unclear and imprecise. Even if we were to go by the Gender Budget Statement, the total budgetary allocations have remained at less than 5 per cent of the union budget for the past 15 years since the exercise began.[55] Unfortunately, gender budgeting has remained a casual mechanical exercise with little attention to enhancing the budgets of programmes that benefit women.

The government needs to enhance budgets for women's programmes across sectors. For example, there should be higher allocations in the police budget to ensure women's safety or prevent crimes against women, significant allocations for making mobility safer for women, and skill development for women beneficiaries. Similarly, allocations to the women and child development department's programmes that benefit women, like working women's hostels and crèches, have remained small. The 2020–21 budget for working women's hostels was a mere ₹0.15 billion. Similarly, the women's skill development programmes and the National Crèche Scheme have had static outlays of ₹2.1 billion and ₹0.75 billion, respectively.[56] Recent programmes launched by the government, such as the

Mudra loan scheme for women entrepreneurs and the Start-up India program, also have had tiny outlays and minimal impact.[57] Only two schemes have somewhat sizeable budgets – the scheme for empowerment of adolescent girls had an allocation of ₹2.5 billion in 2020–21 and the maternity benefit scheme (Pradhan Mantri Matru Vandana Yojana) had an allocation of close to ₹25 billion.[58]

It must be noted that budget allocations to benefit the LGBTQIA+ community have been entirely overlooked. Budget allocation should cover a comprehensive bouquet of programmes aimed at improving safety, skill development, support to entrepreneurs, measures to create safe workspaces, fair wages, better provisioning for health and nutrition, specific provisions for the LGBTQIA+ community, and, most critically, for spreading awareness about gender equality.

It is high time that the government goes beyond tokenism and makes a firm commitment to equity and an equal position for all citizens. This requires enlightened leadership. Only then can the country hope to move towards gender justice and realize the demographic dividend. Fostering a change in mindset and behaviour is a formidable challenge. However, much can be achieved if governments, civil society, women's groups, and employers work in close collaboration. Along with this, there is a need for an enabling environment for enhancing female participation at work at higher levels of the value chain which would improve the dignity of women and the quality of their lives and have a multiplier impact on economic growth.

Notes

1 Kofi Annan Foundation website. https://www.kofiannanfoundation.org/our-work/gender-equality-and-inclusion/.
2 Malala Yusuf Zai, "I am Malala", *Memoirs, 2013.*
3 SRS Statistical Report 2018, Office of the Registrar General & Census Commissioner, *Government of India,* 2018. https://censusindia.gov.in/vital_statistics/SRS_Report_2018/4.Executive_Summary_2018.pdf; date of access September 2, 2021. A major cause for worry is that the sex ratio has not been showing any improvement. In fact, according to the SRS Report of 2018, the sex ratio declined marginally from 906 in 2011 to 899 in 2018.
4 Ayesha Banu, "Human Development, Disparity and Vulnerability: Women in South Asia," *UNDP,* 2016. http://hdr.undp.org/sites/default/files/latest_edited_banu_template_gl_1_august.pdf; date of access August 24, 2021.
5 Diva Dhar, Tarun Jain & Seema Jayachandran, "Intergenerational Transmission of Gender Attitudes: Evidence from India," *The Journal of Development Studies,* 55:12, pp. 2572–2592, 2019.
6 Archana Shukla, "Attitudes towards Role and Status of Women in India: A Comparison of Three Generations of Men and Women," Psychological Studies, Volume 60, page s119–128, *Springer,* 2015. https://link.springer.com/article/10.1007/s12646-015-0298-6; date of access April 5, 2020.
7 Rohini Pande, Jennifer Johnsson, and Eric Dodge, "How to get India's Women Working? First, let Them Out of the House," *IndiaSpend,* 11 April 2016.
8 National Family Health Survey (NFHS-4), 2015–16. http://rchiips.org/nfhs/nfhs-4Reports/India.pdf.

9 Kumar Das and Bijeta Mohanty, "The Growing Concern Around Violence Against Women In India – Where Do We Stand?" *International Growth Centre*, 25 November 2020. https://www.theigc.org/blog/the-growing-concern-around-violence-against-women-in-india-where-do-we-stand/; date of access January 5, 2020.

10 Seema Jayachandran, "The Roots of Gender Inequality in Developing Countries," *The Annual Review of Economics*, 7:63–88, 2015. https://faculty.wcas.northwestern.edu/~sjv340/roots_of_gender_inequality.pdf; date of access February 5, 2020.

11 Sunny Jose, "Women's Paid Work and Well-being in Rajasthan", *Economic and Political Weekly*, vol. 47, no. 45, pp. 48–55, 10 November 2013.

12 Nisha Srivastava and Ravi Srivastava, Women, "Work and Employment Outcomes in Rural India," *Economic and Political Weekly*, vol. 45, no. 28, pp. 49–63, 10–16 July 2010.

13 Ranjeet Kaur, "An Assessment of Quality of Life of Working Women in Ludhiana District of Punjab," *Punjab Agricultural University*, Ludhiana. https://krishikosh.egranth.ac.in/displaybitstream?handle=1/5810006247&-fileid=64a7bf10-f277-4eb9-8e5b-ebfb2176bdf3; date of access January 2, 2020.

14 Anita Kumar, 'Women in Workforce: What it Would Take to Achieve Gender Parity in India", *YS Journal*, 9 October 2018. https://yourstory.com/journal/women-in-workforce-what-it-would-take-to-achieve-g-pre59syolk/amp; date of access March 5, 2021.

15 Isabelle Attane, "Being a Woman in China Today: A Demography of Gender," *Open Editions Journals*, 2012/4. https://journals.openedition.org/chinaperspectives/6013; date of access March 10, 2021.

16 Usha Chandran, "India China Neighbours Strangers", A Woman's World, *India International Centre Quarterly*, vol. 34, no, 3/4 pp. 288–301, Spring 2010.

17 Isabelle Attane, "Being a Woman in China Today: A Demography of Gender," *Open Editions Journals*, 2012/4.

18 Rachna Chandira, "10 NGOs Working For Women's Empowerment That You Should Know," *Shethepeople*, 2 November 2018 https://www.shethepeople.tv/news/10-ngos-working-womens-; date of access January 4, 2021. The Self Employed Women's Association (SEWA), promoted in 1972 by Ela Bhatt, has empowered women by giving them identity as informal workers and taking up women workers' rights issues. Today, they have close to 2 million women members. Snehalaya, established in 1989, works for women in vulnerable contexts, including commercial sex workers. The North East Network (NEN), set up in 1995 as part of the Beijing World Conference on Women, actively promotes gender justice across all the North-Eastern states. The Azad Foundation works for poor women living in urban India who face abuse. CREA, founded in 2000, has provided a platform to challenge oppressive norms and increase self-confidence in women. Vimochana, founded in 1979, is a Bangalore-based women's activist group. The Bharatiya Grameen Mahila Sangh (BGMS), founded in 1955, is a major national organization for rural women. The Mahila Kissan Adhikar Manch (MAKAM) has been at the forefront of the fight for the rights of landless women farmers. Janodaya has completed 34 years working for the socio-economic development of destitute women, including former prisoners. Jagori (meaning 'awaken, women!') is an NGO whose mission is to empower women in innovative ways, including psychosocial counselling. Women's organizations of political parties include the All India Democratic Women's Association (AIDWA), the National Federation of Indian Women (NFIW), and the All India Mahila Congress (AIMC).

19 Jensen, R., & Oster, E., "The Power of TV: Cable Television and Women's Status in India," *Quarterly Journal of Economics*, 2009, 124(3), 1057–1094.

20 Seema Jayachandran, *Annu. Rev. Econ.* 2015. 7:63–88.

21 Farah Naqvi and A. K. Shiva Kumar, "India & The Sex Selection Conundrum," *The Hindu*, 24 January 2012. https://www.thehindu.com/opinion/op-ed/india-the-sex-selection-conundrum/article2826252.ece.

22 Deshpande and Gupta, "Nakusha: Son Preference, Unwanted Girls, and Gender Gaps in Schooling," *Ideas for India*, 25 September 2020. https://www.ideasforindia.in/topics/social-identity/nakusha-son-preference-unwanted-girls-and-gender-gaps-in-schooling.html.

23 Farah Naqvi and A. K. Shiva Kumar, *The Hindu*, 24 January 2012.

24 Vaishaka Saxena, "10 Sexist Slurs That Show How Ridiculous Indian Politicians Can Be," *India Today*, 20 July 2016.

25 Tracy Ann, "8 Times Our Netas Casually Said the Most Offensive & Disrespectful Things About Women," *Diva*, March 2021. https://www.idiva.com/news-opinion/opinion/sexist-misogynistic-statements-indian-politicians-made-recently/18018557; date of access: August 5, 2021.

26 Peter Dizikes, "Leading by Example: The Presence of Female Politicians Boosts Aspirations, Educational Achievements of Young Women," *MIT News Office*, 13 January 2012. https://news.mit.edu/2012/female-politicians-0113; date of access March 5, 2021.

27 Chattopadhyay, R. and E. Duflo, "Women as Policy Makers: Evidence from a Nationwide Randomized Experiment in India," *Econometrica*, 72, 1409–1443, 2004.

28 A few women role models immediately come to mind: Ruth Manorama, women's activist; Brinda Karat, politician; Sania Mirza, tennis player; Gita Gopinath, economist; Vrinda Grover, lawyer; Mallika Srinivasan, entrepreneur; Shuba Mudgal, singer; and Vinita Bali, corporate CEO.

29 "5 Indian Women Ahead of Their Time," *Jaagore*, www.jagore.com.

30 Shivangi Singh, "Inspiration, My Story, Sexism and Patriarchy," *Society*, 3 May 2019. https://www.youthkiawaaz.com/2019/05/heres-why-i-believe-that-gender-education-can-help-attain-un-sdg-5-gender-equality/; date of access April 5, 2021.

31 Urvashi Sahni, "Teaching Boys to Examine Gender in Patriarchal Societies," *Brookings*, 2019. https://www.brookings.edu/blog/education-plus-development/2019/04/10/teaching-boys-to-examine-gender-in-patriarchal-societies/; date of access April 7, 2021.

32 Suman Sachdeva, "7 Principles for Empowering Teachers to be Architects of Girls' Empowerment," *Brookings*, 2018." https://www.brookings.edu/blog/education-plus-development/2018/07/18/7-principles-for-empowering-teachers-to-be-architects-of-girls-empowerment/; date of access April 11, 2021.

33 Susana Gonsalez-Perez, Ruth Meteos de Cabo and Milagros Sainz, "Girls in STEM: Is it a Role-Model Thing?" *Frontiers in Psychology*, 10 September 2020.

34 Seethalakshmai S. "Law Schools Set Aside 30% Quota For Girls, *Times of India*," 2 February 2008. https://timesofindia.indiatimes.com/india/law-schools-set-aside-30-quota-for-girls/articleshow/2749920.cms?from=mdr; date of acess March 5, 2020.

35 "Digging the NIRF Law School Rankings", *Legally India*, 16 June 2020.

36 Bansari Kamdar, "India's Women Bear the Burden of Unpaid Work", *The Diplomat*, 2 November 2020. According to the 2019 NSS time-use survey, women spend 243 minutes on unpaid housework against a mere 25 minutes spent by men – this works out to 19.5 per cent of the time spent by women in a day compared to only 2.5 per cent of the time spent by men.

37 Saumya Uma, "Game Changer or Trojan Horse," Aditya Kamath, *Economic & Political Weekly*, 16 May 2020. https://www.epw.in/journal/2020/20/review-womens-studies/gamechanger-or-trojan-horse.html.

UNSHACKLING GENDERED MINDSETS

38 Rohini Pande, Jennifer Johnsson and Eric Dodge, "How to get India's Women Working? First, let Them Out of the House," *IndiaSpend*, 11 April 2016.

39 "53% Working Women Fear for Their Safety: Assocham," *Mint*, 9 October 2008. https://mcKinseyfor-their-safety-Assocham.html; date of access April 5, 2021.

40 Jayshree Bajoria, "No Me Too for Women Like Us," *Human Rights Watch*, 14 October 2020. https://www.hrw.org/report/2020/10/14/no-metoo-women-us/poor-enforcement-indias-sexual-harassment-law; date of access May 3, 2021.

41 Section 149 of Companies Act, 2013 read with Rule 3 of Chapter XI – Companies (Appointment and Qualification of Directors) Rules, 2014. http://ebook.mca.gov.in/Actpagedisplay.aspx?PAGENAME=18078; date of acess May 7, 2021.

42 "India Ranked 12th in the Women Number Presence in Companies," *Economic Times*, 8 March 2020.

43 Amendments to the Maternity Benefit Act, 1961. https://pib.gov.in/newsite/PrintRelease.aspx?relid=148712; date of access April 4, 2020.

44 Namrata Gupta, "Indian IT Industry Attracts More Women, But Many Exit Within First 5 Years in the Job," *The Print*, 20 February 2020. https://theprint.in/pageturner/excerpt/indian-it-industry-attracts-more-women-but-many-exit-within-first-5-years-in-the-job/368504/; date of access April 4, 2020.

45 Sona Mitra, "Patterns of Female Employment in Urban India: Analysis of NSS data (1983–1999/2000), Vol.41, No. 48, *Economic & Political Weekly*, 2–8 December 2006.

46 Alexis Krivkovich, Marie-Claude Nadeau, Kelsey Robinson, Nicole Robinson, Irina Starikova, and Lareina Yee, "Women in the Workplace 2018," McKinsey, 23 October 2018. https://www.mckinsey.com/featured-insights/diversity-and-inclusion/women-in-the-workplace; date of access April 10, 2020.

47 Rachel Brulé, "Empowering Effects of Women in Politics," *Hindu Business Line*, 29 January 2019. https://www.thehindubusinessline.com/opinion/columns/empowering-effects-of-women-in-politics/article26122124.ece; date of access May 7, 2020.

48 Agarwal, B., Anthwal, R. and Malvika, M., "Which Women Own Land in India? Between Divergent Data Sets, Measures and Laws," GDI Working Paper 2020-043, *The University of Manchester*, 2020. https://hummedia.manchester.ac.uk/institutes/gdi/publications/workingpapers/GDI/gdi-working-paper-202043-agarwal-anthwal-mahesh.pdf; date of access June 5, 2021.

49 "LGBT Rights in India," Wikipedia.

50 "Living with Dignity: Sexual Orientation and Gender Identity Based Human Rights Violations in Housing, Work, and Public Spaces in India," *International Commission of Jurists (ICJ)*, June 2019. https://www.icj.org/wp-content/uploads/2019/06/India-Living-with-dignity-Publications-Reports-thematic-report-2019-ENG.pdf; date of access June 4, 2021.

51 Charles Kenny and Dev Patel, "Norms and Reform: Legalizing Homosexuality Improves Attitudes," Working Paper 465, *The Center for Global Development*, October 2017. https://www.cgdev.org/sites/default/files/norms-and-reform-legalizing-homosexuality-improves-attitudes.pdf; date of access June 5, 2021.

52 Cyril Amarchand Mangaldas, "Will an Indian Workplace Ever be 'Inclusive' Towards 'Transgenders'?" Bloomberg Quint Opinion, Bloomberg, 12 December 2018. https://www.bloombergquint.com/opinion/will-an-indian-workplace-ever-be-inclusive-towards-transgenders; date of access June 11, 2021.

53 Statement 13, Gender Budget, Expenditure Profile 2021–2022. https://www.indiabudget.gov.in/doc/eb/stat13.pdf; date of access December 2, 2021.

54 Ibid.

55 Aasha Kapur Mehta, "Union Budget 2020–21: A Critical Analysis from the Gender Perspective," *Economic and Political Weekly*, vol. 55, issue no. 16, 18 April 2020.

56 ₹2,110 million of total four skill development schemes for women, Statement 13, Gender Budget, Expenditure Profile 2021–2022, *Government of India*. https://www.indiabudget.gov.in/doc/eb/stat13.pdf; date of access March 2, 2022.
57 Uma, "Women Missing in India: By Choice or by Disparities," Women and Development: Issues and Challenges, *Elite Publishing House*, 2018.
58 Union Budget 2021–22, Ministry of Women and Child Development, Government of India. https://www.indiabudget.gov.in/doc/eb/sbe100.pdf; date of access March 2, 2022.

8

PROMOTING PLANNED URBANIZATION

> Urbanization is not about simply increasing the number of urban residents or expanding the area of cities. More importantly, it's about a complete change from rural to urban style in terms of industry structure, employment, living environment, and social security.[1]
>
> **Li Keqiang**, Premier, People's Republic of China

Rising Urban Neglect

It is predicted that over 70 per cent of future GDP growth in India will be from urban areas.[2] In this context, in Chapter 6, we emphasized the need for an urban-centric approach to livelihoods, adopting a well-planned urban cluster model development.

India's towns and cities currently rank amongst the lowest on quality-of-life indicators. The foreign visitor goes back with horrific memories of filth and squalor, unhygienic crowded markets, and extreme traffic congestion. A herd of cows standing around a mountain of garbage or stray dogs dotting the sidewalks is a typical sight that meets the eyes of overseas travellers, leaving them with a sense of disbelief about the apathy of local authorities as well as citizens.

India's urbanization is much more extensive than indicated by the 2011 census figures.[3] It is distressing that not only have urban areas expanded haphazardly, but they have also witnessed a sharp rise in poverty, particularly since the onset of the Covid-19 pandemic. Urban poverty levels are at least double those of the last official urban poverty 2011 estimate of 13.7 per cent. Loss of employment and income has been the sharpest in the informal sector, especially amongst migrant labour. Also, most of them live in slums despite their share in employment being as high as 90 per cent.[4] An estimated 35 per cent of India's urban population lives in slums.[5]

The poor in the slum settlements have a Damocles sword hanging over their heads – both their slum tenements and the occupation of spaces from where they peddle their goods are technically 'illegal'. Drinking water and

DOI: 10.4324/9781003346258-8

159

electricity connections and even 'protection to live' are provided by the nexus of local slum lords and local authorities.

Slum settlements have seen little improvement as there is no pressure from the rest of urban society. The wealthier sections are happy with flyovers and metro systems and perceive waste, sanitation, road congestion, and slums as someone else's problem. That they are the principal beneficiaries of the cheap labour from these slum areas is a truth conveniently ignored. They are also unaware that the near absence of sewerage and sanitation systems in slum settlements may be the principal factor for the prevailing high disease burden in cities and towns.[6]

Against the above background, we examine five critical issues plaguing urban areas: the lack of urban planning; the gross neglect of housing for the urban poor; the pathetic urban sanitation situation; the appalling solid waste management; and the urban mobility crisis. Addressing the challenges in these vital areas is particularly critical for improving the quality of life of urban residents. Equally, it is a crucial enabler for setting the country on the path of rapid economic growth. Based on the analysis, we identify an integrated set of public policy actions to remedy the situation in each of these five focus areas, prioritizing the infrastructure and financing requirements of industrial cluster towns that we discussed in Chapter 6.

Urban Planning: Divorced from Reality

In India, the inhabitation of cities has almost always preceded any actual urban planning.[7] In the early post-Independence years, due to a lack of foresight, low-density housing was planned in cities like Chandigarh and Delhi. Unsurprisingly, as the urban population has risen exponentially, master plans have been followed more in violation than in compliance.

These plans ignore ground realities and have become obsolete and irrelevant. Moreover, these plans are neither forward-looking nor consider the urban infrastructure requirements of poor households and the rising numbers of migrant labour. However, despite the lack of housing and urban services, cities attract migrants in search of better employment opportunities.[8] Further, vested interests have vitiated the planning process. Buildings constructed in violation of the plan often get regularized due to the influence exerted by builders, while slums are frequently demolished. In contrast, the existence of slums is always uncertain, and they remain in danger of demolition.

Under pressure from a vocal, resurgent middle class and builders, governments have focused on providing new dwelling units, drinking water, roads, and commercial spaces to accommodate the needs of the relatively wealthy sections of the rapidly growing urban population. Swanky hospitals have come up, but public health has remained neglected. As a result of limited budget allocations and a lack of sensitivity of governments and local bodies, the poor have remained acutely bereft of even the essential urban services.

Yet, the numbers of urban poor continue to grow. They live on the fringes and constantly struggle to claim their rights as citizens. As seen in the COVID-19 pandemic, their voices have been largely ignored.

Urban planners acknowledge the presence of slums in cities but seldom integrate this reality into their plans. As a result, urbanization has become almost synonymous with slum growth. The larger cities are now more like urban sprawls. Comparisons between the master plan and actual land use show shocking divergence between the planned land use and the actual land use.[9] For example, the findings of a land-use study in Andheri East, a suburb of Mumbai, reveal two striking deviations– rampant commercialization in violation of the master plan and the mushrooming development of slum settlements. Slums had occupied 17 per cent of the total land, many of them along highways and pipelines. Interestingly, the master plan had earmarked most of the slum areas for housing; but it was not meant to be in this random and unplanned manner.[10]

Near Absence of Housing for the Poor

The 2011 census registered 17.3 million houses in slums, with 68 million residents in these settlements.[11] The urban slum-dwelling population is now well over 100 million. According to a study, the proportion of slum residents in 19 cities with a million-plus population is 25 per cent.

Mumbai typifies the appalling situation of housing for the urban poor. The state government created the Maharashtra Housing and Area Development Area Authority (MHADA) as far back as 1978, with the mandate to redevelop slums and build a sizeable stock of affordable homes in the city. But by 2018, it had built only 30,000 homes in Mumbai, while the slum population has grown from 1.5 million to 9 million.[12] Dharavi, the largest slum in Asia, is home to over 1 million residents. Ironically, in 2019, Mumbai recorded an unsold inventory of 0.3 million ready-to-move-in homes that could cater to 1.5 million citizens. Unfortunately, as these houses are priced beyond the reach of most people, they have no takers.[13]

Lack of Sanitation Arrangements

Most urban areas lack access to proper sanitation, with sewerage networks largely limited to metro cities.[14] A sewerage system links only one-third of urban households in India, and only 300-odd towns and cities in India have even a sewerage network. Within these 300, cities with one million-plus population alone account for 85 per cent of the sewerage networks, while the metros account for 70 per cent of the entire sewerage network in the country.

Sewerage networks, where they exist, are poorly maintained with frequent blockages, acute siltation, and many missing manhole covers and gully pits. Preventive maintenance and repairs to the sewerage system are undertaken only in situations of crisis. Data from 1,400 cities indicates that sewage collection efficiency is merely 10 per cent.

Deficits in wastewater treatment are even more humongous. In Class I and Class II cities, the existing wastewater treatment capacity stands at only 30 per cent of the actual requirement, and effective treatment of wastewater could be as low as 22 per cent. Another study, which includes smaller towns, puts treatment capacity at a much lower 5 per cent. Even the existing sewage treatment plants function inefficiently for various reasons, due to lack of electricity, poor maintenance, and diversion of industrial wastewater to plants designed for treating domestic waste. Most of the treatment capacity is in Class I cities. There are 211 treatment plants in Class I cities compared to only 31 in Class II cities and 26 in all the remaining towns. Only 2 per cent of the nearly 8,000 towns have both sewerage systems and sewage treatment plants (STP). In most small towns, the treatment capacity is as low as 5 per cent, and most STPs do not conform to discharge standards.[15]

In the absence of sewerage networks, most urban homes have a septic tank or pit latrine.[16] Often such on-site arrangements have no soakaways; hence, the effluent flows into open drains without any faecal sludge treatment. A Central Pollution Control Board study found that organic matter and bacterial population of faecal origin due to discharge of untreated sewerage are the primary sources of pollution of the country's rivers and groundwater.[17]

Meanwhile, of an estimated 60 million urban households, as many as 10 million still defecate in the open, 2 million have no access to proper sanitation, and 5 million have access only to public toilets.[18] Public toilets are usually unusable as they lack proper water facilities and are poorly maintained in the absence of buy-in from users. Further, as most of them are unlit, women are wary of using such facilities and are left with no option but to urinate and defecate in the open. In both open defecation and public toilets, women and girls experience a loss of dignity and are left exposed to the risk of sexual abuse and harassment.

This abysmal state of household sanitation in India is a reflection of the casteist bias and historical mindset, revealing a strange paradox: most Indian homes are spotlessly clean while their surroundings are disgustingly dirty. The *Manu Samhita*, the ancient sacred text of Hindus that includes instructions for morning ablutions, helps us understand the paradox. The *Manu Samhita* earmarks open places for defecation and urination some distance away as they were considered environmentally safe and the odours dissipate. Deep-rooted in *Manu Samhita* is the notion that only a few lower castes, such as the Bhangis and Valmikis, should be engaged in collecting and disposing of faecal matter. These lower castes have been pushed into a separate system of existence and are restricted to three occupations – cleaning toilets, sweeping, manual scavenging, and handling of dead bodies.[19] The practice of assigning by force all aspects of cleaning, waste collection, and waste disposal to one small section of society, and building social barriers to confine its members within its limits is at the root of India's sanitation and waste management problems.

In India's early history, this arrangement did not disturb the ecology or create any crisis. The cleaning community remained the weakest and most exploited section of Indian society, and caste barriers ensured that they had no way out. Cleaning became a compulsion for the cleaning community and not a shared responsibility. The situation altered radically when economic growth and urbanization brought in a huge explosion of household consumption; the resulting explosion of waste was way beyond the capacity of the small cleaning community. The centuries-old conditioning that higher-caste households should not share any sanitation and waste management responsibility has led to a system breakdown.[20]

Pathetic Solid Waste Management

If sanitation arrangements are deplorable, the situation is even more so with solid waste management. India generates an estimated 115,000 tonnes of municipal solid waste per day – the third largest quantity globally. Waste management requires an enormous amount of organizational capacity, specific skills, and the use of technology, from collection to disposal. Yet, due to our cultural and caste biases, the entire onus of waste collection rests on the shoulders of the small cleaning community who are paid bare minimum wages and armed with nothing more than rusted wheelbarrows, pails, and brooms. This system was bound to fail as it functioned without tools, technology, or resources.[21]

Till recently, Indian cities had taken a hub-and-spoke approach to waste collection. Households threw their garbage at a designated dumping place with no penalties or fines for non-compliance. If housemaids or residents found the designated place to be far away, they dumped the waste in empty plots, and such unassigned areas became garbage hills.

Much of the urban municipal waste dumped in designated spaces or collected from households does not even reach assigned landfills – a significant quantity is diverted into an unregulated, informal industry that employs millions in exploitative, filthy, and dangerous working conditions. This informal recycling sector does not have the technical knowledge or capacity to process the tonnes of waste collected in this manner.[22] Vast amounts of plastic and glass bottles, polybags, batteries, and almost all the old newspapers and magazines are picked up by an estimated 3 million rag pickers – many of them children – before the waste is burnt in the open or taken to landfills. These rag pickers have the lowest form of human existence while government and civic authorities remain mute spectators.

In the first decades after Independence, India's waste composition and quantum were small and benign enough for open landfills, informal recycling, or open combustion. With economic liberalization, along with the growth of household consumption, the consumption basket has also changed dramatically. While the earlier urban consumption basket mainly comprised a few categories such as food, apparel, furnishing, and consumer durables, several new items such as e-waste now account for a significant chunk of the waste and are causing significant ecological damage.

In contrast to India and much of the Third World, First-World countries shifted to an efficient system of collecting waste at its source in containers, standardizing the process over 50 years ago. Standardization ensured the sharing of responsibility for waste collection between local bodies and citizens, with households mandated to install garbage bins on prescribed lines. Over time, colour-coded bins for different types of waste were introduced. Sadly, India is decades away from these practices, even in the major metros.[23]

Distorted Urban Mobility Arrangements

Urban mobility plans should provide for people to commute easily from place to place rather than the present vehicle-centred focus. In the absence of foresight and vision, public transport systems have remained woefully inadequate in all towns and cities. Deficient transport systems have negatively impacted the economic efficiency of cities and the well-being of citizens.

As bus services are unreliable, are of poor quality, and have failed to keep pace with urban requirements, people have had little choice but to turn to personal vehicles, such as mopeds, scooters, motorcycles, and cars. Other intermediate modes like autorickshaws, tempos, and taxis have also grown exponentially. Motorized vehicles occupy 90 per cent of urban roads, even though only 10 per cent of the urban population own cars and 35 per cent have two-wheelers.[24] Against the marginal population increase of 2 per cent of cities, the growth rate of registered vehicles has been as high as 11.7 per cent per annum.[25] In the category of motorized vehicles, buses have a negligible share even though they occupy a fraction of the road space per person compared to personal vehicles, and cause much less air pollution. Rather than improving bus transport, there has been an undue focus on metro systems in recent years, the most capital-intensive public transport mode.

As a result of the rising vehicular density, most Indian cities face acute traffic congestion, leading to dangerously high levels of air pollution.[26] What exacerbates the congestion is the brazen encroachment of roads by parked vehicles, the unauthorized extension of houses and shops, and hawkers.[27]

New roads are continuously built, and existing ones are widened to accommodate the surge in vehicles. More road space only results in more vehicles filling that space. This excessive focus on increasing road capacity results in a lopsided public transport system. Authorities fail to recognize that road congestion is primarily due to the gross imbalance in the modal

PROMOTING PLANNED URBANIZATION

split and not an inadequate road network. Expansion of road capacity also results in further shrinking the already limited pedestrian paths. The dwindling pedestrian paths drive more and more people into a vehicular mode of transport even to travel walkable distances. This flawed policy affects the mobility requirement of low-income households, who are entirely dependent on public transport or commute by foot. The inadequacy of pedestrian paths and public transport particularly compromises the safety of women commuters.

Urban Planning: A Fresh Approach

Urban planning in India must become participatory and inclusive, involving all stakeholders. The vital issues of housing for the poor, sanitation and public transport need to occupy centre stage. Each of the plans in the existing 8,000 towns and cities needs to be reviewed and replaced by those that are forward-looking. The plans need to be dynamic and allow frequent corrections.[28] In place of being static and divorced from reality, plans should be updated annually and incorporate new data points. Annual modification of plans is entirely possible and is easily done with remote sensing technology and digitalization.

Towns should set clear city/town limits to preclude mindless spatial expansion. Urban plans must have convenient shopping, retail hawking, recreational facilities, and workspaces close to where people live so that trip distances are kept short. 'Towns with shorter travel distances' should be the mantra. Compact townships have multiple benefits compared to urban sprawls. Often, plans grossly underestimate the space requirement for shops and business establishments. As a result, shops and offices mushroom and occupy and encroach upon the main streets. Therefore, plans must scientifically estimate the future requirement for various services.

Housing for the urban poor must be at the core of such planning; it must include an action plan to improve the living conditions of those in slum settlements, as well as plan housing for the future influx of migrant labour. In this context, let us again turn our attention to Birsa and Rasika's family.

> We noted in Chapter 6 that Birsa and Rasika are in perpetual debt and, if they remain in the village, see little hope of seeing any improvement in their lives. Birsa does dream of one day breaking away from this vicious cycle of poverty migrating to a city or town such as Hyderabad or Ranchi where he has been told the earnings are much higher than his casual agricultural labour earnings. But of those who migrated, some have come back and told others of city life. They relate how living conditions are much worse than in the village, and that even in slum settlements, rents are high and there is neither water nor any place for defecation, with garbage strewn all over the place. One of the persons from Birsa's village who had

165

PROMOTING PLANNED URBANIZATION

got a job as a casual factory worker spoke of spending close to two hours commuting by the uncertain bus services in the city to his workplace. Moreover, employment is uncertain. During the COVID-19 pandemic, most of the people from Birsa's village lost their jobs and had a difficult time getting back to the village. With such depressing news, Birsa appears reconciled to his fate in his village.

It is not housing alone that is the major issue faced by low-income families such as Birsa and Rasika looking to migrate to towns and cities. Many migrants take up street vending to supplement their income. Therefore, along with housing, plans should earmark adequate and convenient spaces for informal retail and hawking in the proximity of residential areas. Despite a large section of the urban population relying on street-side retailing for their livelihood, existing plans have ignored their existence.[29] Apart from the housing needs of street vendors, their rights to livelihood have also been largely neglected.[30] The central government has introduced PM SVANidhi, a scheme that aims to mainstream street vendors through loans and digital payments. There is evidence that the scheme could help street vendors. However, the scheme has seen only slow progress. This is because the local bodies do not update the lists of street vendors for years, as they face no penalty for non-compliance.[31]

Planning for the 1,000 towns and cities identified for industrial cluster development in Chapter 6 needs to be integrated with the plans for livelihoods and new businesses. These plans and their speedy implementation need to be prioritized as they have the highest potential for livelihood opportunities. This would require the creation of a suitable governance structure. At present, municipal councils have neither the staff nor the urban management and governance skill sets. Fragmentation of the management of various services across multiple agencies and departments results in a lack of convergence. Comprehensive legislation would be required to create an integrated authority and vest it with powers to execute the plan. The government must provide the integrated authority with adequate staffing and financial resources. It must also be authorized to enforce solid and liquid waste management regulations, deal with encroachments on roads and footpaths, act against plan violations, and levy fines and penalties for non-compliance. More importantly, it must have the authority to acquire spaces for housing the poor, hawking, and other essential urban services.

There are several global examples of an integrated approach, such as the programme for the urban poor in Bogotá, the capital of Columbia. There was a simultaneous focus on affordable housing, public transport, comprehensive road maintenance, and inter-agency coordination to improve the urban well-being and quality of life of the urban poor.[32] Similarly, in India, preparing and speedily executing integrated plans in these 1,000 identified growth clusters would give an impetus to a wider dispersion of urbanization and ensure lower levels of migration to the metros and large cities.

166

PROMOTING PLANNED URBANIZATION

Execution of plans in the remaining 7,000 towns would also require strengthening the capacity of local governments and augmenting their financial resources. Along with this, it must be noted that urbanization is also taking place rapidly beyond these towns. Many large villages have already acquired urban characteristics. Therefore, there is a need for the government to reclassify all emerging rural settlements with populations above 10,000 as urban and ensure each of them has appropriate plans.

Housing for the Poor

To provide decent living spaces for the poor, the first step would be to improve the quality of existing slum dwellings. This would entail giving title to the slum dwellers in the space currently occupied by them, to incentivize them to upgrade their homes and give them a sense of security. However, legal rights through the regularization of individual dwellings pose a formidable challenge. This is because many homes are in hazardous areas – below transmission lines, beside sewer lines, and adjacent to busy roads and highways. Further, slum dwellings come up cheek by jowl, with no space for pathways, drains, sewers, or water pipelines.

A well-planned slum settlement would have adequate earmarking of roads, footpaths, water, electricity, sewer lines, stormwater drains, anganwadis and a school, a health outpost, and play areas. In the most optimistic scenario, after allocating spaces for these utilities and services, at best 50 per cent of dwellings can be regularized. The remaining residents would need relocation for which local authorities will need to acquire lands nearby – if the relocation is a distance away, households will not move and are likely to trade the plots for cash. Therefore, the regularization of slums must be scientifically planned with well-thought-out plans for relocating those that cannot be resettled in the same settlement. Execution of the plans must be through dedicated government agencies, manned by professionals.[33] An alternative strategy of permitting private builders to execute redevelopment of slum settlements through private participation and in partnership with slum residents has been experimented with in Mumbai but has not been met with much success. Here, it would be relevant to look at Manila's model for slum improvement. (See Box 1: Manila: Innovations for Poor Housing).

Box 1   Manila: Innovations for Poor Housing

Manila provides a template of a possible approach to low-income housing. Its slums are spread over 526 communities across Metro Manila, housing 2.5 million people on unused private or public lands, usually along rivers, near garbage dumps, along railroad tracks, under bridges, and beside industrial establishments. Slums proliferating even

---

167

next to mansions in affluent residential areas are not an uncommon sight. Although there are relatively large slum communities in Metro Manila, many urban poor settlements are dispersed and come up wherever there is space and opportunity.

Metro Manila consists of 12 cities, 5 municipalities, and 1,694 barangays, administered by local government units that are relatively autonomous. The Metropolitan Manila Development Authority (MMDA) ensures the effective delivery of metro-wide services, including the rehabilitation and development of slums, and the provision of housing facilities and essential social services. Along with increased decentralization, the participation of non-governmental and people's organizations in planning, implementing, and monitoring the local unit-led projects of MMDA has increased.

The Urban Development and Housing Act of 1986 provides the overarching framework for comprehensive and integrated urban development and housing. Under the community upgrading scheme, the government can allot land to residents after developing the site and putting in place basic services and facilities. In addition, the government has established a viable home financing system through financing institutions. Insurance funds have also been deployed to finance long-term mortgages even for those below the poverty line.

The strength of Metro Manila's approach lies in its holistic metro-wide action for slum improvement and regularization, housing finance, poverty alleviation, and partnerships with non-government organizations. The long-term success of this approach, despite the enormity of Manila's slum issues, shows that persistent adherence to a metro-wide policy can lead to desired outcomes.[39]

'Housing for All', the oft-stated vision for housing policies in India, is mostly understood to mean house ownership for all citizens. This singular focus on ownership has been part of programmes from the early 1970s. The government has failed to recognize that there is a wide range of housing tenures that can contribute to a viable, sustainable housing market.[34] Where housing for the poor is concerned, ownership of housing is a highly flawed policy. Most low-income households cannot buy houses, irrespective of how 'affordable' they might be. Most low-income families live in rented accommodation, and solutions must, therefore, centre around creating a vibrant and truly affordable rental housing market for the poor.

In the above context, let us examine the central government's scheme of the Affordable Rental Housing Complexes (ARHCs) announced in July 2020. The scheme envisages the participation of private builders on a large scale to build homes for migrants and low-income families.[35] The scheme's implementation is through three channels: converting government-funded housing into ARHCs through public-private partnership (PPP); outsourcing the construction and management of the complex to a concessionaire; and incentivizing manufacturing units, industries, institutions, associations, as well as government organizations to develop and operate the ARHCs on their lands.

While the idea of rental complexes is good, as migrant labour and most poor households cannot buy homes themselves, the scheme does not appear to have received any response so far and is unlikely to garner interest in its present form.[36] Given that rental income from residences in residential complexes typically gives only a 2–3 per cent return on investment, considerable tweaking of the scheme is required to attract private companies and investors. Relaxation in the floor area ratio (FAR) provided in the ARHC scheme is not sufficient to guarantee returns. The scheme requires several structural changes. To begin with, complexes must be located within a convenient distance from commercial and workplaces. To ensure wide participation, PPP projects under the scheme must have an adequate component of viability-gap funding. Also, the government must permit builders to sell the residential units to anyone willing to buy them, with no restrictions on the individual's income status. This relaxation will require a change in mindset as present regulations permit only low-income families to buy Economically Weaker Section (EWS) units. Finally, there should not be excessive regulation in the fixation of rents; over time, as many complexes come up, the rentals will get rationalized.

In designing such complexes, it would be helpful to look at the traditional 'chawl' system, which worked well for several decades and is the foundation upon which Mumbai exists today.[37] However, the absence of any arrangement for their maintenance and upkeep is a significant drawback of the existing chawls. Therefore, the government must not just ensure compliance of designs and specifications as appropriate to such complexes, but the builder must also be made responsible for the maintenance of the complexes and be empowered to collect the prescribed maintenance fees from each resident.

In addition to ARHCs, the government is implementing the Pradhan Mantri Awas Yojana (Urban) [PMAY (U)] which aims to construct 11 million housing units for the urban poor and for slum households by 2022. The programme envisages a total investment of ₹734 billion, of which the centre would contribute 25 per cent, states 20 per cent, while beneficiaries finance the remaining 55 per cent. The progress of the programme has been satisfactory, but it helps only those who already own a site; it helps neither those whose property title is not clear nor the surging migrant labour population.[38]

Apart from budgets for PMAY (U), the central and state governments have sizeable budgets for urban housing, including for housing government employees. As the private housing market is well-developed, it makes sense to divert the government housing budget of cities and towns to fund low-income housing. The reallocation of funds should include the current budgets for low-income group (LIG) housing schemes as, in any case, these units are beyond the means of the intended beneficiaries. With substantial inventory lying unsold with private builders, it also does not make sense for governments to continue housing programmes for the middle class or their employees. Government employees not allotted government housing can be compensated by a higher house rent allowance to enable them to rent private homes.

Sanitation: Prioritization Along the Value Chain

Neither civic bodies nor governments have taken due cognizance of the enormous value of sanitation. Sanitation is a public good and vital to the well-being of the population. The World Health Organization notes that investment in sanitation delivers nine times in social and economic benefits for every dollar spent.[40] Sanitation vastly improves the quality of drinking water and thus people's health. For example, diarrhoea incidence reduces by at least 30 per cent with sanitation, even without any measure to promote hygiene behaviour. Sanitation improvements also have many non-health externalities, such as enhanced productivity, comfort and convenience, safety for women and children, dignity, and societal status. Sanitation is also closely connected with nutrition. Thus, there is a very strong case for investing in sanitation. [41]

The Swachh Bharat Mission (Urban), the government's flagship programme, covers over 4,000 towns. It aims to provide 10 million household toilets and 0.5 million community and public toilets.[42] While the goals are ambitious, the tragedy is that most toilets built under the programme are not linked to a sewerage system or to treatment plants and there is no arrangement for the collection of faecal sludge. Building toilets has become a numbers game, with little thought to creating a supportive sanitation infrastructure. Contrary to government claims, despite the construction of millions of toilets, open defecation is rampant.[43] Perhaps, at some level, the government perceived the construction of toilets as coterminous with sanitation. The point is that when toilets are not linked to a sewage treatment plant (STP) or sewerage system, the faecal sludge flows into and contaminates rivers, lakes, or drains.[44]

Therefore, the focus has to be on the entire sanitation value chain.[45] While a sewerage-based sanitation system would be ideal for all cities and towns, for smaller habitations and slum settlements a sewerage system may be neither feasible nor cost-effective. In such areas, end-to-end on-site arrangements are required. The planning for sanitation must contend with many factors, including low priority accorded to sanitation by stakeholders themselves, dated technologies, and the logistical challenges in providing sanitation services in slums.[46] What is needed is for the Swachh Bharat Mission to look at complete solutions, rather than ad hoc piecemeal interventions such as building toilets. A vital component of the strategy must be a massive education and awareness drive to foster behavioural change so that the demand for sanitation gets generated from the bottom up. In this awareness campaign, the involvement of local leaders is critical to influencing people to develop sustainable, responsible, and informed sanitation behaviour.[47]

Along with building sewerage networks, the scientific treatment of urban wastewater is critical to prevent contamination of underground water, rivers, and lakes. The existing STPs are too few, and even those that exist function way below their capacity. Unfortunately, because of a lack of integrated planning, standalone STPs are often set up without their integration with the sewer system.

The preceding analysis suggests two policy imperatives. First, the policy needs to address gaps in the entire waste management cycle, with particular attention to service provisions for the urban poor. Second, the state needs to extend functional sanitation systems to all towns and cities, irrespective of size. While doing so, priority should be accorded to filling up existing gaps and completing incomplete projects. However, given the scale and enormity of the challenge, there is a need to begin by taking up works in the identified 1,000 cluster towns and cities.

The government can ill afford to delay the investments required to quickly expand sewerage networks, improve sewage collection, and set up STPs in all towns and cities. However, there is a severe financing deficit for urban sanitation. The estimated cost to build a sewage grid and treatment system across India's cities and towns is ₹30–50 billion, at least ten times higher than existing sanitation investments.[48]

The existing policy discussions focus on addressing this financing deficit by bringing in additional sources of funding. While massive investments are required, technology adoption and meticulous and systematic planning could rationalize some costs. At several locations, it may become prudent to go in for on-site systems; for example, a study showed that operating expenses for sewer-based systems were 1.5 times higher than on-site systems.

In this context, it is important to reiterate that sanitation must be recognized as a shared responsibility of citizens and the state. Therefore, a substantial part of the financing will need to come from a cost-based user fee. Though sectoral experts have been advocating a cost-based user fee for some time, most towns and cities have not introduced user fees to cover sanitation costs. The fees must not only cover a portion of the capital cost but a major part of the operational costs including sanitary workers' salaries, equipment, vehicles, and system maintenance.[49]

Mindset Change in Solid Waste Management

In 1994, the plague epidemic in Surat shook citizens, the government, and the local authority alike out of their slumber. Following this health crisis,

Surat took a series of steps to transform what was once called the 'city of floating sewage' into one of the cleanest cities in India. The success of the measures undertaken can be largely attributed to the exceptional leadership provided by the then municipal commissioner of Surat.[50] The country requires such extraordinary steps and enlightened, dynamic leadership immediately at all levels. It also requires buy-in from the citizens. Therefore, reconditioning the Indian mind on public hygiene and cleanliness must become the lynchpin of the new approach towards waste management.

The central government's Swachh Bharat Mission (Urban) has the objective of making the country clean and litter-free with scientific solid waste management (SWM) in 4,041 towns and cities. In respect of 1,000 of these towns and cities, the implementation of 100 per cent door-to-door waste collection and transportation of waste has been targeted.[51] By March 2019, at least on paper, 76,101 wards (out of a total of 84,420 wards) had 100 per cent door-to-door collection. Over half of the waste generated in these 4,041 towns and cities is currently being processed, and slightly more than 60 per cent of wards are practising source segregation.[52] However, while there has been some visible improvement in waste collection, segregation and disposal remain neglected. Overall, of the 62 million tonnes of urban waste generated every year, less than 60 per cent is collected, and only 15 per cent of waste is processed.[53]

Apart from the lackadaisical attitude of civic authorities, the major reason for the deplorable state of SWM is the continuance of the age-old practice of solely assigning this humongous task to the small sweeper community, who have remained a lowly lot. There are many ways of introducing practices so that waste collection gets its due respect, as has happened in hotels and airports. More importantly, government and civic authorities must shift from a sweeper system to one where waste collection adopts technology and modern equipment and casts on citizens their share of responsibility in both segregation and collection. Along with this, bulk generators of waste – such as industrial units, hospitals, and residential and commercial complexes – must be mandated to segregate, treat, and facilitate transportation, recycling, and safe disposal of waste.

The experience of the cleanest countries of today reveals that they deployed three instruments to ensure their communities toe the line in respect of SWM – education, legislation, and education. By the end of World War II, sanitation inspectors in the First-World countries were going from door to door educating people and advising them on good practices of hygiene and waste collection. From the start, penalties were used both as an effective deterrent and an enabler for the enforcement apparatus. Along with sustained awareness campaigns, there is a need for strict enforcement. Over time, this approach changed social behaviour, and the regulations have now become internalized. This approach takes away individual discretion while freeing the bandwidth of local bodies to upgrade their operating standards and infrastructure to collect waste.

The central government notified the Municipal Solid Waste (Management and Handling) Rules, 2016 (superseding the rules notified in 2000), along with the E-Waste (Management) Rules, 2016, under the powers vested under the Environment (Protection) Act, 1986. These provide a set of guidelines for solid waste management and have provisions for the imposition of penalties and fines for non-compliance. However, the rules remain unenforced, except partially in a few urban pockets and are devoid of the desired specificity that could pack an operational punch. The rules are skewed more toward prohibition rather than guidance. There should be a clear legal framework that sets out the responsibilities of enforcement bodies. The rules need to be practical and enforceable based on scientific knowledge of sustainable waste management.

The implementation capacity of local authorities will also need to be vastly augmented. Staff will have to be well trained in the technical aspects of solid waste management and a new cadre of managers with domain knowledge brought in. Equally, awareness generation is critical to evoke a sense of ownership in stakeholders so that they become active participants in implementing the regulations. Finally, there must be continuous monitoring by the central and state governments on technical, economic, and social parameters with specified benchmarks.[54]

Waste collection is the first crucial step towards an effective waste-management response. There are two other vital elements to a complete SWM system – waste segregation and waste disposal. Waste segregation into dry waste, recyclable waste, and wet waste should be made compulsory in all urban areas and rigidly implemented under the rules, backed by effective enforcement machinery. Moreover, waste can be reduced through composting solutions, which can be strictly enforced in all formal residential colonies and mandated for implementation by all resident welfare associations and large establishments.

India must wake up to the impending dangers of inadequate and rudimentary waste disposal methods. Landfills and incineration are not sustainable solutions for the disposal of waste. Waste collection and disposal must cover construction and demolition waste. In emerging cities such as Gurgaon in Haryana, the unsightly mess of construction waste dumped in any available public space is all too common. There is also a need for a customized response through user fees to handle waste collection from mass events such as public rallies, weddings, social and religious functions, and temporary bazaars. As in the First-World countries, India will need to ensure that rules are comprehensive and are applied uniformly without exception.

Apart from a legislative push and a massive communication campaign, waste disposal requires a policy push, capital, scale, and expertise. The sector offers immense opportunities for the deployment of private capital and formal employment. Well-planned waste disposal systems will not only address the existing ad hoc informal employment but also meet the objective of safe waste disposal.[55] The First-World countries have been through a long journey to get to the present level of scientific waste management. We can learn from their experience and bypass many stages to quickly leapfrog and be on par with their waste management systems. We can also benefit from the success stories in waste management that abound both within India and outside (See Box 2: Waste Management – Success Stories).

There are two key lessons for India from the experience of First-World countries. The first is effective enforcement to foster a new normal in the sanitation behaviour of society.

Box 2   Waste Management – Success Stories

In Alappuzha, Kerala, mounds of stinking garbage were a common sight. This threatened the town's status as a tourist destination and exposed residents and visitors alike to the risk of disease spread by flies and mosquitoes. In 2014, protests by residents led to the closure of the city's landfill site, forcing the authorities to address waste management through a decentralized system. Biodegradable waste is now segregated at the ward level and treated in small composting plants; it provides many of its 174,000 residents with biogas for cooking. For its efforts, Alappuzha has received the Clean City award from the Centre for Science and Environment.

In an area within Pune city, an innovative, cost-effective waste management model is being used by the Seva Sahakari Sanstha Maryadit (SWaCH), a cooperative wholly owned by self-employed rag pickers and waste collectors. In 2008, SWaCH entered into a contract with the Pune Municipal Corporation, and its 2,100 SWaCH members now provide door-to-door waste collection services to over 360,000 homes in the city. The waste is segregated into recyclables and wet waste for composting.[56]

Among major cities, Chandigarh is a success story of city-wide, end-to-end solid waste management.[57] In 2017, a municipality in the town of Nawanshahr, near Chandigarh, adopted a decentralized approach to solid waste management, with a three-pronged focus on infrastructure, intensive citizen engagement, and integration of waste workers in the waste management chain. With 100 per cent source segregation and door-to-door collection, the city has become almost bin-less.[58] Then again, with the support of Tata Trusts, Ahmedabad has used data analytics and technology to upgrade its existing solid waste-management systems.[59] Interestingly, Panchgani in Maharashtra converted a dumping ground into an attraction for tourists and residents by putting red mud on heaps of naturally made compost to serve as a foundation for planting trees.[60]

There are also many global examples. Penang, in Malaysia, turns the island's waste into fertilizer through large-scale composting for use on farmers' fields, which has significantly reduced the pressure on the limited landfill space and prevented pollution of its waterways.[61] Cajicá, in Columbia, undertook a five-year awareness-raising campaign and the town now has a recycling rate of 30 per cent and has reduced its landfill tonnage by 25 per cent.[62] India can also learn from the 19 cities identified across the world for excellent practices in the recycling of waste management. These cities follow a stepwise hierarchical approach, namely prevention, reuse, recycling, and disposal.[63]

The second is to ensure the availability of sufficient resources for SWM. Unfortunately, urban local bodies are starved of funds and have given SWM a low-order priority. This is true even of large metros. For example, of Bangalore's Municipal Corporation's annual expenditure of over ₹50 billion, the spend on SWM is not even 10 per cent. What's more, of this 10 per cent over 80 per cent goes towards the salaries of sanitation workers.[64]

To augment the financial resources of local bodies, as in the case of sanitation, the costs of SWM should also be substantially recouped through user fees from the citizens on actuals. To reiterate, such urban services cannot continue to be treated as an absolute right with no obligations. Such user fees should also be charged to all bulk waste generators, such as large industrial units, medical establishments, hotels, and large commercial and residential complexes. Strangely in India, bulk waste generators expect payment for waste – as if waste were a commodity – and hence the entire revenue flow is backward: the waste generator gets payment from the local collector, who in turn gets paid by middlemen, who finally get paid either by the government for dumping or by the recycler for supplying raw materials for the recycling process. This perverse system needs to be reversed: the bulk generator pays the local collector who is also reimbursed for transportation of the waste to the designated location to recycling and disposal sites. This is the common practice widely followed across many countries today. There should be strict penalties for non-compliance by citizens, bulk generators, collection agents, etc.

In addition to the introduction of user fees, local authorities will have to accord higher priority to SWM. Given the manifold benefit of SWM, there will need to be a quantum jump in the budgetary support by the central and state governments to the urban local bodies (ULBs). Disbursal of funds to ULBs should be made conditional on performance against set targets. ULBs failing to achieve the targets could be penalized by way of cuts in their budgeted allocations.

Performance targets for ULBs should be especially fixed for the processing and recycling of waste. Unfortunately, only two cities, Pune and

Bengaluru, currently have made some progress in the processing of waste. The rest of the country has continued to dump waste in earmarked landfills, as well as random sites.

Buses Need Prioritization

Buses cause less pollution per passenger per kilometre than personalized modes of transport and occupy less road space.[65] Bus services have low capital expenditure and operating costs. Worldwide, 80 per cent of commuters who depend on public transport use a bus. However, bus systems exist only in a few cities; there, too, they are woefully inadequate and inefficient. In most Indian towns and cities, bus transport is altogether absent.[66]

The focus of local and state governments has been building and widening roads to accommodate the ever-rising number of cars and two-wheelers. The inadequacy of efficient bus services has led to an increased demand for taxi services. Such a rampant increase in taxis puts pressure on roads and hogs most of the parking areas and even empty spaces.

This lopsided priority persists even though the National Urban Transport Policy, 2014, stresses planning for people rather than vehicles.[67] So, ideally speaking buses should be given priority as, for most commuters, they are the primary means of transport. It was against this background that the Jawaharlal Nehru National Urban Renewal Mission (JNNURM) proposed to finance 50 per cent of the cost of the purchase of buses for city transport in 63 cities. State governments were required to chip in 20 per cent, and the balance 30 per cent was to be contributed by municipal corporations, transport corporations, or the private sector through public-private partnership (PPP). However, in practice, besides the low budgetary allocations under JNNURM, new buses are only bought as replacements for the ageing fleet rather than for augmenting the public transport capacity. Also, the state government and transport authorities have failed to exploit the PPP option to augment their bus fleets.[68]

As with several other public utilities, bus transport systems will need large subsidies by the centre and the state, as ULBs are starved of resources. Cities can also learn from and replicate the successful Surat and Indore models, which have largely outsourced bus services to the private sector and have profitable city transport corporations. Furthermore, there is a need to incentivize bus deployment, for example, through GST and motor vehicle tax exemptions on the purchase of buses. To compensate for the loss in revenue from these sources, a congestion tax can be levied on all private vehicles, a rapidly growing trend in many countries.[69]

However, to increase the use of buses by vehicle owners, buses need an image transformation. Buses are neither attractive nor appealing, as they are poorly maintained. Their image can be changed. What is needed is a set of quality protocols that are rigidly implemented for the upkeep and maintenance of the bus fleet, as also the timely scrapping of old unserviceable buses. In addition, the share of well-maintained, air-conditioned buses will have to substantially increase so that metro travellers and vehicle owners are inclined to shift to buses. The objective should be to provide bus services on par with the metro system. Private fleet owners should also be incentivized and permitted to operate and given reasonable freedom to operate along with the flexibility to fix fares.

Technology deployment can also transform the image of the humble bus through, for example, digital signage at bus stops to indicate the time of arrival of the next bus and digital ticketing. Ahmedabad has successfully applied the Internet of Things approach to building a smart bus system.[70] Similarly, Mumbai's local software companies have created an app to enable commuters to locate their bus and estimate its arrival time and use the app to pay the bus fare in advance.

Cars have long symbolized wealth and status around the globe. These attitudes are changing. Familiarity with the car has also robbed it of novelty. This trend is visible in the First World. In 2002, 77 per cent of US adults less than 25 years old owned a car. By 2011, this figure had dropped to 66 per cent. Younger populations are more likely to switch from personal to public modes of transport. With the increase in online shopping, the use of personal vehicles for shopping has been declining. Rather than going out to restaurants, online ordering of food is growing exponentially. India must quickly take advantage of these trends that indicate a waning interest in personalized modes of transport and put in place bus transport systems that offer efficient, convenient, and seamless travel experiences.

Metro Systems Distort Priorities

The success of the Delhi Metro rail system has sparked demands for setting up similar services in other large cities – Bengaluru, Chennai, Mumbai, Ahmedabad, and Pune. The frequency, quality of infrastructure, and punctuality of metro services have attracted commuters in huge numbers leading to a rapid expansion of services across cities. Far-flung areas even beyond the city's boundaries have become connected, and office-goers can commute as much as 50 km to work with comparative ease. Such intra-city services have also spawned demand and connected cities and suburban towns as far apart as Noida and Gurgaon. Such expansion could have perverse outcomes as employees no longer need to have homes close to their workplace. Rather than developing self-contained towns, the metro could contribute to turning cities into large urban sprawls.

Despite its growing popularity, the Delhi Metro has the lowest share of commuters walking to or from stations, compared to elsewhere in the world. This is because of the lack of wide, well-laid, encroachment-free, well-lit, and safe pedestrian paths. Thus, there is a high usage of motorized modes to access the metro in Delhi. In addition, there is evidence that, for a given duration of access and egress, trips in the metro take longer than trips

PROMOTING PLANNED URBANIZATION

by bus.[71] Further, metro services require exceptionally high capital costs, leaving little resources for bus transport and pedestrian paths. Phase III of the Delhi Metro is estimated to cost an astronomical ₹5,520 million per km.[72] In sharp contrast, a high-quality city bus (say, Volvo brand) would cost only ₹7 million. Thus, limiting a metro line by just one kilometre could finance the purchase of 800 buses.[73] The capital cost could have been justified if metro services see high ridership. However, metro ridership in most cities has been comparatively low vis-a-vis the capital cost. Apart from the near absence of serviceable pedestrian paths, a major reason for the low ridership is the lack of integration with feeder bus services. Unfortunately, multi-modal integration suffers from a multiplicity of agencies each working in silos. For example, in Delhi, bus transport is managed by the Delhi government, while the Delhi metro is operated by an independent entity, the Delhi Metro Rail Corporation (DMRC). At present there is little coordination between the two agencies, leading to low ridership due to a lack of proper route planning and inadequate feeder services. Therefore, there is an urgent need for a city-wide transport authority agency that can coordinate all forms of public transport within a city, including taxis and private fleet operators.[74] Such integrated authorities have been set up in several cities that have an efficient public transport system. For example, London's transport authority has integrated a wide range of services including the bus, the Underground, local and light rail, river services, private hire cars, bus coaches, cycle hire, and road and traffic management.[75]

Finally, to ensure that metro services do not contribute to an unplanned expansion of cities, they should be confined to transport within city boundaries. Metro services should not get extended to inter-city rail services, which should be planned and managed separately. The present trend of extending metro services in cities like Delhi to suburban towns such as Gurgaon, Noida, and Meerut is blurring this distinction.

The bottom line is that existing transport systems have failed to address the needs of the urban poor, particularly women, thus restricting them from fully participating in economic activities. Therefore, a transformative public transport policy is imperative with the central focus of urban mobility on the poor and women.

Ensuring Rights of Pedestrians and Cyclists

In many cities around the world, a sizable proportion of the population walks to work. In New York, this figure is 11 per cent and 26 per cent in London. In Hong Kong, it is as much as 45 per cent, while in Mumbai it is even higher at 55 per cent. Thus, walking remains a simple yet essential mode of commuting within cities. Moreover, this pollution-free mode provides exercise and costs nothing.

Cities that have efficient, well-planned pedestrian systems end up cleaner, less congested, and safer streets. Walking can also be the fastest mode for short trips. Sadly, in Indian cities, investments in pedestrian paths have been accorded way lower priority than investments in roads and flyovers. There are numerous instances of pedestrian paths being appropriated for road widening. Paths are also getting massively encroached upon by shopkeepers, illegally parked vehicles, and street vendors. There should be heavy penalties imposed for such encroachments and illegal occupation of pavements and pedestrian paths. Investment in public transport will come to nought if the last-mile linkages to homes and workplaces do not have clean, safe walkways. In planning for pedestrian paths, the gender dimension is vital. Women are often wary of walking, especially at night, because these paths are neither well-maintained nor well-lit.

Along with walking, cycling has captured the interest of commuters in many cities across the world. In the Netherlands, 27 per cent of all trips are by bicycles.[76] Bicycle-sharing across the globe is emerging as one of the best low-cost smart transport solutions. Velib in Paris was the first to launch a bicycle-sharing scheme in 2007, initially operated by a private company as part of a concession agreement with the city's municipal authority. The name Velib is derived from two French words – *velo*, meaning bicycle, and *liberte*, meaning freedom.[77] Velib's success led to the introduction of similar schemes, most of them in Chinese cities. This model requires setting docking stations at convenient locations nearby. With dedicated cycle paths and docking stations, travel time by bicycle can be the same as by car; this would involve no hassle of parking, no expense, in addition to being environmentally friendly.

Unfortunately, Indian cities are seeing a reverse trend. Over years, bicycle usage has declined with large segments of the population shifting to motorized transport.

Manifold Budget Enhancements

Financing urban development is one of the most formidable challenges that India faces in planning for urbanization. The central government has abdicated its responsibility in financing states and ULBs for the provision of urban services, by taking shelter in the Seventh Schedule of the Constitution, which lists urban development as a state subject. However, urban citizens – comprising 40 per cent of the population and generating over 60 per cent of the country's income – deserve a better deal.

The 74th Constitutional Amendment has contributed to the neglect of the urban sector. Already in poor financial health, the amendment has further weighed down ULBs with additional responsibilities without providing them the requisite financial resources. In addition, the autonomy of ULBs to generate their revenues is also very limited. Their capacity and authority to deliver urban services are similarly constrained.[78] Also, as municipal councillors get overwhelmed by local issues, they are unable to see the larger picture and create a vision for the city.

Though the central government has attempted to give an impetus to urban transformation through multiple programmes, budgets allocated for these have been dismal, given the enormity of the challenge. The budgetary spend of ₹70 billion across all central urban development schemes over the entire 2015–2020 period, translates into a paltry ₹1200 per capita for the country's 40 per cent urban population.[79]

Not only does the centre require to enhance budgets for urban development, but the states too should match this increase. They also must be accompanied by measures enabling ULBs to become financially healthy. This can be achieved by empowering them to raise resources through levy of user fees and congestion charges, raising resources through financial instruments such as municipal bonds, and ensuring that they get a reasonable share of all taxes raised in the urban areas by the states, such as vehicle registration and excise duties. State governments need to ensure that ULBs get fulsome financial support, as towns and cities are the major contributors to the dynamism and growth of a state.

We believe that a concerted focus by the central and state governments on the vital issues highlighted in the chapter would materially transform the physical and economic well-being of citizens living in urban areas. These priority areas include the introduction of an inclusive and dynamic planning framework, priority to low-income housing, and attention to the neglected areas of sanitation and SWM, along with reordering the priority of urban areas from roads to public transport and pedestrian paths The government will have to complement these measures with the implementation of the proposals given in Chapter 6 to widen livelihood opportunities in towns and cities, especially for women, and to provide the much-required impetus to economic growth.

Notes

1 "Li Keqiang, Urges Deeper Urbanization to Support China's Growth", *Independent*, November 22, 2012. https://www.independent.co.uk/news/world/asia/li-keqiang-urges-deeper-urbanization-to-support-china-s-growth-8343013.html; date of access March 22, 2021.

2 i) Amit Kapoor and Harshula Sinha, "View: India's Urbanisation Challenges and The Way Forward," *Economic Times*, 27 November 2020. https://economictimes.indiatimes.com/news/economy/policy/view-indias-urbanisation-challenges-and-the-way-forward/articleshow/79443872.cms.
ii) "The Future is Urban: Is India Prepared?" *Hindustan Times*, 20 August 2019. https://www.hindustantimes.com/real-estate/the-future-is-urban-is-india-prepared-notes-on-a-2030-realty-report/story-UpVeNpZ5acseup4KYAFYYO.html.

3 Pronab Sen, "Puzzles of Indian Urbanization," *Economic and Political Weekly*, May 2018. The census definition of 'urban' is among the most stringent globally, involving three criteria – population size, population density, and the proportion of adult males employed in agricultural activities. If one of these criteria is relaxed, the urban population in 2011 itself would have jumped to well over 40 per cent against the official estimate of 32 per cent.

4 "India Habitat III National Report 2016," Ministry of Housing and Urban Affairs (MoHUA), Government of India, 2016.

PROMOTING PLANNED URBANIZATION

5 "Population Living in Slums (% of Urban Population)," *World Bank*, 2018. https://data.worldbank.org/indicator/EN.POP.SLUM.UR.ZS?locations=IN date of access July 10, 2021.
6 Ganesh Kumar and Nitin Joseph, "Drainage and Sewerage System in Urban India: Need for Action," *Indian Journal of Occupational and Environmental Medicine*, September 2016.
7 Ankur Bisen, Chapter 3, "Urban Planning," *Wasted*, Macmillan, 2019.
8 Lalit Batra, "A Review of Urbanization and Urban Policy in Post-independence India," WP Series, Centre for the Study of Law and Governance, *Jawahar Lal Nehru University*, CSLG/WP/12, April 2009.
9 Abhay Pethe, Ramakrishna Nallathiga, Sahil Gandhi, and Vaidehi Tandel, "Re-thinking Urban Planning in India: Learning from the Wedge Between the De Jure and De Facto Development in Mumbai," *Cities*, Elsevier. Volume 40, pages 120–32, August 2014. https://www.**academia**.edu/6748322/Re_thinking_ urban_planning_in_India_Learning_from_the_wedge_between_the_de_jure_ and_de_facto_development_in_Mumbai; date of access July 20, 2021.
10 Ibid.
11 Dr C. Chandramouli, "Housing Stock, Amenities and Assets in Slums – Census 2011," Registrar General and Census Commissioner, *Government of India*.
12 Ankur Bisen, Chapter 3, "Urban Planning", *Wasted*, Macmillan, 2019.
13 Ashwini Kumar Sharma, "Half of Unsold Ready-to-move-in property in Mumbai Unaffordable," *Mint*, 27 September 2019.
14 Myles F. Elledge and Marcella McClatchey, "India: Urban Sanitation, and the Toilet Challenge," *RTI Press*, September 2013.
15 Kavita Wankhad, "Urban Sanitation in India: Key Shifts in the National Policy Frame," *Environment & Urbanization*, Vol 27 No 2, October 2015. https:// journals.sagepub.com/doi/pdf/10.1177/0956247814567058; date of access August 2, 2021.
16 Sama Khan, "Swach Bharat Mission (Urban); Need vs Planning," Policy Brief, *Centre for Policy Research*, June 2018.
17 Chaitanya Mallapur, "70% of Urban India's Sewage is Untreated," *India Spend*, 27 January 2016.
18 Kavita Wankhad, Urban Sanitation in India, 2015.
19 Santosh Mehrotra, Deboshree Ghosh, "Addressing the World's Worst Sanitation problem: A Program to Redesign to Use and Not to Just Build Toilet," Institute of Applied Manpower Research, IAMR Occasional Paper, no. 2/2013, Planning Commission, *Government of India*, August 2015.
20 Ankur Bisen, Chapter 3, "Urban Planning," *Wasted*, 2019.
21 Ankur Bisen, Chapter 5, "Waste Collection – They Don't Really Care About Us," *Wasted*, 2019.
22 Ibid.
23 Ibid.
24 Population Research Bureau, *Government of India*, March 2012.
25 Annual Report 2018–19, *MoRTH and Road Transport Year Book 2016–17* (latest available as of April 20), Government of India.
26 Sriraman, "Urban Transportation Planning and Investment in India", Emerging Challenges, Cities and Sustainability, *Springer Proceedings, Business and Economics*, 2013. A survey carried out in 2017 showed that the 42 million-plus population cities had 73 million vehicles, close to 30 per cent of all registered vehicles in the country. Delhi had the highest number – 10 million vehicles – followed by Bengaluru (7 million), Chennai (5 million), Ahmedabad (4 million), Greater Mumbai (3 million), and Surat (3 million). These six cities accounted for 44 per cent of the total registered vehicles amongst the million-plus population cities.

27 Sanjay Kumar Singh, "Urban Transport in India: Issues, Challenges and the Way Forward," *European Transport*, Issue 52, 2012.
28 Abhay Pethe, Ramakrishna Nallathiga, Sahil Gandhi, Vaidehi Tandel, "Rethinking Urban Planning in India: Learning from the Wedge between De jure and De Facto Development in Mumbai," Elsevier, pp. 120–132, *Cities* 39, 2014.
29 Mila Friere, "Urban Planning: Challenges in Developing Countries," *World Bank*, 2006.
30 "Do Street Vendors have a Right to the City?" CCS, Innovative Governance of Large Urban Systems. https://ccs.in/sites/default/files/do-street-vendors-have-a-right-to-the-city-iglus.pdf; date of access August 12, 2021. The Street Vending Act, 2014 provides hawkers protection. Despite the regulatory provisions, municipalities have registered very few street vendors – most continue to be treated as 'encroachers' and face the usual extortion, harassment, and eviction. State authorities and local administrations are in contravention of the law by evicting vendors and creating no vending zones. Unfortunately, the courts mostly side with the government and upheld evictions.
31 Avishek G Dastidar, "Explained: How Scheme for Street Vendors will Help Alleviate Poverty," *Indian Express*, 3 November 2020. https://indianexpress.com/article/explained/street-vendors-scheme-explained-6920235/.
32 Mila Friere, *World Bank*, 2006. https://www.worldbank.org/en/results/2015/08/13/better-transport-water-and-sanitation-for-the-urban-poor-in-bogota; date of access June 10, 2021.
33 Pronab Sen, "Puzzles of Indian Urbanization," May 2018.
34 Anindita Mukherjee, Shubhagato Dasgupta and Aparna Das, "State of Urban Poor Rental Housing in India and Emerging Policy Trends, 2020," *World Bank Conference on Land and Poverty*, 2020. https://scifi.cprindia.org/sites/default/files/11-01-Mukherjee-786_paper.pdf; date of access August 12, 2021.
35 Jagan Shah,"What If Our Migrant Workers Had Safe Homes in Cities? Just Imagine," *The Quint*, 16 May 2020. https://www.thequint.com/voices/opinion/covid-urban-affordable-housing-govt-migrant-workers-welfare-research-development; date of access July 2, 2020.
36 "Urban Transformation Through Housing for All: 1 Crore and More," MoHUA, Government of India, 27 December 2019.
37 Ankur Bisen, Chapter 3, "Urban Planning", *Wasted*, 2019.
38 "Housing for All by 2022," PMAY(U)-PMAY-HFA, *Government of India*.
39 Junio M. Ragragio, "Understanding Slums, Case of Metro Manila," 2003.
40 Myles F. Elledge and Marcella McClatchey, 2013.
41 Madhumita Dobe, "The Role of Sanitation in Malnutrition," pp. 7–14, Vol. 36, *Journal of Public Health*, February 2014.
42 "Country Paper India," Sacosan Vi Dhaka, *Government of India*,1-13 January 2016.
43 Myles F. Elledge and Marcella McClatchey, 2013.
44 Madhura Karnik, "Toilet, Toilet Everywhere in India, But Where Does All the Shit Go?" 2016. https://qz.com/india/661119/toilets-toilets-everywhere-in-india-but-where-does-the-shit-go/; date of access May 4, 2020.
45 Shubhagato Dasgupta and Prashant Arya, "Beyond 2019: Why Sanitation Policy Needs to Look Past Toilets, 2017," *CPR Policy Brief*, March 2017. https://www.cprindia.org/system/tdf/policy-briefs/beyond%202019%20Why%20sanitation%20Policy%20needs%20to%20look%20past%20toilets%200407%20(1).pdf?file=1&type=node&id=7012&force=1; date of access July 5, 2021.
46 J. B. Isunju et al, *Public Health*, June 2011.

47 Jain, S., Khurana, N., & Bajaj, B., "Involvement Led Attitudes Towards Responsible Waste management under Swachh Bharat campaign: a study of government employees working in National Capital Region of India," *International Journal of Indian Culture and Business Management*, 16 (4), 384, 2018.

48 Kavita Wankhad, "Urban Sanitation in India: Key Shifts in the National Policy Frame," 2015.

49 Levying a sewerage fee will face resistance. As Chairman of the Bangalore Water Supply and Sewerage Board, Bangalore, I had proposed the levy of a modest sewerage fee as a percentage of the water rate. This met with such fierce resistance from local elected representatives that the entire proposal had to be dropped.

50 Ankur Bisen, Chapter 5, "Waste Collection," *Wasted*, 2019.

51 "India Habitat III National Report 2016", MoHUA, *Government of India*.

52 "MoHUA Annual Report 2018–19," *Government of India*.

53 Mathangi Swaminathan, "How Can India's Waste Problem See a Systemic Change?" *EPW Engage, Economic & Political Weekly*, 2018. https://www.epw.in/engage/article/institutional-framework-implementing-solid-waste-management-india-macro-analysis; date of access July 17, 2021.

54 "Sustainable Sanitation and Water Management: Strengthening Enforcement Bodies," https://www.sswm.info; date of access June 10, 2021.

55 Ankur Bisen, Chapter 6, "Waste Disposal – Missing the Obvious," *Wasted*, 2019.

56 https://www.wiego.org/blog/india-pune%E2%80%99s-poorest-operate-world%E2%80%99s-most-cost-effective-waste-management-models; date of access June 5, 2021.

57 Namita Gupta, Rajiv Gupta, "Solid Waste Management and Sustainable Cities in India: The Case of Chandigarh, Environment & Urbanization," *International Institute for Environment and Development*, 2015.

58 "Transforming urban landscape 2014–2019," MoHUA, *Government of India*. http://mohua.gov.in/upload/5c987f9e0fcecUTBook25March2019compressed compressedcompressedmin11.pdf; date of access August 2, 2021.

59 "Using Data to Improve & Mechanize Door to Door Waste Collection: Learnings from Ahmedabad," July 2019.

60 "Transforming Urban Landscape, 2014–2019," MoHUA, *Government of India* http://mohua.gov.in/upload/5c987f9e0fcecUTBook25March20191compressed compressedcompressedmin11.pdf; date of access May 10, 2021.

61 "Solid Waste Management in the World's Cities," United Nations Human Settlements Programme, *UN Habitat*, 2010.

62 "Solid Approach to Waste: How 5 Cities are Beating Pollution," Story Green Economy, UN Environment Program, 22 November 2017.

63 "Success Stories for Recycling of MSW at Municipal Level: A Review," Waste and Biomass Valorization, October 2015. The cities with the highest ranks include the towns and cities of Palo Alto and San Fransisco in the US, Dogliani and Cappanori in Italy, Argentona, Verdu and Hernani in Spain, Schweinfurt in Germany, Kamikatsu in Japan, Gloucester in England, Limerick in Ireland, Boras in Sweden, and Flanders in the Netherlands.

64 Ankur Bisen, Chaptter 5, "Waste Collection," *Wasted*, 2019.

65 Sanjay K. Singh, "Review of Urban Transportation in India," *Journal of Public Transportation*, Vol. 8, No. 1, 2005.

66 "City Bus Transport: Need to Chart a New Route," *Indian Express*, 11 June 2016.

67 India Habitat III National Report 2016, MoHUA, *Government of India*.

68 Sriraman, Business and Economics, 2013.

69 Sanjay K. Singh, "Review of Urban Transportation in India," 2005.
70 "Moving Towards an Intelligent Transportation System, IOT driven buses in Ahmedabad, Case Study," July 2019, https://smartcities.data.gov.in/sites/default/files/Case5_Ahmd_ITMS.pdf; date of access July 4, 2021.
71 Rahul Goel and Geetam Tiwari, "Access–egress and Other Travel Characteristics of Metro Users in Delhi and its Satellite Cities," *IATSS Research*, 39, 164–172, 2016.
72 James Clark, "Comparison of Cost and Construction Times of first Metro Lines in Asia, *Future Southeast Asia*, Dec. 17, 2019. https://futuresoutheastasia.com/comparison-of-first-metro-lines-in-asia/; date of access March 10, 2021.
73 "All Volvo Bus Models with Price List in India, 2021," *Machinephd*. https://www.machinephd.com/all-volvo-bus-models-with-price/; date of access August 3, 2021.
74 O. P. Agarwal, "Compulsion to Choice: How Can Public Transport in India be Transformed?" *Economic & Political Weekly*, Vol. 54, Issue No. 4, 26 January 2019.
75 Venkat Sumantran, Charles Fine, and David Gonsalves, The Future of the Car and Urban Mobility, *The MIT Press*, Cambridge, Massachusetts, England, 2017.
76 Patrick Collinson, "On your Bike: The Best and the Worst of City Cycle Schemes," 25 February 2017.
77 "Velib," *Wikipedia*, https://en.wikipedia.org/wiki/V%C3%A9lib%27; date of access April 10, 2021.
78 India Habitat III National Report, MoHUA, *Government of India* 2016.
79 Author's calculation.

9

THE WAY FORWARD

Principles, Actions, and Sustainability

The Macro Framework

We began our discussion in Chapter 1 against the backdrop of the crises arising from the misguided and poorly implemented economic and social policies resulting in the neglect of the quality of life, equity, and well-being of citizens. It was noted that inadequate attention to social and human development indicators is not only highly deleterious to sustainable economic growth but also tantamount to a breach of the State's obligations to ensure fundamental human rights. Furthermore, as the COVID-19 pandemic has led to massive disruptions in economic activity, livelihoods, and well-being, a radical course correction has become imperative.

India has a small window in the next two decades to utilize the potential of its young population and reap the benefits of the demographic dividend. However, it can do so only by according the highest priority to improving the quality of life of citizens and providing them with decent livelihoods. It is in this context that we identified seven interconnected areas that directly and critically impact the well-being and livelihoods of citizens. These areas are public health, food and nutrition security, the young child, school education, livelihoods and jobs, gender, and urban development. Based on an in-depth analysis of the causative factors for sub-optimal outcomes issues in these identified areas, a holistic and integrated approach has been taken to make recommendations to tackle the country's formidable development challenges.

In this final chapter, the main elements of the new approach and the design principles that underpin this new development framework have been spelt out. The recommendations have considered the opinions of sectoral policy experts and well-proven practices as also the author's extensive first-hand experience and learning. The comprehensive holistic approach has the potential to materially enhance the quality of life and livelihoods of the people if efficiently implemented. This chapter delineates the overall vision and the essence of our proposals for each sector.

DOI: 10.4324/9781003346258-9

185

Undoubtedly, the implementation of these proposals will require enhanced budgets. Therefore, needless to state, the fiscal sustainability of the recommendations needs to be addressed. So, reasonable back-of-the-envelope estimates of the additional funds required to implement the recommendations have been provided at the end of the chapter. But where will the money come from? Will there be a need to cut back on other development priorities, such as economic infrastructure, or other national imperatives such as defence, internal security, or high-cost petroleum imports? We demonstrate in this chapter that the economy has the financial capacity to support the enhanced expenditures required without paring the budgets of other critical sectors.

Approach and Design Principles

The analysis of current government policies and schemes has revealed that systemic design flaws and the inevitable faulty implementation have led to sub-optimal outcomes even in programmes with sizeable budgets. Thus, if budgets are enhanced without correcting the systemic flaws, there may be only a marginal improvement in outcomes and well-being. Our approach rests on two fundamental principles: one, a clear understanding of poor households; and second, the design of programmes that are cost-effective and implementable by government structures.

Thus, each proposal considers its programme's adoption by people, especially low-income families. In this context, while designing proposals we have been acutely conscious that most Indian households come with their baggage of faith and beliefs. This often prevents people from making correct and rational decisions and taking full advantage of government interventions. Added to this, gender prejudice born from patriarchal attitudes is an obstacle to the implementation of government schemes. Therefore, to counter entrenched belief systems and gendered mindsets of households, sustained communication, advocacy campaigns, and intensive engagement with families are vital and integral elements in our proposals. The proposals take cognizance of the fact that poor households are so entangled in their daily struggles that their response to government interventions is slow. For example, poor households are the least likely to get their children vaccinated and are most irregular in antenatal care visits. Similarly, many poor families do not access health services even when available, preferring local health providers Also, they often fail to send their children to anganwadis or schools. Low-income families take time to change their perspectives and attitudes; our interventions recognize that the poor need a lot of support, handholding, and patience.

The proposals address other major reasons for the poor outcomes of government programmes. First, there are just too many government schemes. The plethora of poorly and hurriedly designed and inadequately funded programmes has sapped the energy of the implementation agencies. My own experience, and that of most civil servants, bears this out. Government systems work well when the focus is clear, as evidenced by the efficiency of the government's electoral system, emergency flood or drought works, or in the implementation of the few programmes that are closely monitored and prioritized by the government. Given the limited governmental bandwidth available, the number of schemes must be small and limited to critical areas that matter most. Therefore, in place of the existing laundry list of schemes, interventions are recommended in those areas that are most vital and within the government's implementation capacity. Further, given the vast diversity within the country, it has been suggested that there should be considerable flexibility given to states in the implementation of central schemes.

The second reason for sub-optimal outcomes has been that, along with multiple schemes, each government scheme that targets poor families draws up its list of beneficiaries. This naturally complicates overall implementation and leads to vested interests and erroneous beneficiary lists. Therefore, in our approach, we have advocated the adoption of a single consolidated list of low-income families for all programmes for the poor. It is possible to adopt a uniform list in specific areas – the PDS, health insurance, credit, housing, and direct cash transfer schemes – with the beneficiary families being the poorest 30 per cent households at the national level. We recognize that measuring poverty is not an exact science, and economists hold widely divergent views on the criteria and methodology to be adopted for measuring poverty. The measurement of poverty is further complicated by the fact that poverty is not a static concept; for example, since March 2020, the fallout of Covid-19 has impoverished millions of households, pushing large numbers of people below the poverty line.[1] The challenge is even more formidable when governments attempt to identify and physically enumerate poor households on the ground. And yet, at the local and community level, there is generally a consensus on which families are poor. Therefore, we have suggested that it makes practical sense to have the list of beneficiary families screened and vetted by village and local assemblies. Of course, errors will remain, and there should be an annual update and revision to the list of poor families based on open discussions at the local and village levels.

The third reason for poor outcomes has been the neglect of service quality. Governments have focused on quantitative targets, for example, the number of toilets built, loans sanctioned, and children enrolled in schools. Similarly, government policy has prioritized access and expansion of government facilities such as anganwadis, schools, colleges, health centres, and hospitals. As a result, the quality of services, and the maintenance and upkeep of government institutions, have been relegated to the backburner. In contrast, our recommendations have a clear focus on the maintenance and upkeep of infrastructure, the quality of assets, and service delivery. A critical recommendation, among other things, is the professionalization of the workforce, ensuring a full complement of staff with quality standards benchmarked to well-run private facilities.

The fourth reason for programme failure is systemic design flaws, stemming from rigid bureaucratic mindsets, resulting in a lack of openness to revisions or new ideas. These attitudes have been challenged in the book and redesign of programmes recommended based on research evidence and best practices. The book also emphasizes the inter-connectedness of different sectors and the need for government ministries to work closely and in coordination with others. Therefore, the book presents an integrated agenda, cutting across all the vital development areas. We hope that the adoption and success of the proposals would change mindsets among policymakers and encourage them to be open to new ideas. This openness should lead to intensive engagement and meaningful collaboration with civil society and the provision of greater autonomy to local governments.

Finally, government programmes have failed to generate much-needed employment, as there has been an over-reliance on market forces. Leaving job creation to the market has left millions unemployed and has led to extreme livelihood uncertainty for vast sections of people. Therefore, our approach makes livelihoods and job creation the cornerstone of development strategy. In this context, we have recognized the limitations of agriculture in providing employment and improving livelihoods and advocated an urban-centric approach through planned urbanization to fuel economic growth and generate jobs.

The Economic Environment

A supportive economic environment is vital for ensuring that implementation of the recommendations results in improved well-being and livelihoods. The increasing trend towards crony capitalism and increased 'tax terrorism' is disturbing and must be checked. While economic reforms since the 1990s have undoubtedly brought in multiple benefits to the economy, these have been skewed in favour of a few large companies; many smaller businesses have floundered or collapsed. Further, as noted, income inequality has grown, while poverty levels have remained high. Though there has been economic growth it has not resulted in concomitant enhancement in livelihoods or job creation for the vast majority of people.

However, this situation should not lead us to conclude that a reversal of economic reforms is required. On the contrary, the private sector must remain the principal player across all economic sectors. The current complex regulatory structure with multiple rules and licenses thwarts enterprise and innovation and must be replaced with an open, transparent oversight framework based on trust; this expectation will, for the present, remain on our wish list! We recognize that private enterprises are in the business of profit and the creation of financial value for their shareholders; employment is, at best, a side-effect. Therefore, our livelihood strategies have focused on giving a stimulus and providing profitable avenues to labour-intensive enterprises. We have also countered the conventional hypothesis that the government should not be in the business of direct job creation. Instead, we have proposed that millions of new productive government jobs be created in the social sector for promoting development and implementing livelihood programmes.

The Vision and the Road Map

We strongly believe that implementing the proposals made in this book would vastly improve overall well-being and provide the stimulus and opportunities to enhance livelihoods. The overarching vision is of a caring and responsive polity that ensures the physical well-being of all its citizens in terms of health, education, and nutrition, and provides equal opportunities for women and men to access jobs and meaningful livelihoods. The road map delineated in this book would enable the country to realize this vision and attain human development indicators and poverty reduction levels benchmarked to the best in the world, and provide productive employment to each citizen.

The healthcare system would rest on the foundation of well-functioning primary healthcare services closely connected to the community. The priority would be preventive and promotive services through an efficient surveillance and screening system and well-structured IEC activities. Effective referral and quality management systems at all levels of healthcare would be the hallmark of curative services.

The transformed primary healthcare system would have fully staffed PHCs housed in refurbished and well-maintained buildings, with the required medical equipment and other infrastructure. A motivated and professional cadre of female health workers and ASHA workers would engage intensively with the community to counsel and guide poor households. There would be an adequate supply of free medicines and round-the-clock services at PHCs and community hospitals. A vastly strengthened National Health Mission would prioritize maternal and child health. A fully staffed and trained male health cadre would form the backbone for surveillance and screening for illnesses and diseases. There would be overarching public health legislation and regulatory oversight for the early detection and management of infectious diseases, including pandemics such as COVID-19.

Instead of building new hospitals, the focus would be on upgrading existing institutions, providing sufficient staff and resources, enhancing capacity, and ensuring service quality through rigidly implemented standard operating protocols. Thus, all CHCs and hospital buildings would undergo extensive upgrades and renovation. All rundown medical equipment would be replaced, and diagnostic facilities expanded.

The strengthened public healthcare system would reduce the pressure on private hospitals. Furthermore, a reformed Ayushman Bharat would provide BPL households with a health insurance scheme that offers flexibility and a wider choice of insurance policies to ensure cashless access in both government and private hospitals. Government policy would clearly distinguish between philanthropic/non-profit institutions and private hospitals running on purely commercial lines. The former would get support, encouragement, and autonomy, while the latter would be more closely regulated.

Food insecurity and malnutrition would be tackled through a paradigm shift in strategy. Food insecurity due to income-poverty amongst the poorest households, the Antyodaya Anna Yojana beneficiaries, would be addressed through cash transfers, financed via savings in food subsidy through PDS reform. PDS reform would focus on two fundamental objectives – food grain price stability by maintaining buffer stocks and prioritizing food security for BPL households. Thus, the 30 per cent of poorest households would continue to be provided food grains at highly subsidized rates. The remaining families could avail themselves of the universal PDS and purchase an assured quantity of food grains at around 50 per cent of the market price. Nutrition of women and children will get closer attention under the strengthened POSHAN Abhiyan. Intensive education counselling campaigns would address critical aspects of malnutrition such as nutrition imbalance and the emerging trend of obesity.

The four vital aspects of the young child's well-being – health, nutrition, cognitive development, and care – will be prioritized. For this, the ICDS, instead of being confined to anganwadis, would adopt a community outreach approach and get support from the vastly strengthened POSHAN Abhiyan. The neglected areas of ECCE and childcare would become a primary focus, and crèches opened to cater to vulnerable households. Anganwadi workers would be trained to become full-time professional community childcare workers with enhanced remuneration. Monitoring of growth parameters of each child, parental counselling, nutrition education, and awareness programmes would be essential responsibilities of anganwadi workers.

School education reform will address the alienation of both children and parents of poor households from the system and look at issues from their perspective. The starting point for improving the quality of schools will be a near single-minded focus on learning outcomes. Teacher training would guide teachers away from rigidly following the curriculum and rote-learning methods. Instead of simply completing the syllabus, teachers would prioritize learning by ensuring that teaching is at each child's level, to the extent possible. Teacher motivation and accountability would be achieved through reforms in teacher recruitment and transfers and addressing teachers' pain points while providing them effective academic supervision. Children

THE WAY FORWARD

studying in government schools and others from poor households would receive extensive remedial support to compensate for the lack of a learning environment at home. Government schools would undergo an image makeover with adequate resources earmarked for the proper upkeep of school buildings and other infrastructure. Private schools managed through not-for-profit institutions would be provided autonomy and space to innovate in pedagogy and curriculum.

The proposed livelihood and job creation strategies are far-reaching and cover all principal household categories. Thus, as noted, the most impoverished families comprising the bottom consumption decile would be the beneficiaries of cash transfers. Migrant labour would get covered under an effective social security scheme. Reforms in agriculture insurance would give insurance companies the flexibility and autonomy to customize their products, leading to wider farmer coverage.

A slew of measures is proposed to widen women's livelihood opportunities and access to jobs. First, women will get livelihood finance through generous financial support from credible microfinance institutions. Second, legislative provisions such as the Maternity Benefit Act will be amended to incentivize employers to hire women and create a woman-friendly work environment. Third, governments will be encouraged to provide reservations in government jobs, including the police, the judiciary, and public administration. Fourth, skilling programmes will specifically target women, especially those wishing to re-enter or join the workforce after marriage or after their children enter school. Fifth, setting up crèches would create an effective support system for childcare, and ease the burden of women who wish to go out for work. Additionally, there would be satisfactory arrangements for their safe commute to and from the workplace.

Small businesses that have a vast potential for generating new jobs would be promoted through a recast of the Mudra loan scheme. This, along with equity support, would enable such businesses to hire professional talent, compete with organized players, ensure standardization and quality, and employ skilled workers. The proposed urban-centric approach would exploit the potential for setting up new businesses and creating jobs in cities and towns. Industrial infrastructure would be developed in selected 1,000 towns and cities where there is potential for job creation. In such towns and cities, the infrastructure would cater to enterprises in two or three identified sectors, to exploit the advantage of clustering. In addition, institutional and financial arrangements would support each identified town and city for planning, handholding, skill development, and credit support to potential entrepreneurs. Entrepreneurs will get adequate equity through a professionally managed large investment fund. Along with revamping the manufacturing sector through focused cluster development, trade and manufacturing policies will complement each other and facilitate technology adoption on a large scale. The traditional handicrafts and textile sectors would get transformed into new-age production systems through technology, skill training, modern equipment, and contemporary designs to cater to the fast-changing domestic and global consumer market.

Direct job creation by the government for expanding social infrastructure and basic services as we propose would have a multiplier impact on livelihoods. Government recruitment on a large scale would take place to meet the requirement of the health, school education, nutrition, and livelihood sectors and for urban services. This would be a reversal of the current neglect and apathy by the government in the provisioning of public services. The implementation of proposals would create 5 million government jobs alone in the seven development sectors identified.

Apart from job creation in the public sector, the impetus to businesses, especially in the 1,000 cluster towns, would open up employment opportunities in the private sector as well as provide self-employment opportunities. The vision is to create 60 million livelihood and employment opportunities outside agriculture. An expanded employment guarantee programme to include urban areas would be in place and support livelihoods till an adequate number of stable and secure jobs get created.

A vital component of the development agenda proposed in the book would be changing traditional patriarchal mindsets to ensure equal rights for women. Country-wide, massive, bold, and ongoing communication campaigns to counter deep-seated gender prejudices would replace the current ineffectual schemes. The education policy would promote gender equity and encourage and facilitate women to make non-stereotypical education and life choices. Amendments to labour laws and the Factories Act would ensure gender-friendly policies. Gender equity would become a key element in the government regulation and oversight of companies. Asset and cash transfers to only female members of a family instead of the male would empower women. Given that gender discrimination cuts across all sectors, gender budgets and gender action plans would be implemented and closely reviewed by all government ministries. The gender equity roadmap would include policy and legislative recognition of the rights of the LGBTQIA+ community unequivocally and unambiguously.

In pursuing the urban-centric approach, the focus will be on improving living conditions in urban areas, through inclusive and dynamic plans and prioritizing the provision of basic urban services – such as housing, sanitation, solid waste management, and mobility. Slum resettlement and housing for the poor would be an integral part of urban planning. An innovative, affordable rental housing policy attractive to investors would be implemented. In sanitation, the focus would be on the entire value chain. Reconditioning the Indian mindset on public cleanliness would be the lynchpin of the approach to solid waste management. Modern systems and practices for waste collection and disposal would facilitate the shift from a sweeper-centric system to one where citizens share responsibility. The development of the identified 1,000 cluster towns and cities would get high priority, with each having well-resourced and adequately funded integrated planning, implementing, and enforcement authorities. In the remaining 7,000 towns too, the central focus would be on bettering the financial health of urban local bodies through capacity development and financial support.

Augmentation of bus fleets and their image transformation through rigidly implemented protocols on upkeep and maintenance would get high priority. Metro rail systems would be provided solely within city boundaries and be seamlessly integrated with feeder bus and last-mile services. Rather than widening our roads or adding to the road length, taking cognizance of the rights of pedestrians and cyclists, there would be well-laid and well-lit pedestrian paths to ensure that women feel safe at all times of the day.

Transforming Lives of Poor Households

Our vision and road map has accorded the highest priority to the well-being and livelihoods of low-income households. Let us now visualize what difference it could make to the lives of Birsa and Rasika and their children. We fast forward to seven years after the central government adopts most of the proposals made in the book (hopefully not an altogether hypothetical situation).

> Birsa and Rasika have been beneficiaries of the income transfer scheme, which has enabled them to pare away most of their debt. Along with this regular cash transfer and much greater engagement of ASHA and anganwadi workers at the household level, nutrition and health indicators of the three children as well as the parents have improved appreciably.
>
> Rasika continues to borrow money through the SHG; though no longer for meeting basic consumption needs, but rather to purchase fabric for her home-based tailoring business, which she runs on a part-time basis. Since agricultural labour continues to be their primary income source, the family income has not seen much improvement. This is despite employment guarantee works now being available regularly, and Bindu and Rasika being assured of employment whenever they are out of work.
>
> Over the previous three years, Birsa had heard a lot from villagers who had gone to try their luck in Ranchi, about the growing job opportunities in the city. Birsa finally decided to move there to seek better prospects. Initially, he got employment as casual labour but has since honed his skills as a trained mason. For the past year, he has been employed by a building contractor as a mason. On a visit to his village, he had discussed with Rasika the possibility of migration, and they decided that it was perhaps time for the entire family to make a move.

Rasika and the children have now joined Birsa at Ranchi. The family has rented a house built under the new affordable housing scheme. The house has a functioning toilet, tap water, a sewer connection, and a kitchenette!

Their children have been enrolled in the local government school that has a high school section. Komal, who is now 15 years old, is particularly looking forward to attending the high school, which has a much better infrastructure than in the village. Komal, who had earlier not been inclined to go to school, got interested in studies when classroom teaching at the village school became interactive, and she began receiving personal attention. She and her two siblings, Bindu and Shibu, who are now 11 and 8 years old, respectively, have also regularly attended the remedial classes in the village school. The village school building, which was earlier a dilapidated and ill-kept structure, has since been refurbished, with toilets and running water. It now has its playground. The children do miss their friends in the village but will make new ones.

Birsa travels by bus to his workplace. Rasika, who had brought along her sewing machine, has received a few tailoring orders for making garments but is now looking for a full-time job as the children have grown up. There is a garment export factory 7 km away that hires women but occasionally requires them to work a late evening shift. There is a reliable bus service to and from her workplace and well-lit pedestrian paths everywhere. However, Rasika will need to upgrade her skills to be able to work on the modern sewing machines in the factory. Birsa has encouraged Rasika to enrol in the training programme available in the local government skill development centre.

Birsa and Rasika have learnt that their household ration card, though issued at their village address, is valid in Ranchi too. Moreover, their BPL card entitles them to free hospitalization even in the nearby private hospital, but they may not choose to go there. Recently, when Shibu fell ill, they had gone to the local urban PHC and were provided satisfactory treatment.

Birsa and Rasika are gradually forgetting their dreary past and feel hopeful as they discuss their improved lives and the possibility of a reasonably bright future for their children.

The Political Environment

Before we lead ourselves to believe in an optimistic future for India, especially for poor families such as that of Birsa and Rasika, we need to ask a crucial question: What are the chances that the government would adopt the proposals in the book? We had noted in Chapter 1 that if the proposals do not have political resonance then they would remain only confined to academic discourse. Therefore, the question arises: Along with vastly improved development indicators, would the development agenda also promise electoral dividends? Certainly, it will; for example, the creation of millions of employment opportunities, with over 5 million jobs in the government alone, would have strong electoral appeal. Equally, small firms and the self-employed would feel motivated and energized with a government that provides fulsome support for their business.

Would citizens not feel satisfied when they get prompt treatment and free medicines in government hospitals and PHCs? Would not the poorest households vote for a government that provides them substantial income transfers? Would not poor households support a government that provides them food and nutrition security, quality education for their children? Would women not support a government that prioritizes gender equity and equal opportunities in the workplace? Would the urban citizens not be pleased when they find their towns and cities free of garbage and the sanitation system working well? Would they not be happy with an efficient and modern public transport system, and well-lit and paved pedestrian pathways? The answer to these and all such questions would be a resounding YES.

Fiscal Sustainability

However, even if the political will is present, there appears to be a stumbling block – where do we find the money? Sizeable budget allocations would be required to ensure that development policy is steered towards the development of human capital, urban development, gender, and social equity, and to grow livelihood opportunities. It would have to be ensured that these budget allocations are not at the cost of other critical sectors.

Over the years, development sector experts have estimated budgetary requirements. For example, health sector advocates have sought enhancement of the health budget from the current 1 per cent to 3 per cent of GDP.[2] Similarly, educationists have suggested raising the education budget to 6 per cent of GDP and the NEP 2020 corroborates this proposal.[3] In addition, the State of the Young Child in India Report 2020 has sought to earmark 20 per cent of social sector budgets for young child programmes.[4] Further, given the loss of livelihoods due to the COVID-19 pandemic, economists have recommended an additional government spending of 2 per cent of GDP to bring the economy back on track.[5]

While the foregoing suggestions have considerable merit and justification, many would feel that the centre and the states may not have the fiscal capacity to implement them may be constrained. In this context, we carried out an exercise and arrived at a back-of-the-envelope figure of the budget required to implement the proposals made for the seven sectors covered in the book. It will be observed that our estimate of the requirement for the identified sectors is quite modest compared to estimates of sectoral experts. In any case, government capacity to rapidly absorb funding in these sectors must also be considered. Therefore, some essential expenditures have been spread over 4–5 years. To implement the proposals in this book, the centre would need to increase its annual spending by ₹4,000 billion, which amounts to a modest 2 per cent of GDP, and 15 per cent of the central budget and is within the fiscal and implementation capacity of the government. The break-up of the additional sectoral outlays required, across the seven identified sectors, along with the assumptions made, is given in the Appendix at the end of this chapter.

For the health sector, the additional annual requirement of ₹678 billion, represents a 90 per cent increase over the current health budget. Over 40 per cent (₹296 billion) of this amount is for meeting the human resource requirement for primary healthcare, and for meeting the current shortfall of staff at sub-district and district hospitals. Of the total outlay proposed 30 per cent (₹208 billion) is for medicines and equipment and 18 per cent (₹124 billion) is for the renovation, refurbishment, and new facilities. The balance outlay of ₹50 billion is earmarked for IEC.

According to our estimate, will see an annual saving of ₹1,500 billion in food subsidy through two sets of reforms of the PDS reforms: one, the sharp targeting of the poorest 30 per cent households for supplying highly subsidised food grains; two, raising the issue prices for the remaining families in the PDS to 50 per cent of the economic cost. These savings are proposed to be deployed to directly address the income poverty of the 10 per cent of most impoverished households through the 'basic income' cash transfer scheme. (This amount is reflected in the Appendix in the budget estimate of the livelihoods and jobs sector.) The food and nutrition sector would, however, require intensive engagement and outreach to households. Therefore, an additional provision of ₹100 billion has been indicated as the outlay towards IEC for this sector and nutrition.

The implementation of the proposed young child programmes would require an additional ₹245 billion annually: ₹103 billion for restructuring and strengthening the ICDS and enhancing community outreach; ₹50 billion for supporting POSHAN Abhiyan; and ₹92 billion for establishing crèches. This requirement is 122 per cent higher than the current central budget outlay for the sector.

For improving school education, it is estimated that the central government needs to earmark an additional ₹770 billion annually – 83 per cent higher than the existing outlay for the sector. Of this outlay, 65 per cent (₹500 billion) is for the annual renovation and refurbishment of existing schools. The remedial 'catch-up' programme would require ₹84 billion annually, while ₹126 billion is for supporting games and sports teachers.

An estimated ₹50 billion is required for IEC campaigns focusing on the education of the girl child and SC/ST children while ₹10 billion is earmarked for setting up good quality teacher-training institutions and systems.

The annual fiscal requirement for implementing livelihood and job creation strategies is an estimated ₹2750 billion – 137 per cent more than the current central government allocation for the rural development and industries sectors. This allocation includes the basic income transfer of ₹1,500 billion to 10 per cent of most impoverished households (re-allocated out of the savings from food subsidy). An estimated ₹200 billion is for expanding the farmer coverage under agricultural insurance (through redesign and flexibility of the scheme). The recast and expansion of MGNREGA to cover urban settlements would cost an estimated ₹200 billion annually. The creation of livelihood and job opportunities via cluster development of the identified 1,000 towns and cities and promotion of new enterprises would cost an estimated ₹850 billion annually. After accounting for ₹1,500 billion savings from PDS restructuring, the net annual increase in the budget for livelihoods and job creation is ₹1,250 billion.

For promoting gender equity and changing patriarchal mindsets, the estimated additional requirement to run sustained massive campaigns is ₹100 billion, a 285 per cent increase over the current budget of ₹35 billion for women's schemes.

The total additional budgetary requirement for urban development as per recommended strategies would require an additional annual allocation of ₹959 billion, against the centre's current outlay of ₹550 billion (a hike of 175 per cent). An annual provision of ₹112 billion is estimated for basic urban services (sanitation, solid waste management, and housing) in the identified 1,000 cluster towns, while ₹640 billion is the requirement for the remaining 7,000 towns. For augmenting bus transport, an additional ₹167 billion is required annually, while ₹40 billion is the estimated additional annual requirement for the provision of pedestrian and cycle paths.

The additional annual outlay of ₹4,000 billion, translating to 2 per cent of the country's GDP, may not appear astronomical given the enormous returns, but the money would need to be found. There is huge potential in mobilizing revenues by reviewing the existing tax base. Moreover, rationalizing subsidy schemes, discontinuing dysfunctional programmes, and reviewing allocations would yield sizeable savings which can then be channelized into the identified sectors.

The centre's tax revenues have been hovering at around 10 per cent of GDP, while the combined tax revenue of the centre and states in India stands at about 17 per cent of GDP.[6] Many research studies, including one undertaken by the International Monetary Fund (IMF) for the Fifteenth Finance Commission (XVFC), have indicated the large gap in tax collections – over 5 per cent of GDP – compared to the potential.[7] Budget collection efficiency is another problem highlighted by the XVFC; the central government's tax collections during the period 2010–19 were, on average, 4 per cent less than budgeted.[8] It is reasonable to view this gap as unrealized revenue potential. The XFVC has therefore estimated that India's tax revenues are short of the potential by about 4 per cent of GDP. The National Institute of Public Finance and Policy has forecast that India's tax-GDP ratio would increase from 18.91 per cent in 2016–17 to 22.84 per cent in 2030–31.[9]

A review of the current total revenues reveals that the total tax revenue of the centre is only ₹22,000 billion. Of this, direct taxes (₹5,500 billion each of corporation and income tax) account for only 50 per cent of total revenue.[10] Given the extreme income inequality and the relatively progressive nature of direct taxes, there is huge potential in mopping up additional tax revenues from corporation and income taxes; there is currently a vast amount of tax evasion and direct tax rates are below those in developed countries. Thus, the centre can collect, if it has the will, an additional ₹8,000–10,000 billion in taxes (4–5 per cent of GDP), especially from direct taxes.

It may be noted that the development agenda proposed in the book requires only 50 per cent of the tax potential of 4–5 per cent of GDP. Also, central outlays are likely to be matched, at least partially, by state-level spending on the suggested programmes. Thus, the estimated additional annual revenue of ₹4,000 billion to transform the lives of our people can be raised, and that too without reducing the budgets of other sectors.

The strategies and steps recommended in the book can, in the next ten years, secure an enhanced quality of life, meaningful livelihoods, and dignity for each citizen. Of course, the immediate challenge is for the government to overcome the economic and unemployment crisis faced by the country on account of the COVID-19 pandemic. As noted, several economists have suggested the massive scaling up of expenditures that directly reach the affected population to boost consumption. Several of the measures suggested in the book would place more money in the hands of those that need it most.

It is hoped that the analysis of – and policy recommendations for – the seven most vital areas of development would trigger a healthy and vibrant debate amongst policymakers and development practitioners. It is also expected that civil society and NGOs would add their voices in support of these proposals. It should then be in the realm of possibility to imagine that the proposals garner political support and the recommendations find a place in the election manifestos of political parties. Thus, there is ample reason to be optimistic that the proposals made in this book would lead to the actual framing of programmes and their implementation on the ground.

THE WAY FORWARD

Appendix: Estimated Annual Budget Requirement to Implement Proposals

Sl. No.	Proposal	(₹ billion)	Notes/Assumptions
2	**Chapter 2: Health**		
2.1	Additional 0.5 million ASHA workers	60	@ ₹10,000 monthly salary.
2.2	Enhanced remuneration to existing ASHA workers	72	Additional monthly salary of ₹6,000 to 1 million ASHA workers.
2.3	Human resource requirement	124	The aggregate of sub-components of 2.3 (all shortfall figures from Rural Health Statistics 2020).
	ANM/Health worker (M)/Health assistants at SCs and PHCs; Nursing staff at PHCs and CHCs; Para-medical staff at CHCs /sub-division/ district Hospitals	66	Shortfall: ANMs – 26,950, health worker (M) – 16,085 @ ₹25,000 monthly salary; nursing staff at CHCs/PHCs – 11,222 @ annual salary of ₹3,00,000; para-medical staff – 22,585 at CHCs/ sub-division/ district Hospitals @ monthly salary of ₹25,000.
	Doctors/specialists/ GDMOs at PHCs, CHCs and sub-district/district hospitals	29	Shortfall: PHC doctors – 2,757 @ ₹7,00,000 annual salary; CHC Specialists – 21,466 @ ₹10,00,000 annual salary; CHC GDMOs – 1,280 @ annual salary of ₹8,00,000; Sub-district/ district hospital doctors @ ₹8,00,000 annual salary.
	Radiographers, lab technicians and pharmacists at CHCs	9	Shortfall: Radiographers, lab technicians, and pharmacists – 29,184 @ annual salary of ₹3,00,000.
	Running PHCs on a 24×7 basis	20	@ ₹1.2 million to PHCs to function 24×7. This provision includes salaries of 3 additional staff nurse/health workers for emergency care, additional infrastructure for conducting deliveries in the night shift @ a monthly salary of ₹25,000, and @ ₹3,00,000 for infrastructure.
2.4	Renovation and refurbishment	70	Provision for all PHCs (30,000), CHCs (5000), Sub-division/ district hospitals (2000) @ ₹7.5 million, ₹15 million and ₹25 million per facility respectively spread over 5 years.
	PHCs	45	
	CHCs, SDH and DH	25	

(*Continued*)

199

THE WAY FORWARD

Sl. No.	Proposal	(₹ billion)	Notes/Assumptions
2.5	Medicines, equipment, and diagnostic infrastructure	208	@ ₹5 million, ₹7.5 million, and ₹25 million respectively to each PHC, CHC, sub-district/district hospital.
	PHCs	150	
	CHCs, SDH and DH	58	
2.6	Training of healthcare workforce and healthcare professionals	40	The estimate is more than the Fifteenth Finance Commission recommendation of ₹133 billion for the training of the 5 million healthcare workforce and includes provision for training infrastructure.
2.7	New health facilities	54	Shortfall: 2,000 new PHCs (1,000 each in rural and urban areas); 1,000 new CHCs in low-income urban pockets @ ₹20 million per PHC and ₹30 million per CHC for initial infrastructure, spread over 5 years. The provision includes an annual budget of ₹10 million and ₹20 million towards drugs and equipment.
	PHCs	28	
	CHCs	26	
2.8	IEC health	50	The annual amount of ₹50 billion is proposed towards IEC and awareness health campaigns.
	Annual additional outlay for the health sector	678	
3	**Chapter 3: Food Security and Nutrition**		
3.1	IEC: Food security and Nutrition	100	The annual spend at present in IEC on food security and nutrition is negligible. An annual expenditure of ₹100 billion represents a manifold hike.
3.2	Transforming the public distribution system	−1,600	The 2021 budget for TPDS is ₹2,430 billion If highly subsidized grains are limited to the poorest 30 per cent households at a central issue price of ₹5 and ₹7 for wheat and rice respectively, while other households will be supplied at around 50 per cent of economic cost, the estimated budget requirement is ₹830 billion, resulting in an annual saving of ₹1,600 billion

(*Continued*)

THE WAY FORWARD

Sl. No.	Proposal	(₹ billion)	Notes/Assumptions
	Net potential savings on food security and nutrition	1,500	
4	**Chapter 4: Young Child**		
4.1	POSHAN Abhiyan	50	In the 2021–22 budget, Saksham Anganwadi and POSHAN 2.0, ₹200 billion has been allocated. An additional 25 per cent is proposed.
4.2	Additional salary to Anganwadi workers	50	Additional monthly salary @₹3,000 to 1.4 million anganwadi workers (figs. rounded up)
4.3	Training for ICDS (including ECCE)	15	Additional training budget for 1.4 million anganwadi workers and supervisors (@ 1 supervisor for 25 workers) @ ₹10,000 per trainee.
4.4	IEC budget for outreach to parents	10	No explicit IEC budget exists at present. An annual outlay of ₹10 billion is proposed.
4.5	ECCE equipment to anganwadis	28	Additional budget for ECCE equipment @ ₹20,000 each to 1.4 million anganwadis.
4.6	Crèches	92	For conversion of 10 per cent of anganwadis to crèches @ one additional crèche worker + two helpers at a monthly salary of ₹12,000 and ₹8,000, respectively to each of the 1, 40,000 crèches will cost ₹50 billion annually. A lumpsum amount of ₹3 billion (@₹20,000 per person) for training and ₹7 billion (@ ₹50,000 per crèches) for equipment is proposed. ₹35 billion is the estimate for additional meal and nutrition @ ₹50 per day per child assuming 250 working days in a year and 20 children per crèche (figs. rounded up)
	Additional outlay for Young Child	245	

(*Continued*)

THE WAY FORWARD

Sl. No.	Proposal	(₹ billion)	Notes/Assumptions
5	**Chapter 5: School Education**		
5.1	Repairs and refurbishment of schools	500	@ ₹5,00,000 per school annually for the existing 1 million government schools in India. (Government of India's UDISE 2019–20 reports 1.03 million government schools in India).
5.2	Strengthen teacher-training systems and institutions	10	An additional annual outlay of ₹10 billion is proposed.
5.3	Volunteer-based remedial 'catch up' programme	84	@ ₹7,000 monthly honorarium to each of the two teachers deployed to the 1 million government schools for 6 months a year.
5.4	Games, music, and dance teachers	126	@ ₹7,000 monthly remuneration to each of the two art/ sports teachers deployed to the 1 million government schools for 9 months a year.
5.5	IEC - education and schooling (with focus on SCST, Girl child)	50	An additional annual outlay of ₹50 billion is proposed.
	Additional outlay towards school education	770	
6	**Chapter 6: Livelihoods and Jobs**		
6.1	Protection scheme for impoverished households and migrant labour	1,500	Income transfer to the bottom 10 per cent households: @ ₹5,000 per month to the bottom 25 million households will cost an additional ₹1,500 billion.
6.2	Income protection for agricultural households	200	The additional outlay is proposed as redesign will increase existing farmer coverage beyond the present 15 per cent. The existing outlay towards PM Fasal Bima Yojana is ₹160 billion.
6.3	Recasting the employment guarantee act	200	The existing MGNREGA outlay is ₹730 billion. The additional outlay is proposed for extending MGNREGA to urban settlements.
6.4	Women's livelihoods and their access to jobs	50	The additional outlay is for supporting MFIs for livelihood finance.

(Continued)

202

THE WAY FORWARD

Sl. No.	Proposal	(₹ billion)	Notes/Assumptions
6.5	Promoting labour intensive modern enterprises in the newly proposed urban cluster towns	500	@ Annual support of ₹10 million per unit to 50 enterprises per cluster.
6.6	Equity support for small businesses	300	20 per cent of the present Mudra Loan credit outlay of ₹1,500 billion is proposed.
	Additional outlay towards livelihoods and jobs	2,750	
7	**Chapter 7: Gender**		
7.1	IEC Budgets: Gender	100	An annual additional IEC gender-equity budget of ₹100 billion is earmarked. This includes campaigns to change mindsets and the role perceptions of women and attitudes towards the LGBTQIA+ community and support to companies for promoting gender diversity.
	Additional outlay for tackling gender issues	100	
8	**Chapter 8: Urban Planning**		
8.1	New 1000 cluster towns: sanitation/ solid waste management/ new posts	112	@ ₹50 million per 1,000 cluster towns annually, for solid waste management and sanitation. In addition, the budget for creating 50 new posts in each of these 1,000 municipal corporations @ an average monthly salary of ₹20,000.
8.2	Existing towns: solid waste management and sanitation infrastructure	640	₹40 million additional budget to each of the existing 8,000 towns and cities.
8.3	Urban bus transport.	166	Provision of 100 buses in each of the new 1,000 towns, @ ₹5 million per bus and spreading the capital expenditure over 3 years.
8.4	Pedestrian and cycle pat	40	A lump sum amount of ₹20 billion each is proposed for both existing and new towns.
	Additional outlay: urban planning	959	
GRAND TOTAL		4,000	This translates to an additional outlay of 2 per cent of GDP.

Notes

1 Rakesh Kochar, "In the Pandemic, India's Middle Class Shrinks and Poverty Spreads While China Sees Samaller Changes," *Pew Research Centre*, 18 March 2021. https://www.pewresearch.org/fact-tank/2021/03/18/in-the-pandemic-indias-middle-class-shrinks-and-poverty-spreads-while-china-sees-smaller-changes/; date of access July 17, 2021.

2 Shankar Prinja, Pankaj Bahuguna, Andrew D. Pinto, Atul Sharma, Gursimer Bharaj, Jaya Prasad Tripathi, Manmeet Kaur and Rajesh Kumar, "The Cost of Universal Health Coverage in India: A Model-based Estimate," *PLOS*, 7(1), 2013.

3 Niti Kiran, "Spending 6% of GDP, Doubling Enrolment 2 Lofty Targets of National Education Policy 2020," *Business Today*, 13 August 2020.

4 Chapter 6, "Fiscal Allocations and Expenditure for Child Development," State of the Young Child in India, Mobile Creches, *Routledge*, 2020.

5 "COVID 19 Pandemic Impact: Here's What Eminent Economists Suggest About India's Economic Recovery", *CNBCTV18.com*, 2 June 2021.

6 "Fifteenth Finance Commission Report", Ministry of Finance, *Government of India*, October 2020. India's revenue -to-GDP ratio has virtually remained stagnant in the last decade and is much lower than that of its peers. The tax-GDP ratio improved from 10.2 per cent to 11 per cent of GDP during the period from 2011–12 to 2018–19, i.e., by only 80 basis points. This ratio is based on the gross tax revenue of the Union government. The ratio slid to 10.9% for FY 2019–20 and to 9.8% for the FY 2020–21. The Fifteenth Finance Commission's analysis reveals the untapped revenue potential in major direct and indirect taxes and concludes that, with appropriate corrective measures in tax administration and policy, the tax to GDP ratio could, in time, be raised by 5 percentage points. The recommended corrective measures bear the potential of yielding revenue gains from GST, personal and corporate income taxes, as well as property taxes at the local government level. The Fifteenth Finance Commission's report has also noted that there is great scope for improving efficiency in public spending, and the immediate reason for fiscal pressures faced by governments stems from the inability to mobilize adequate non-debt resources.

7 "India's GST Collections are Below Potential: IMF Team," *Times of India*, 17 February 2020.

8 "Fifteenth Finance Commission Report", Ministry of Finance, *Government of India*, October 2020. "This prediction error leads to ad hoc expenditure management, typically in the second half of the financial year that includes cuts in developmental expenditure creating uncertainties for implementing agencies, reneging on contractual obligations and payments, and significant carry-overs of liabilities."

9 M. Govinda Rao and Sudhanshu Kumar, "Envisioning Tax Policy for Accelerated Development in India," *NIPFP Working Paper series*, No. 190, 2017. https://www.nipfp.org.in/media/medialibrary/2017/02/WP_2017_190.pdf; date of access September 10, 2021.

10 "Budget at A Glance, Ministry Of Finance, *Government of India*, 2021" https://www.indiabudget.gov.in/doc/budget_at_glance/budget_at_a_glance.pdf; date of access June 10, 2021.

SELECT BIBLIOGRAPHY

Aasha Kapur Mehta, "Union Budget 2020–21: A Critical Analysis from the Gender Perspective", *Economic and Political Weekly*, Vol. 55, Issue No. 16, 18 April 2020.

Abhijit Banerjee and Esther Duflo, "*Poor Economics*", Random House, 2011.

Abhijit Banerjee and Esther Duflo, "*Good Economics for Hard Times*", Juggernaut Books, 2019.

Abhijit Banerjee, Raghuram G. Rajan, Gita Gopinath and Mihir S. Sharma, "*What the Economy Needs Now*", Juggernaut, 2019.

Abhijit Sen, "Report of the High-Level Committee on Long Term Grain Policy", Government of India, July 2002.

Abhijit Vinayak Banerjee, Pranab Bardhan, and Rohini Somanatan, T. N. Srinivasan, "*Poverty and Income Distribution in India*", Juggernaut Books, 2017.

Ajay Chibber, and Salman Anees Soz, "*Unshackling India*", Harper Collins, 2021.

Ajay Khera Sila, Robert Johnston, Praween K. Agrawal, Sowmya Ramesh, Nizamuddin Ahmed, Porwal Avina, and Swarna Rajib Acharya, "Children in India: A Statistical Appraisal", Ministry of Statistics and Programme Implementation, Government of India, 2018.

Alain de Janury, Elisabeth Sadou, and Nong Zhu, "*The Role of non-farm Incomes in Reducing Rural Poverty and Inequality: India, and China*", Department of Agricultural and Resource Economics and Policy, University of California, Berkeley, March 2005.

Amartya Sen, "*Development as Freedom*", Knopf, 1999.

Amartya Sen, "*Commodities and Capabilities*", Elsevier Science Publishing Company, 1985.

Angus Deaton and Jean Drèze, "Food and Nutrition in India: Facts and Interpretations", *Economic & Political Weekly*, Vol. 44, Issue No. 7, 14 February 2009.

Ankur Bisen, "*Wasted*", Macmillan, 2019.

Ayesha Banu, "*Human Development, Disparity and Vulnerability: Women in South Asia*", UNDP, 2016.

Diane Coffey and Dean Spears, "*Where India Goes*", Juggernaut, 2017.

"Early Years", Annual Status of Education Report (ASER) Report, *Pratham*, 2019.

India Habitat III National Report 2016, Ministry of Housing and Urban Affairs, Government of India, 2016.

Indrani Gupta, "*India: International Health Care System Profiles*", The Commonwealth Fund, 5 June 2020.

SELECT BIBLIOGRAPHY

Isabelle Attane, "*Being a Woman in China Today: A Demography of Gender*", Open Editions Journals, 2012/4.

Kavita Wankhad, "Urban Sanitation in India: Key Shifts in the National Policy Frame", *Environment and Urbanization*, Vol. 27 Issue No. 2, pp. 555–572, 1 October 2015.

K.P. Kannan, and G. Raveendran, "Jobless to Job-loss Growth", *Economic and Political Weekly*, Vol. LIV Issue No. 44, pp 40–43, 9 November 2019.

Mila Friere, "*Urban Planning: Challenges in Developing Countries*", World Bank, 2006.

Monica Das Gupta, B.R. Desikachari, Rajendra Shukla, T.V. Somanathan, P. Padmanaban, and K.K. Dutta, "How Might India's Public Health Systems be Strengthened? Lessons from Tamilnadu", *Economic and Political Weekly*, Vol. 45, Issue No. 10, pp. 46–60, 6–10 March 2010.

Myles F. Elledge and Marcella McClatchey, "*India: Urban Sanitation, and the Toilet Challenge*" RTI Press, September 2013.

Nandan Nilekani, *Imagining India*, Penguin, 2008.

National Family Health Survey (NFHS-4), 2015–16, Government of India.

National Family Health Survey- 5 (NFHS-5), 2019–21, Government of India, 2021.

N.K. Singh, Fifteenth Finance Commission Report, Government of India, October 2020.

NRHM MIS (HMIS) Data Base – Rural Health Statistics, Department of Health and Family Welfare, Government of India, 2019.

Prabhu Pingali, Anaka Aiyar, Mathew Abraham, and Andaleeb Rehman, "*Transforming Food Systems for a Rising India*", Palgrave Macmillan, 2019.

R. Chattopadhyay, and E. Duflo, "Women as Policy Makers: Evidence from a Nationwide Randomized Experiment in India", *Econometrica*, Vol. 72, 1409–1443, 2004.

Sanjay K. Singh, "Review of Urban Transportation in India", *Journal of Public Transportation*, Vol. 8, Issue No. 1 pp. 79–97, 2005.

Savita Bhaskar, Richa Shankar, Shrikant Kale, Soumya P. Kumar, and Ravi Kumar, "Comprehensive National Nutrition Survey (CNNS)", National Report, Ministry of Health and Family Welfare, Government of India, UNICEF, and Population Council, 2019.

Sendhil Mullainathan, and Eldar Shafir, "*Scarcity*", Penguin Books, 2013.

Sriraman, "*Urban Transportation Planning and Investment in India, Emerging Challenges, Cities and Sustainability*", Springer Proceedings, Business and Economics, 2013.

"State of the Young Child in India", Mobile Creches, Routledge, 2020.

T. C. A. Ranganathan and T.C. A. Srinivasan, "*All the Wrong Turns*", Westland Publications, 2019.

"Transforming Urban Landscape, 2014–2019", Ministry of Housing and Urban Affairs, Government of India, 2019.

"Unified District Information System for Education Plus (UDISE+), 2019–20", Government of India.

Usha Chandran, "A Woman's World", *India International Centre Quarterly*, Vol. 36, Issue No. 3/4 pp. 288–301, 2009. http://www.jstor.org/stable/23006419.

Vimala Ramachandran, "*Inside Indian Schools*", Social Science Press, 2018.

Vimala Ramachandran, "*The Elementary Education System in India*", Routledge, 2009.

INDEX

Aadhar card 49
AAP government 95–96, 101
Abhay Bang 18
Abhijit Banerjee 1, 7–8, 28, 41, 87, 118
Abhijit Sen 48
adult height 40
agriculture in India 114–116;
    agricultural insurance 121–122,
    191; agricultural productivity
    114–115; agriculture households
    111; agriculture market 14, 114–115;
    farm gate price 45; farm laws
    44, 114–115; Minimum Support
    Price (MSP) 44–45, 48, 114–115;
    opportunities in agriculture 114–
    115; PM Kisan Samman Nidhi 120,
    122
Amartya Sen 2
Angus Deaton 40
Arvind Panagriya 20
Ashok Gulati 43, 149
Atamnirbhar 128; Make in India 128
Aya Kimura 45

Bangladesh 14, 26, 38, 49, 119, 127
BASIX 119, 123
beliefs and practices 26, 112–113, 137,
    142; cultural beliefs 112, 137, 161;
    patriarchal mindset 5, 113, 136, 146,
    192
Beti Bachao Beti Padao 60, 141
Bharat Ramaswami 49
Bhore Committee 21
Birsa & Rasika 7–8, 18, 58, 62, 85,
    110–111, 138, 165–166, 193–194

cash/income transfer 49–50, 115,
    120–121, 151, 190, 196
census, 2011 86, 159

childcare in India 4, 63–72, 147;
    anganwadi 63; anganwadi-cum-
    creche 63, 73; anganwadi training
    69; anganwadi worker 61, 63–64,
    67–69; caring environment 62;
    childcare arrangements 62; child
    diseases 59–60; child health 25,
    66; child height/stunting 40; child
    indicators 4, 25, 57–58, 64; child
    illness 59–60; child nutrition 4, 39,
    57–58; child well-being 4, 57–58,
    190; creches/day care 62, 65, 72–74,
    147; disadvantaged children 57,
    60; Early Childhood Development
    (ECD) 58–61, 65, 70; girl child 57,
    60; infant and child mortality 57,
    59; Integrated Child Development
    Services (ICDS) 46, 57–58, 63–65,
    68–69; National Creche Scheme
    63, 73; National Nutrition Mission
    (NNM) 68; POSHAN Abhiyan 46,
    68; State of the Young Child in India
    Report 57; supplementary nutrition
    64; take-home ration 64
China 39, 92, 96, 116–117, 127,
    129–130, 139
climate change 4, 115
corruption 3, 83
COVID-19 2, 4, 14–15, 22, 24, 26–27,
    38, 43, 51, 58, 64–65, 88–90, 111,
    121, 137, 150
Cuba 15, 27, 31

Dean Spears 40
demographic dividend 5, 185
developed/first-world countries 14, 148,
    164
developing/third world countries 14,
    170–171

207

INDEX

development agenda for India 3, 6, 11, 198; alternative development agenda 11; multi-sectoral approach 74; 'people-first agenda 2, 10–11; road map/way forward 186–190; urban-centric approach 110, 192
Diane Coffey 40
drinking water 32, 160

Early Childhood Care and Education (ECCE) 70–72; early learning 61; ECCE Task Force 71–72; preschool curriculum 71; preschool education 60–62, 70, 88
economic distress 102, 109, 185
economic growth/GDP growth 1–2, 159; economic environment 188–189; job-loss growth 2, 111–112
economic reform 1, 119, 188–189
Eldar Sharif 8
employment 111–112, 187; guarantee 130; opportunities 111; rate 2, 111–112; Mahatma Gandhi Rural Employment Guarantee Act (MGNREGA) 48, 130–131; self-employed 111; women's employment 111–112, 123–124, 139; youth unemployment 111
Essential Commodities Act 114
Esther Duflo 1, 7–8, 41, 118
exports 128; trade policy 128

Factories Act 147–148
family planning/fertility control 25
Felix Muchomba 44
Fifteenth Finance Commission 197–198
first-world/developed countries 148, 173–174
fiscal capacity 195–198; fiscal sustainability 195–196, 198; tax revenue/potential 198
food security in India 41–43; calorie deficiency 41–42, 45; food-grain stocks 43–44; food subsidy budget 43, 48, 195; National Food Security Act 43; savings in food subsidy 48, 120, 195–196
freedoms 3

Gabriela Mistral 57–58
gender issues/women's issues 50–51, 136–139; actions by companies 148–150; constitutional provisions 123; discrimination 5, 112, 136–137,

139, 148; gender bias in education 146; gendered mindset/prejudice 92, 136, 144, 186; gender inequity 136, 148; gender sensitisation 146; gender wage gap 112; girl child 60; Global Gender Gap Index 5; Maternity Benefit Act 62–63, 124, 147, 149; National Commission of Women 141; sexist statement 143–144; sex ratio 136; sexual abuse 143; Sexual Harassment of Women at Workplace Act 149; skilling programmes 124; son preference 137, 142; triple burden 138–139; violence against women 137; women centred education 149; women empowerment/movement 5, 140–141; women role models 141, 144–145; women's education 113, 146; women's well-being 137–138
Global Hunger Index (GHI) 38
governance structure 3, 10
government budgets in India 195–196; additional budgets 197, 199–203; child budget 74, 196; education budget 86–87, 102–103, 196; fiscal sustainability 186; food budget 43, 196; gender budget 153–154, 197; health budget 14, 22, 31; livelihoods and jobs budget outlay 197; nutrition budget 51; sanitation and solid waste management budget 171, 197; tax revenue 197; urban budget 179–180, 197
government policies/programmes 3, 7, 10–11, 186–187; design flaws 2, 10–11, 187–188; design principles 186; integrated approach/inter-connectedness 6, 50, 65, 188; policy making 10; policy mindset 45; poor outcomes 187; programmes for poor 8
Gro Harlem Brundtland 38

healthcare system 4, 14–16, 189–190; accredited social health activist (ASHA) 17–18, 24, 67–69, 145; All India Institute of Medical Sciences 28; anaemia 39, 45; anaesthetists 27, 191; antenatal care (ANC) 17, 66; auxiliary nurse midwife (ANM) 17, 23–24, 67; Ayushman Bharat 15, 23–24, 28–29, 31, 190; child health 24–25; child health indicator 3–4; Clinical Establishments Act 21, 30; Commissioner Health & Family

208

INDEX

Welfare 19, 22; community-based health care 26–27; community health centres (CHCs) 19; curative services 15; diagnostic equipment 191; disease management/programme 21–22, 26; district hospital 20, 27; Epidemic Diseases Act 21; gaps in public health care 20; government hospital 20–21, 27–29; health education 26; health household expenditure 21, 23, 31; health infrastructure/refurbishment 16, 19–20, 27–28, 189–190; health insurance 28–29, 190; health outcomes/indicator 14; health policy 15, 20; health regulation/legislation 15, 21, 30; hospital beds 6, 19; hospital management 19–20; immunization 4, 60, 66–67; life expectancy 24; local health provider 18–19, 30–31; male health worker 26; maternity mortality 14; medicines and drugs 23; morbidity 4; mortality rate 4; National Health Mission (NHM) 17, 30–31; National Health Policy 20; National Medical Commission 30; non-communicable diseases (NCDs) 4, 26; obesity 26; preventive and promotive healthcare 15, 21; primary healthcare 16, 22–23, 26; primary health centres (PHCs) 16–17, 23, 66–67; private health sector 20, 30; private/local health provider 30–31; Public Health Act 21; public health care 15–16, 21–22; referral system 27; refurbishment of hospitals 189–190; subcentres (SCs) 17, 23; universal health coverage 31; Universal Immunization Programme (UIP) 66–67; wellness centres 23–24, 28; women's health 4, 24–25, 39
household savings 123

income inequality 1; Gini Coefficient 1
income protection 120
indebtedness 123; debt 118; money lender; perpetual debt 110
industrial cluster development 126–127, 129
Information, Education and Communication 47; awareness/media campaigns 26, 141–144
International Labour Organisation (ILO) 112
investment fund 127; private equity 127; private sector investment 129

Jan Dhan account 110, 123
Japan 94, 96, 113, 148–149
Jean Dreze 40
job creation 112, 189, 191–192; government jobs 130, 191–192

Khap Panchayats 143
Kofi Annan 80, 136
Krishna Kumar 72, 83, 88

labour force 110–111, 116; casual labour 112; Female Labour Work Participation rate (LFPR) 112–113, 137; Labour Force Participation Rate 111; labour laws 121; landless labour 111, 120; migrant labour 6, 110, 117, 121, 191; Periodic Labour Force Survey 111; working population 111
labour-intensive enterprise 111, 125
labour laws 120–121
Le Keqiang 159
Lesbian, Gay, Bisexual, Transgender, Queer, Intersex, Asexual + (LGBTQIA+) 137, 151–153
livelihoods 109; livelihood opportunities 191; traditional livelihoods 116, 127, 191–192; women's livelihood 5, 122, 191

Make in India 128; Atmanirbhar 128
Malala Yousafzai 136
Manila 167
manufacturing sector 127–128, 191
Manu Samhita 162
markets, over reliance 109
Michael J. Dowling 114–115
micro-credit 118–119
micro finance institutions (MFIs) 118–119, 123; livelihood finance 123, 191
Mobile Creches 71, 73
money lender 7, 110, 118–119
Mudra loan scheme 125

National Bank for Agriculture and Rural Development (NABARD) 118
National Family Health Survey (NFHS) 25, 39, 61
National Sample Survey (NSS) 9, 112
Neeraj Kaushal 44
Nelson Mandela 80
Niti Aayog 1, 9, 44, 115
non-farm sector in India 115–116

209

INDEX

non-government organisation (NGO)/ civil society 11, 24, 46, 63, 90–92, 153, 198

nutrition in India 4; calorie deficiency 40–42; Comprehensive National Nutrition Survey (CNNS) 39; hidden hunger 42; malnutrition 39, 41; maternal nutrition 40; National Nutrition Mission 68; nutrition imbalance 4, 39–40; nutrition indicator 38, 40; nutrition outcome 41; obesity 41; squeezed budget 42; voluntary hunger 42

Paulo Friere 89

politics 10, 195; electoral appeal 10; electoral benefit 194; political environment 195, 198

poor households/low-income households 6, 8–9, 23, 41–42, 50, 59, 62, 67, 90, 186–187, 193–194; Antyodaya families 120, 147; below poverty line (BPL) 8, 43; beneficiary families 8; daily struggles 7–8; enumeration/identification 8–10, 187; understanding the poor 7

poverty 110–111; poverty estimate 110, 187; poverty trap 111, 118; understanding poverty 7; urban poverty 159

Pratham 71, 90, 93

processed foods 39

Programme for International Student Assessment (PISA) 19, 93–94

public distribution system (PDS) 8, 38–39, 42–43, 47–50; Antyodaya Anna Yojana 43, 50, 190; BPL card/ ration cared 42–43; leakage/diversion 43; PDS reform 47–49, 51, 190; universal PDS 48

quality of life 185

Rani Bang 18

rural credit 118, 123; bank credit 118 rural output 116

scarcity mindset 8

school education in India 4, 45, 80; Annual State of Education Report (ASER) 62, 80–82, 85–86; catch-up/ remedial programme 90, 191, 196; child population 96; commissioner of schools 94, 96, 98, 100; counselling 98; curriculum 89–90, 95, 100; digital education 89; District Primary Education Programme (DPEP) 87, 90; dropout rate 81, 96; education of children of poor households 82–83, 85, 90, 97; education reform 87–88, 99, 102, 190; education system , 83–84, 87–88, 99; Eklavya 90–91; elementary education 96; English education 86, 180; enrolment 81, 85; enrolment gap/rate 80–81; girls' enrolment/ gender gap 81, 113; government schools 81, 83–84, 90–91, 95–96; high schools/secondary education 87, 96–97; household expenditure on education 103; inequity 81; innovations in school education 91–92; international initiatives in education 92–94; language issue 100; learning outcomes/ level 82, 88, 102, 190; literacy 81; Nali Kali 90–91; National Education Policy, 2020 (NEP), 70–71, 86, 90, 102; Operation Blackboard 87; pedagogy 88–89; Pratham 82; primary elementary education; private schools 85, 100–102; Right of Children to Free and Compulsory Education Act (RTE Act) 70, 80–81, 87, 97, 101; rote learning 83, 88; quality of education 5; quality of schools; Sarva Shiksha Abhiyan 87; school facilities/school infrastructure 95; school network 81, 85, 96; school performance 5, 84, 101, 197; secondary education/high schools 96–97; teacher absenteeism 84; teacher motivation/performance 82–83, 97; teacher posting and transfer 97–98; teacher recruitment; teacher training 83, 88, 90–91; tuition fees 101; vocational education 97

Science, Engineering, Technology, and Maths (STEM) 146

SC/ST families 9–10, 60, 81, 120

self-help groups (SHG) 110, 118–119, 123, 125

Sendhil Mullainathan 8

service quality 7, 16, 19, 187

SEWA 73, 123

skilling programmes 128

210

INDEX

Small Industries Development Bank of India (SIDBI) 127
solid waste management (SWM) 163, 171–175; E-Waste 173; landfills 163; municipal waste 173, 176; success stories 174; waste collection and disposal 173–174
Sri Lanka 14, 26, 31
street vendors/hawkers 166
sub-Saharan countries 14, 38, 40
Surjit Bhalla 49

technology adoption 128
textile sector 117, 127
Thomas Piketty 1
tiny & small businesses 125, 128
traditional livelihoods 116–117; artisan 116; handicrafts 116–117, 127; handlooms 117, 127
trickle-down effect 2

Ukraine war 44
United States (US) 14, 26, 148–149
urban housing 167, 192; affordable rental housing complexes (ARHCs) 168–169; housing conditions 160; housing for the poor 6, 161, 165, 167, 169; housing market 6, 168; Pradhan Mantri Awas Yojana (Urban) 169–170; slum population 161; slum settlement 160–161, 167
urban mobility 164, 176–179, 192; bus services 164, 176–177; cars 177; congestion charge/tax 176; cycling 179; Jawahar Lal Nehru National Urban Mission (Urban) 176; metro services 177; motorised vehicles 164; National Urban Transport Policy

176; pedestrian paths/walkways 178–179; roads 176; women's mobility 147–148
urban sanitation 50, 161, 170–171; cleaning community 20; faecal sludge 170; open defecation 40, 50, 58, 162, 170; public toilets 161; recycling of sewage waste 170–171, 173; sanitary infrastructure 161; sanitation system 161–163, 170–171; sewage treatment plants 171; sewage/waste water treatment 162, 170–171; sewerage network 161; Swach Bharat Mission (Urban) 170, 172; toilets ,170; user fees 171
urban sector in India 6, 159, 192; Atal Mission for Rejuvenation and Urban Transformation (AMRUT) 126; Maharashtra Housing and Area Development Area Authority (MHADA) 161; unliveable conditions/unclean surrounding 6, 159; urban cluster development 125–126, 129, 166, 191; urbanisation 159; urban local bodies 176–177, 179–180; urban neglect 159; urban planning 6, 160–161, 165–167; urban sprawl 161
Usha Chandran 139

Vijay Mahajan 119
village panchayat/local community 24, 144–145

well-being 3; women's well-being 137, 146
World Bank 16, 27, 122, 126
World Health Organization (WHO) 66

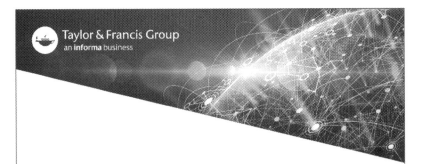